ADVANCE PRAISE FOR

Dialogue for Student and Teacher Development

"Working autobiographically, Saeed Nazari provides a powerful illustration of the journey to teach, from the historical circumstances—familial, institutional, and political—that drew him to education, in the first instance, to the role of *currere* in opening up new ways of interacting with his educational present. This work undercuts any simple story of becoming a teacher. It invites consideration of the importance of history and dialogue in teacher development."
—Anne M. Phelan, Professor, Department of Curriculum and Pedagogy
Centre for the Study of Teacher Education,
University of British Columbia, Vancouver, Canada

"Saeed Nazari's story is as fascinating as it is informative. Many of the trials and tribulations that educators encounter on their route to teaching are present in this text. For example, Saeed's accounts of his earliest days of competitive education to his most recent immersion in *currere* are rich with challenge, opportunity, serendipity, and complexity. His various stories are filled with passion, fraught with tension, and brimming with adventure."
—Anthony Clarke, Professor, Department of Curriculum and Pedagogy,
Centre for the Study of Teacher Education,
University of British Columbia, Vancouver, Canada

Dialogue for Student and Teacher Development

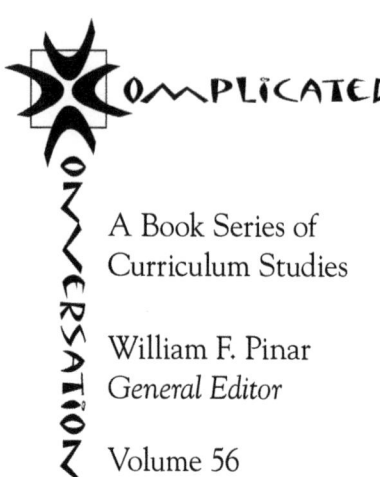

A Book Series of
Curriculum Studies

William F. Pinar
General Editor

Volume 56

The Complicated Conversation series is part of the Peter Lang Education list.
Every volume is peer reviewed and meets
the highest quality standards for content and production.

PETER LANG
New York • Bern • Berlin
Brussels • Vienna • Oxford • Warsaw

Saeed Nazari

Dialogue for Student and Teacher Development

My Persian *Currere*

PETER LANG
New York • Bern • Berlin
Brussels • Vienna • Oxford • Warsaw

Library of Congress Cataloging-in-Publication Data

Names: Nazari, Saeed, author.
Title: Dialogue for student and teacher development: my Persian currere /
  Saeed Nazari.
Description: New York: Peter Lang, 2021.
Series: Complicated conversation: a book series of
  curriculum studies; vol. 56 | ISSN 1534-2816
Includes bibliographical references and index.
Identifiers: LCCN 2020028289 (print) | LCCN 2020028290 (ebook)
  ISBN 978-1-4331-8250-1 (paperback) | ISBN 978-1-4331-8285-3 (ebook pdf)
  ISBN 978-1-4331-8286-0 (epub) | ISBN 978-1-4331-8287-7 (mobi)
Subjects: LCSH: Education—Biographical methods. | Teacher-student
  relationships. | Reflective teaching.
Classification: LCC LB1029.B55 N39 2020 (print) | LCC LB1029.B55 (ebook) |
  DDC 370.72—dc23
LC record available at https://lccn.loc.gov/2020028289
LC ebook record available at https://lccn.loc.gov/2020028290
DOI 10.3726/b17370

Bibliographic information published by **Die Deutsche Nationalbibliothek**.
Die Deutsche Nationalbibliothek lists this publication in the "Deutsche
Nationalbibliografie"; detailed bibliographic data are available
on the Internet at http://dnb.d-nb.de/.

© 2021 Peter Lang Publishing, Inc., New York
80 Broad Street, 5th floor, New York, NY 10004
www.peterlang.com

All rights reserved.
Reprint or reproduction, even partially, in all forms such as microfilm,
xerography, microfiche, microcard, and offset strictly prohibited.

For Nasrin, Nima, and Ana

An Unexamined Life Is Not Worth Living.

—Socrates—

CONTENTS

Foreword	xiii
Preface	xv
Acknowledgments	xvii
Introduction	1
The Point of Entry: Autobiography and Self-Education	1
My First Comprehensive Exam Experience: A Narrative	3
Lost in School Curriculum	4
Falaka in Primary School	5
Revolution and Imposed War	6
In Quest for Quality Education: Dialogue to the Rescue	7
Overview of the Chapters	9
Chapter 1. *Currere* and My Educational Experience	13
Introduction	13
An Excerpt from My Educational Experience	14
Autobiography as a Cross-Contextual Journey	15
Voice	18
Place	25

The Curriculum Reconceptualization Movement	32
The Movement and Tylerian Proceduralism Standardization	33
The Autobiographical Method of *Currere*	34
The Significance of Subjectivity in Curriculum Studies	40
Subjectivity and Evaporation of False Ego (Superficial Self)	43
Free Association and *Currere*	47
Bracketing	49
Temporality of *Currere*	52
Concluding Notes	55
Chapter 2. Autobiography and Teacher Development	59
Introduction	59
Problematizing Education	60
Autobiography in Teacher Education	67
Teachers' Biographical and Autobiographical Research	68
Attunement and Self-Understanding	74
Temporality of Autobiography	78
Concluding Notes	82
Chapter 3. Dialogue and Teacher Professional Development	85
Introduction	85
Background	86
Dialogue in Teacher Professional Development	87
Dialogue in Critical Pedagogy	91
Dialogue as Reflective Practice	93
Hermeneutic Reflexivity and Dialogue	96
Dialogue for Preparation of Teachers	97
Dialogue and Plurality in Teacher Development	100
Dialogue and Individuation	104
Dialogue on Faith for Teacher Professional Development: A Narrative	105
Writing Our Interfaith Dialogue into TESOL	107
Concluding Notes	109
Chapter 4. Gadamerian Dialogue	113
Introduction	113
Gadamerian Hermeneutics and Questions	116
Hermeneutic Understanding and Subjectivity	120

Gadamerian Hermeneutics and Teaching	122
Dialectic Nature of Knowledge	123
The Art of Conversation	125
Gadamerian Hermeneutics and Language	127
Concluding Notes	134
Chapter 5. Gadamerian Dialogue and Student Voice	137
Introduction	137
Background	138
Language and Open-Mindedness	139
Teacher Intervention	141
Becoming Attentive	143
Interpreting Students' World Meaning	144
Concluding Notes	151
Chapter 6. Conclusion	153
Summary	153
Return to Research Questions	156
Research Achievements and Contributions	163
Limitations of the Study	164
Further Research	165
Index	169

FOREWORD

What might I learn from my students today? This humble refrain sums up the openness and curiosity that permeates Saeed's work and is an attitude he encourages all educators to adopt within the context of their own classrooms, lecture halls, gymnasiums, laboratories, or wherever their teaching takes place. At the core of this question is the centrality of selfhood; an abiding sense of who I am as an educator and how I might enable the fullest learning potential of those in my care.

Saeed's story is as fascinating as it is informative. Many of the trials and tribulations that educators encounter on their route to teaching are present in this text. For example, Saeed's accounts of his earliest days of competitive education to his most recent immersion in *currere* are rich with challenge, opportunity, serendipity, and complexity. His various stories are filled with passion, fraught with tension, and brimming with adventure.

Perhaps the most important contribution this text has to offer is the importance of dialogue and what this *practice of engagement* has to offer to those who are willing and attentive to its possibilities. While self-assuredness, confidence, and certitude are often valued as indicators of success in today's world, Saeed's work reminds us that uncertainty, confusion, doubt, and above all humility are equally important as we encounter and engage with both self and other.

Finally, Saeed's text provides an important lesson in what and how being attentive to one's 'inner world' is essential to the practice of teaching and that without this attentiveness, teacher professional development is considerably constrained and limited. The value of self-knowledge is exemplified in each of the chapters in this text as Saeed articulates and makes explicit his assumptions about the world; a world where sometimes the self is absent or denied and at other times explored and celebrated. The crucial message from *Dialogue for student and teacher development: My Persian Currere* is that knowing oneself is a defining feature of teaching as a professional practice.

Anthony Clarke, Ph.D.
Professor, Department of Curriculum and Pedagogy
Co-Director, Centre for the Study of Teacher Education
University of British Columbia, Vancouver, Canada

PREFACE

This book is an original, independent, and novel work by Saeed Nazari.

ACKNOWLEDGMENTS

I express my sincere gratitude to Dr. William F. Pinar who kindly granted me the opportunity to learn from his scholarship in the department of Curriculum and Pedagogy. Without Dr. Pinar's exemplary patience, insightful guidance, encouraging comments, and devoted commitment, this book would not be possible. He kindled the light of self-knowledge and ingrained the art of self-education, self-understanding, and self-actualization in me—an innovative meaning of life-world which will remain for my whole personal and academic life.

I would like to sincerely thank Professor Anthony Clarke, and Professor Carl Leggo who offered unceasing support in creating this work. Dr. Clarke kindly invited me to the community of curriculum theorists and provided caring support and constant encouragement from the onset of my doctoral program. As a dedicated mentor, he patiently, wisely, and enthusiastically opened the mesmerizing world of teacher development and transfixed the true character of a devoted scholar in my mind. Dr. Leggo unleashed the power of self in me through his aesthetic and poetic scholarship. His *Creative Writing* talent taught me the way to understand and value my creative voice as an educator and to transcend my prescriptive writing as an English language teacher. His courageous and fearless narratives invited me to find the light within and transform from a caterpillar to a butterfly.

I owe my sincere gratitude to Dr. Anne Phelan who provoked my thoughts in *Introduction to Curriculum Issues and Theories* by opening the world of subjectivity in teacher education towards me. I offer my enduring gratefulness to Dr. Stephen Petrina who caringly and patiently guided me in his course *Doctoral Seminar in Curriculum and Pedagogy*. Last but not least, I express my humble thankfulness to my genius student, Elham Khoshkam, whose dedicated contribution to creating the index of the book was exemplary.

INTRODUCTION

The Point of Entry: Autobiography and Self-Education

In her engaging paper "On the Virtues of *Currere*[1]", Baszile (2017) refers to one of her favorite quotes in *I Love, Therefore I Am*—the book she reads every morning: "Education will transform the world. *Self-education* will transform education" (Abundantlee, 2016, p. 3; quoted in Baszile 2017, p. vi). Understanding my inner call, I reflect on Baszile's citation as the point of entry into my study; I am wondering which goal one might consider for education other than *self-education*. Why should education promote self-education to transform itself? Why should education be committed to self-exploration and self-actualization of teachers and students? In what way can self-education foster self-transformation, self-fulfillment, and self-wellbeing? Can educators explore their life-world and educational experience to transform education and why should they do that?

Having been practising the autobiographical method of *currere* for over 20 years, Baszile (2017) is wondering why it is so difficult to define *currere* in absolute terms: "it is, after all, like any art, or science for that matter, subject to the idiosyncrasies of the subject. It would be, however, more than a shame for people to shy away or run away not because they disagree with the premise, but simply because they don't know the premise" (p. vi). I can understand Baszile's concern and am wondering why procedural education with a mere focus on tasks and learnt skills which pays scant attention to the learner's self-exploratory learning experience, imagination, and fantasies might have alienated people and thereby lose connection with their selfhood. How might such goal-oriented schooling system have alienated me? And in what way can *currere* come to the rescue to connect me to my shattered self who is calling within?

Currere is self-education, and my engagement with self-reflective writing and inquiring into my educational experience has contributed to my psychological, intellectual, and emotional transformation; it has provided a meaningful understanding of self in education. As my study opens with an autobiographical understanding of my psychological development as an English language practitioner, teacher educator, and emerging scholar, a brief overview of the cognitivist movement and the historical context through which the method of *currere* came into existence will follow later in Chapter 1 of this book.

Britzman (2009) emphasizes that our educational experience can permeate our judgment and disturb our meaning-making process and perceived reality. Understanding that our mind owns the power to reflect on our educational experience enables the autobiographer to observe the source of the disturbance. What *is* the source of disturbance? Anxious understanding of the world and disconnection with the inner world is my disturbance. In my study, I am searching for the peaceful and serene world within and whatsoever obstructs this holistic observation, reflection, and exploration is my disturbance. This observation is voluntarily and unsolicited as is the method of *currere*, and my inner call is the source of this reflective and explorative study. Yet, the question remains in what way we should study our educational experience? Could, for instance, such self-reflective research support teachers who provide care for self and others? Jung (2015, p. ii) in his doctoral dissertation argues that an education centered upon self-care and care-for-others can connect our knowledge and ethics to make "professional judgment" and encourage students who can create their standards for well-being of self, others, of society. What if the teacher knowledge is prejudiced and in what way could they understand that? Without self-study their educational experience through academic research, is it possible for teachers to achieve an unbiased judgment of their knowledge and thereby problematize their professional practices? To me, admitting that there is an unleashing power of subjectivity[2] conditioned and restrained by educational experience makes a convincing reason to initiate this journey. This conditioned self as a byproduct of my educational experience needs growth, development, and unity. That is the main reason why I draw upon the method of *currere* to develop a deeper understanding of my own education and to connect this self-knowledge to teacher professional development, and to student thriving and well-being. I will study, then, in what sense teachers and educators can experience a transformative learning experience using the autobiographical method of *currere* to open creative and critical thinking spaces for themselves and their students. In the following, I will start with my Secondary School experience in Iran to highlight the way teacher dialogue can contribute to teachers and students' development and well-being in a test-centered curriculum.

My First Comprehensive Exam Experience: A Narrative

I remember the time when I was finishing grade eight in Resalat Secondary School (grades six to eight), Tehran, when one of my teachers asked four students including myself to see the school principal during our break. We were not sure what news he was going to disclose in the office. Mr. Naseri was always passionate about the quality of our education. We all knew, however, it was an important meeting as students were rarely called to have a meeting with the principal. In our brief exchange, he informed us that because of our grades and high average scores, we had been selected to take the entrance exam of Alborz High School (constantly ranked as the first or second high school in Tehran). My entrance into Alborz High School could guarantee my admittance into one of the high-ranking universities in Tehran. The teachers were intelligent, knowledgeable, and passionate about students' achievement and were well qualified to prepare them for standardized tests and produce pre-structured educational packages for their students to help them pass the main university entrance exam—called Konkour in Iran—upon successful completion of high school.

What I can recall on the exam day has always been *engraved* in me as a memorable educational experience as it was my first encounter with a comprehensive entrance exam with literally rounds of multiple-choice questions. I started answering the first round of questions believing that I could leave the rough chair on which I was sitting. Then, the second round of the questions came by, and the third, and the fourth! I was quite shocked and wanted to escape. Once I completed the first round of the multiple-choice questions and noticed the second round was coming, I was thinking to myself that this could be just the tip of the iceberg and was wondering what I would experience once I attend Alborz High School. Panicked, I asked one of the invigilators if I could leave the exam setting; he informed me that exam was not finished then and invited me to continue answering the questions until the end. Once I finished answering the questions, I left the school hallway and never returned. I did not even bother contacting the school for my results.

Lost in School Curriculum

When I arrived home, my mother and older sister (who were more engaged with my educational experience than the rest of the family) asked me about Alborz School Entrance Exam experience. I informed them that I was not willing to attend the school at all. This critical decision at times reminds me of the poem "The Road Not Taken" by Robert Frost (Wilcox & Barron, 2000) as it altered the path of my educational experience. As specified by the Iranian Ministry of Education, there were three main fields of study in which students could enroll upon their entry into high school at the age of 15: mathematics, experimental science, and humanities. Although I was interested in humanities, I enrolled in Experimental Science as the career opportunities with satisfactory annual income were appealing (after graduation from a decent program such as medicine). I started grade nine in Be'sat High School as it was near the place where I lived which was a demanding experience with all new subjects such as chemistry, algebra, physics, geometry, and biology among others introduced to the curriculum when I was 15 years old. I could hardly imagine the educational predicament following my nomination for Alborz School Entrance Exam. Overloaded with subject materials, I felt inundated with memorizing daily lessons understanding which could presumably help me flourish and thrive. The procedural schooling method was determined to shape like-minded students whose success was defined and guided by curriculum, reminding me of Pink Floyd's lyrics "We Don't Need No Education".

I loved learning new subjects and felt committed to memorize new themes and ideas, but I experienced some difficulty understanding physics equations, algebraic formulas and even memorizing chemistry tables in the textbooks. I felt dissatisfied with myself memorizing the periodic table although typically

I performed well in all subjects except for physics in grade nine, I recall. On the other hand, I was really into humanities. I enjoyed studying Persian literature, English language, Arabic language, and physical education. Now that I am scanning my high school report cards, I can merely see numerical values out of 20 with no names of teachers or any descriptive values; just ranking scores and figures students were afraid of. We were literally penalized by being ranked by numbers. The competition and comparison in school curriculum constructed learners or better to say rivals competing each other for educational achievements—literally scores. Couldn't education and curriculum provide a more meaningful understanding of our lifeworlds? I am wondering why this brutal policy—guaranteeing self-alienation—is still constantly programmed, engineered, and implemented in Iran's curriculum (as in many other countries), producing superficial students with engineered talents for memorization and rote learning? I am wondering why I was forced to study so many subjects within a year? In what way could chemistry formulas and algebraic expressions contribute to my educational experience and overall well-being? Did I favor quality education nourishing *my selfhood* in school? Why did my curriculum fail to include music, arts, drawing, painting, and philosophy? Did I have satisfying exploration of my own aesthetic and artistic talents at that critical and creative age? Couldn't the curriculum invite me to be in touch with self-education, self-exploration, and self-fulfillment? Was there an intentional disregarding, overlooking, or excluding students' selfhood in their educational experience? And how are those students credentialized yet crazed due to the pressure of coercive schooling and banking education thriving in their personal and public life? As adults, are they now mature grown-ups engaged meaningfully with their self and society?

Falaka in Primary School

Now, I have a flashback to my primary school experience. I understand the source of psychological tensions lies there. Being hyperactive, I can remember how many times I was literally whipped with a piece of water hose or wooden rod on my bare hands, admonished to fit into the prescribed rules such as "walk, don't run", "listen, don't talk", "be still, don't move" in early school years. Our vice principle in Shahid Sadoughi Primary School in District 17 in Tehran was standing near the main entrance with a disciplinary tool in his hands clenched behind. With his thick tailed mustache and gray eyebrow in a navy-blue suit, he was vigilant for nonconformist and guilty students like myself. I am wondering why I break into tears when recalling the memory. I was an innocent, athletic boy full of energy with ruddy cheeks blushing red, typical of a peasant child. I did not intend to bend the rules of school, but I was used to moving than sitting, speaking than listening, running than walking, laughing than crying, and those habits were judged as disobedience and nonconformity. As an individual, my genetic factors and mental orientation coordinated my behavior; school curriculum overlooked those basic aspects of my personality. Physical punishment did hurt indeed, however, the psychological torture and torment I experienced at that young age left scars, signs of deeper wounds in my psyche as we were threatened—frequently—to be struck on the soles of our bare feet using *Falaka (bastinado)*, a traditional method of corporal punishment involving being whipped on the feet by a wooden rod. It was shocking for an eight-year-old kid! Once threatened, I asked my friends what it looked like as I had not seen *Falaka* at school or elsewhere. We never experienced this method of corporal punishment at school; however, this disciplinary method as an emerging threat was deeply carved in our psyche.

Revolution and Imposed War

As autobiography is contextualized in place and time (Barane, Hugo, & Clemetsen, 2018), studying the specific time and place of the Iranian curriculum I experienced as essential for understanding the quality and tensions of education during my primary school. I was born in June, 1975 in Tehran, and by the time I started my first year of primary school in 1981 at the age of seven, Iran had already undergone its Islamic Revolution (starting in 1979—the time of the overthrow of the last monarch of Iran). So, the Iranian Revolution was only two years old when I entered primary school: Shahid Sadoughi (grades one to five). The tensions of Revolution were coupled by imposed war in 1980 when Iraq invaded Iran on September 22. The pressure at the time of war in Tehran was dramatically intense. I recall in my primary school, looking from the windows of the classroom, students, teachers, the principal and co-principal could all see Iraqi missiles flying over, headed to residential complexes, spreading terror among everyone. At nights, I remember when the emergency sirens went off, warning the citizens of the Iraqi attack bombers carrying out airstrikes; people in the neighborhood were shouting "turn off the lights!" so that the aircrafts could not spot our residential neighborhoods in Tehran in utter darkness to attack. To protect students, the government started building underground shelters. By the time I was in Resalat Secondary School in grade seven, nearly all schools in Tehran had completed constructing underground shelters to save students' lives when Iraqi ground to ground missiles and combat aircrafts overhead attack residential targets. When reading *International Handbook of Curriculum Research* (Pinar, 2014), I understand how curriculum is interwoven with history. This is how the subjectivity of my generation was constructed within the history and politics of terror and coercion and how my complicated conversation with myself can register social, political, and historical dimensions of my lived curriculum experience.

In Quest for Quality Education: Dialogue to the Rescue

As I was not satisfied with the quality of schooling in Be'sat High School in grade nine, I attended Motahari High School in my neighboring district in Tehran and studied there in grades 10 and 11 to experience an apparently more caring educational experience. Upon reviewing the scores in my report cards, I notice a steady progress in my achievement during these years, but I am still wondering if my scores are any indication of my self-satisfaction and overall well-being in school? Are my scores an indicator of an experience aimed at self-actualization and self-worth? What kind of learning was valued in my high school experience? In what way did the teachers evaluate our learning progress? Clearly, I am not satisfied with those aspects of my learning experience where I merely followed a procedural, rote-learning, and parrot-fashion pattern following banking education and assessment regime.

One aspect of my learning experience was teacher dialogue, and I would like to dwell on this aspect of what I can imagine as an innovative and progressive curriculum. I remember one of my English language teachers in grade 11, for example, who was a caring teacher as a true gentleman. In our time together in the classroom, he opened a dialogue with all of us about the social and political aspects of education and the way those aspects could influence our selfhood. For instance, he critiqued the socioeconomic status of public-school teachers, a status influencing their quality of teaching. The dialogue provided an empathetic educational opportunity for the students to share their voices in the classroom openly which has given me a memorable learning experience: I could feel worthy when I was engaged in non-judgmental, and genuine conversations with my English language teacher. I recall my Biology teacher in grades 10 and 11 when he talked about his lived experience[3] and shared his uncensored stories with us. As a knowledgeable, devoted, and disciplined teacher, he shared his life stories; I paid undivided attention as I considered that a teacher could be a knowledgeable *human being* with a story to share. I was eager to learn from his engaging stories as well as his knowledge. His real-life stories taught new aspects of learning, and filled the space between the teachers and students.

Not being well-satisfied with the classroom atmosphere in grade 11 in Motahari High School in quest of a higher quality of education, I moved to Ghods High School which was far away from my school catchment in grade 12 where I met another teacher who left a remarkable impression. My Arabic teacher shared his lived stories with us and critiqued the sociopolitical status quo. His teaching method was exemplary: his talent in engaging us with his narratives, and his narrations of his life-world were mesmerizing. Reading history and literature as a hobby, he encouraged us not to be indoctrinated by the mass media and to reflect consciously on our self-development. I am wondering why only a few teachers during my high school experience had the enthusiasm, talent, and self-knowledge to engage us with their stories while others were quite reserved and preferred to stick to their prescribed curriculum. Among all teachers in high school, I mainly remember those who shared their personal stories with us in a dialogic conversation; I feel truly indebted to them as they created an empathetic space of mutual understanding and trust. Not all students thought such personal stories were interesting, though. Sharing teacher personal stories—their otherwise hidden aspect of curriculum—meant caring *for me*. Their narrated stories worked as the main source of inspiring teacher knowledge and understanding—teacher lifeworld—through connecting to my personhood as a student. Those teachers—I believe—did not intend to teach or preach to us, but in sharing their very personal stories they created an animated space of dialogue, connecting their teaching to us. Now I know that sharing teachers' personal stories—using dialogue in a curriculum conceived as complicated conversation—can inspire students and remain in their memories forever. That is the way I now understand the impression they have left on me as they courageously, enthusiastically, and caringly revealed their inner lives, inspiring me thoroughly.

Triggered by my experience with such teachers and understanding self as an autobiographical being, self-explorative and self-reflexive teaching using dialogue has become my passion—a dream that finally came true during my doctoral studies at the University of British Columbia. Prior to my entry into the program, I had discovered the autobiographical method of *currer*, when

I was engaged in an interfaith dialogue with a friend of mine—Joel Heng Hartse—who was an English language educator like myself at that time. (An overview of our duoethnographic dialogue and the resulting publications are referenced at the end of Chapter 3 which can help the readers understand the application of *currere* in dialogue). Long before knowing *currere*, I remember visualizing a bright future (an account of which is presented at the beginning of Chapter 1); however, I was not aware that I was engaged in the progressive phase of *currere* when I was envisioning my vivid dreams. Moreover, my investigation into the historical and political aspects of Islamic Revolution in Iran and the war with Iraq accented the unstable circumstances affecting the curriculum I experienced. Working from within, I will move on to theorizing teacher professional development, emphasizing dialogue. The following questions have guided my research:

(1) In what way has the autobiographical method of currere encouraged an understanding of my educational experience?
(2) How can autobiographical research contribute to teacher development?
(3) In what sense can dialogue nurture teacher professional development?
(4) In what way can Gadamerian dialogue foster teacher professional development?
(5) Could Gadamerian dialogue encourage teachers to value student voice?

To hear, understand, connect with, and empower my narrative story by inquiring into my educational experience, my book starts with the autobiographical method of *currere* in Chapter 1. Then, I take my inquiry into the autobiographical research in teacher development in Chapter 2. Following that, I look into the ways dialogue can nurture teacher professional development in Chapter 3. Finally, Gadamerian dialogue provides an interpretive and hermeneutic insight into teacher professional development; this I detail in Chapter 4. I will contribute to fostering student voice, well-being, and autonomy in Chapter 5.

Overview of the Chapters

In the introduction, I regress—the first phase of the method of *currere*—to remember my high school educational experience to emphasize how opening dialogue and sharing teacher stories in a procedural curriculum—a step-by-step curriculum for acquisition of motor skills by breaking learning materials into small pieces—can leave a particularly positive experience for students once they juxtapose their subjectivity vis-à-vis teacher lived experience. I present the time and place of my curriculum to give an overview of the historical and political context of Iran at the time of revolution and imposed war as well as how my subjectivity was constructed during the period.

In Chapter 1, I regress to recall my educational experience using the autobiographical method of *currere*. I remember my past educational experience and draw upon the related literature to achieve a deeper understanding of my school experience. Informed by past experience and future possibilities, I discuss in what sense my expanded subjectivity mobilizes me to enter the public sphere by learning from pedagogical knowledge.

In Chapter 2, I extend my understanding of autobiographical research in teacher development. I study myself as an educator and examine the way autobiographical knowledge of teachers can contribute to teacher development. I study the ways teachers can reveal untold stories, share pedagogical practices, build communities, transform traditional conceptions of curriculum, and mobilize public and political action.

In Chapter 3, I theorize teacher professional development as a responsibility of individual teachers and the schools in which they work to ensure the highest-quality teaching. I suggest that educators can learn to engage with the humanity and selfhood of other teachers and all students at schools through open and genuine conversations. In the end, I delve into interfaith dialogue as a less explored arena in teacher professional development; I do so within the context of TESOL to provide an intersubjective understanding of faith in pedagogy and practice.

In Chapter 4, I suggest how Gadamerian dialogue can foster teacher professional development as it provides an interpretive understanding of intersubjective knowledge that complements *currere*, adding hermeneutic dialogue to teacher development. My understanding of dialogic knowledge, the arts of conversation, the dangers of prejudice, the mixed legacies of tradition and authority require an ongoing self-examination that supplements the self with a historical understanding of self/other, all in service to teacher professional development.

In Chapter 5, I will expand on Gadamerian hermeneutics to nourish students' voice and study in what sense open-minded teachers can strengthen students' voices by understanding their mistakes, errors, and half-formed arguments as a process of their becoming, thriving, and flourishing. Teachers can provide a supportive space within which students feel more comfortable to move from the familiar (what is known) to the strange (the unknown) and feel at home with their learning experience. Achieving self-fulfillment (what Aristotle called *eudaimonia*), students will learn to express their subjectivity, recognize their own life course, and treasure their individuality in tandem with others in their social space—what I mean by high—quality education.

In Chapter 6, I summarize my findings, specify my contributions, acknowledge limitations, and suggest further research.

Notes

1. *Currere* is an autobiographical method of inquiry into educational experience which constructs the individual's self/other understanding in four phases—regressive, progressive, analytic, and synthetic: [see http://currereexchange.weebly.com, and https://en.wikipedia.org/wiki/Currere].
2. The term 'subjectivity' is the lived sense of self which is associated with circumstances of everyday life from which one's meaning of life is constantly constructed (Pinar, 2009).
3. Heidegger calls it as *lebenswelt*: "the world of lived experience, the preconceptual experiential realm that is usually beyond our perceptual field" (Pinar, 1975b, p. 389).

References

Abundantlee. (2016). *I love therefore I am*. Retrieved March 10, 2018 from https://www.goodreads.com/work/best_book/49455705-i-love-therefore-i-am.

Barane, J., Hugo, A., & Clemetsen, M. (2018). *Creative place-based environmental education: Children and schools as ecopreneurs for change* (English ed.). Stroud, Gloucestershire: Hawthorn Press.

Baszile, D. T. (2017). On the virtues of currere. *Currere Exchange Journal*, 1(1), vi–ix.

Britzman, D. P. (2009). *The very thought of education: Psychoanalysis and the impossible professions*. Albany: State University of New York Press.

Jung, J. H. (2015). *Self-care and care-for-others in education*. Doctoral dissertation, The University of British Columbia, Vancouver, Canada. Retrieved from https://open.library.ubc.ca/cIRcle/collections/ubctheses/24/items/1.0167709

Pinar, W. F. (1975b). *Curriculum theorizing: The reconceptualists*. Berkeley, CA: McCutchan Publications.

Pinar, W. F. (2009). *The worldliness of a cosmopolitan education*. New York; London: Routledge.

Pinar, W. F. (2014). *International handbook of curriculum research* (2nd ed.). New York, NY: Routledge. doi: 10.4324/9780203831694.

Wilcox, E. J., & Barron, J. N. (2000). *Roads not taken: Rereading Robert Frost*. Columbia: University of Missouri Press.

1

CURRERE AND MY EDUCATIONAL EXPERIENCE

> *Currere* is a method that produces a self in relationship to others.
> Nicolas Ng-A-Fook (2005, p. 55)

Introduction

As an English language educator and doctoral student in the Department of Curriculum and Pedagogy, I inquired into my educational experience using the autobiographical method of *currere*. My research question was: In what way has the autobiographical method of *currere* encouraged an understanding of my educational experience? Starting with a brief account of my cross-contextual educational experience to highlight the power of a single short story, I discuss voice and place as commonplace abstractions in biographical and autobiographical literature among others (including community and gender) as they resonate with my cross-contextual educational experience. Only lately have I been able to connect with my voice, time, and place. I will then present an overview of the curriculum reconceptualist movement to trace historically the autobiographical method of *currere*, a method that emerged from the movement to create a transformative understanding of curriculum. I underscore the significance of subjectivity, and explain free association and bracketing phenomenological processes along with the temporality of *currere*. My personal schooling story presents a brief account of my own educational experience across two countries of residence where my educational experience has been constructed and reconstructed—Iran and Canada.

An Excerpt from My Educational Experience

I remember the time when I was walking down the street to Ghods High School in the capital city of Tehran as an eighteen-year-old senior student. I was visualizing a dreamland where I could learn something new every single day and live a peaceful life. I was looking for peace, inner peace. Since my early schooling days, I had always envisioned living in a place based on the new technology, scientific innovations, and sustainable development. The place where I imagined living was like images I watched in movies. What I can recollect are the tidy and neat streets, green surroundings, and friendly educated people walking by with smiles on their faces. What made me fantasize about living in such a place during my schooling years? Did an external experience trigger my dream, for instance, like the way humans started dreaming of flying as they watched birds flying by? Or was it a human innate talent of visualizing the future? How much of my primary and secondary educational experience after Iranian Revolution and following Iran-Iraq war was involved in my visualization?

Years later, as an English language practitioner at the University of British Columbia in Vancouver, I have realized why I dreamed. The education I experienced in my doctoral program provided a deeper understanding of self through the autobiographical method of *currere*. The place where I live on campus is surrounded by the woods and green plants; the educated civilized people in my neighborhood and school are also manifestations of my earlier dreams. Now, I am dreaming new possibilities in education for myself and others. Fantasies are not simply an escape for me anymore. They are being realized. With the confidence achieved through realizing my fantasies, I am envisioning new possibilities in curriculum studies each and every day. And I am wondering in what sense these imagined possibilities have informed my own teaching pedagogy and practice? How can today's visualized realities turn into tomorrow's possibilities?

Autobiography as a Cross-Contextual Journey

As human beings, we are always connected to existing social and political forces; we never live in a vacuum. Our autobiographies, consequently, are written in the contexts of our existence. Morris (2015) notes that autobiography is not simply telling a story because our narratives are closely-knit to a "historical context" (p. 211). My educational account incorporates two historical contexts—one in each of the paragraphs above. In the first paragraph, I have included my secondary school learning experience in Tehran, the cosmopolitan city where I grew up and completed my Bachelor's degree in English Language and Literature in 1998. As I am recalling my memories of undergraduate studies, memorization of subject materials in a pre-structured curriculum was the key component. I remember that there existed two aspects of learning experience; understanding literature and memorizing literary terms and genres. I was mesmerized by understanding literature and meaning-making process as I found myself connected with an exploratory journey experienced by the artist and the artwork. I felt helpless specifically in mid-term and final exams once our instructors demanded our memorized data which made me totally unqualified and uncomfortable. When I was admitted into the program, I was hoping to experience a transformative understanding of lived experience; I wondered why literature could turn into rote learning and parrot-fashion understanding! Miller's (2005) teaching account of her undergraduate teacher preparation courses resonates with my learning experience as an undergraduate student in Tehran.

> Such perspectives had informed my English-major undergraduate studies but had in no way influenced my scant and behaviorally oriented undergraduate teacher preparation or my full-time high school teaching experiences. There, I was pressured to present predetermined, sequential, skills-oriented and measurable versions of "English" to my students - hardly ways to encourage looking "inquiringly and wonderingly on the world. (p. 46)

Inspired by Miller's teaching experience, I am wondering in what way memorization and rote learning have dominated my past educational experience. Although understanding new ideas and words is important, memorization can only be the very first stage of learning and understanding. It was impossible for me to become a successful English language teacher without memorizing new language structures, vocabularies, stress patterns, rhythms, chunking, punctuations, proverbs, and idiomatic expressions of English language. However, what memorization deprives students of is their creative and imaginative understanding of the lifeworld. Once your brain is fragmented into certain chunks and pieces, holistic understanding is virtually sacrificed. I remember cramming for mid-term and final exams when we were forced to memorize a lot of language chunks and subject materials within a short period of time; this has left an unpleasant educational memory in my psyche. I remember when I was teaching English language courses in classes with 50 to 60 students as a full-time faculty member in Arsanjan Azad University—Arsanjan is a small town in Fars Province near Shiraz—between June 2003 and July 2009. As prescribed in their curriculum, my students took mid-term and final multiple-choice tests, required to achieve satisfactory scores in Basic English and General English Language courses. Sadly enough, many failed as they experienced difficulty with understanding English-language grammar and reading comprehension. I am wondering why they had to take multiple-choice tests? Wasn't there a more humanistic, personalized, and holistic way to evaluate their educational experience and final achievement? In what sense has their learning experience in those memorization-based courses contributed to their well-being or their fear of the test manifested in test anxiety?

My learning journey in my doctoral program, however, takes innovative pathways into understanding my educational experience as an educator; there are no chunks or predetermined structures to memorize. I understand that my past educational experience was externally-oriented and procedural. Thinking, living, and learning autobiographically, however, involves in a creative bottom-up processing rather than a static top-down step-wise procedure. The content of learning is being. Considering our life history as the content of learning, the method of *currere* invokes our educational experience in four existential phases by recollecting, envisioning, analyzing, and synthesizing our educational narratives to create new possibilities of education.

To prepare my students for International English Language Testing System known globally as IELTS, I have opened my own language school since I moved to Shiraz following my doctoral graduation in June 2019. Learning the psychoanalytical aspects of education during my doctoral studies and overcoming my own test anxiety due to my self-reflective research, I know the learning anxieties and challenges my students face very well. As all my students have been exposed to test-centered curriculum and parrot-fashion learning to score higher in their competitive educational experience in Iran, they undergo tensions when creating ideas, opinions, and thoughts when answering questions in IELTS test interviews. My understanding of their sources of anxiety and discomfort in test situations as well as my self-reflective and hermeneutic study have enabled me to intervene in their struggles and even help them work through their cultural, contextual, and historical obstacles when possible. Miller (2010a) notes that autobiographical work has the potential to reveal specifically how we have been conditioned by culture, context and history, and it goes beyond simply telling a personal story by students, teachers and educators.

Stories occur within the contexts and history of the autobiographer, so they take on—perhaps in altered form—the contextual and historical attributes. Autobiographers have been informed by their history so they typically communicate with their historical conditions. Regarding cross-contextual educational experience, Miller writes that autobiographical theories highlight that the self-knowledge of individuals can be continuously re-situated in streams of global mobility—a process which has made me more conscious of my existential experience in previous and current countries of residence, especially now that I am involved in my reflective thinking and writing. I am now a bilingual and bicultural educator whose 'subjectivity' has been informed by two languages and cultures and histories, English and Persian. Through reading my autobiographical study, students and teachers might learn from my lived experience, becoming conscious of their own cross-contextual even trans-cultural experience—as reading other autobiographical research made me aware of and curious about my own cross-contextual learning journey.

One might want to go further by reading between the lines in my autobiographical excerpt above and question; what feelings regarding people, place and culture are conveyed in both places of residence? What is the main reason for visualizing a dreamland in my first place of resident? In what way was my visualization triggered by or due to my high school educational experience? In what way might I evaluate my educational experience as a doctoral student, graduate teaching assistant, and graduate research assistant? These phenomenological and existential questions are personal and psychoanalytical, and probing into such questions has provided deeper understanding of my educational experience and they create new meanings of my lived experience. My review of the autobiographical research has revealed that some concepts such as *voice* and *place* are commonly used in autobiography. Drawing on the related literature, I will study these in my own autobiographical account to achieve a deeper understanding of such notions.

Voice

Voice in autobiographical writing emerges as the most appealing and powerful concept for me. To me voice includes two interdependent aspects, physical voice and inner voice. Regarding my physical voice, the strength and power of my voice have improved since the time I reflected on my subjectivity using autobiographical method of *currere*. I relate to my physical voice whenever I speak with my students in my office, on the phone, or other people, specifically strangers. Using direct feedback once teaching IELTS courses, I invite specifically my female students to watch related TED talks on voice training to empower those whose voice might be weakened due to sociopolitical—including gender—circumstances of their time and place, to understand their unique and individual powers. I am more confident when I meet new people who possess different points of views from mine as I am at peace with my own self. I listen to their ideas, opinions, and belief systems non-judgmentally, a practice that supports me as it encourages them to share their personal stories. My autobiographical research has given me confidence with my human voice when talking to people and presenting in academic and non-academic venues. The more connection I create with my inner voice through autobiography, the more clarity I can experience within, and the more concentration I can devote to in my performances in academic and professional arenas. When I reflect on my autobiographical being, I understand my inner voice as an integral part of me, particularly once engaged in thinking and writing this self-reflective book. Autobiographical writing keeps me in touch with my lifeworld and inner voice, and gives me strength, power, and creativity due to the experience of an emerging attachment and continuous connectivity with self and others. I can hear my internal dialogue when revealing my educational stories. When reflecting on tensions arising from my early schooling experience, I can forgive myself for certain inadequacies in my educational experience—for instance being bullied in my primary school due to my accent. I understand how my educational system in early schooling could include individuality in curriculum instead of conformity and collectivity, emphasizing, for instance, inner voice.

Pinar et al. (1995) positions the concept of voice as pivotal in autobiographical and biographical research in the work of Janet Miller, D. Jean Clandinin, and F. Michael Connelly. Miller (1990) argues that instead of proposing an infallible argument, she purposefully creates spaces for the other teachers so that they are enabled to find their voices in ongoing conversations. Educators can create such spaces by providing constant support for other teachers to explore and express their voices. When teachers understand the strength and power of their own inner voices, they can empower other teachers and students so that they experience this transformation. Miller acknowledges the "struggles of position and voice" among university and classroom teachers and students, and with researchers' stance in relation to "subjects, data, and the possibility of interpretations" (Miller, 1990, p. 8). Miller's affirmation of creating space and acknowledging struggle recall my parenting challenges. Happily bonding us together, it has been my contemplative silence that can give sympathetic and supportive space to my family to find their voice and create their space in our continuous dialogue. In my IELTS teaching courses, I strengthen my students' voice by careful listening and understanding their test anxious removing which can invariably support their self-confidence. My autobiographical writing has invited me to listen to others more attentively and to create a space for their dialectic. Creating a receptive mode of being allows a reflective space for understanding other interlocutors by deep thinking and contemplation—a mode of caring consciousness.

Grumet's critique of autobiographical voice—it is, she points out, not a single sound but a chorus—displays the subjectivity of teachers: "Teacher talk is then a defensive move deployed to assert her subjectivity in the face of the objectifying gaze" (Grumet, 1990, p. 279). The term *gaze* calls to mind the process of marginalization during which teacher subjectivity could be deformed to accommodate the demands of onlookers in a sociopolitical context of curriculum. Such social pressure presents itself in one form or the other and in different contexts which marginalizes teachers whose voices are taken for granted by the curriculum. Using autobiography to unravel one's reality, it is possible for teachers to achieve a nuanced understanding of their personal voice vis-à-vis the dominating power of social forces and circumstances surrounding them.

The process of marginalization, however, can be traced back to our early childhood education. In *Bitter Milk*, Grumet (1988) shows how the school curriculum moves the child from a private space of home to the public world as it overlooks the possibility of dialogue between the private and the public, instead imposing an objectified and impersonal understanding of education on the children. In this isolating, bureaucratic, and hurried transition, the child's subjectivity and voice are completely taken for granted while curriculum could virtually be "a temporary and negotiated settlement" (p. xiii) between the private and the public lives. Marginalized teachers, however, can reclaim their voices lost in their childhood curriculum—even during their teacher education coursework—with autobiographical inquiry into their early educational experiences. Autobiography can reconstruct teacher childhood educational experience and eliminate psychological obstructions in teacher subjectivity and voice.

Voice and Biographic Situation. To reclaim their voices, teachers are advised to understand their social, cultural, historical, and political positioning. Once teachers understand their "biographic situation" (Pinar & Grumet, 1976, p. 51) and become conscious of the historical period and cultural tradition in which they are embedded, they can express their autobiographical voice more fully. Being conscious of teacher thinking, knowing, and understanding calls for a self-reflective and self-analytic study of learning experience. Teachers who explore their self-knowledge understand the significance of their subjective narratives. Writing autobiographically, I can relate to my educational experience and connect to my voice what is otherwise missed. Considering its holistic approach to understanding teacher lifeworld, autobiography has contributed to finding my sociocultural, sociopolitical, and historical reality, and overall well-being.

Sharing these stories can facilitate dialogue for our students to reveal their untold stories and encourage them to understand their own biographic voice and situation. Phelan (2005) contends that teachers have hardly been considered as "reflective practitioners" and could be given the liberty to recognize and express their voice:

> [My inquiry] illustrates one teacher candidate's struggle to let go of a conception of knowledge as generalizable formulae that can be readily applied in practice and to become more open to practice itself as a site of learning. Teacher educators can nurture such openness by helping aspiring teachers to appreciate the fragility of knowledge, the epistemological value of feeling, and the priority of the particular, in teaching. (p. 339)

Being brought up in a procedural curriculum based on memorization and formulaic learning, I can relate to Phelan's experience with her teacher candidate. Such educational experience constructs a fragmented understanding of reality rather than a holistic approach to one's lifeworld. Self-reflective understanding of the world, however, can reconstruct our educational experience by deconstructing such instructional fragments into one unified piece to transform teacher reality. Reflective practitioners are conscious of their students' knowledge and fragility of their understanding. Exploring ontological, phenomenological, and epistemological understandings of self-knowledge, teacher candidates can achieve a personalized way of thinking, being, and becoming. Through self-education teachers can analyze and synthesize the formulaic learning and understanding of their methodology and practices by reflecting on their biographic situation. As Phelan asserts, the transition from formulaic learning to epistemological understanding of teacher knowledge is not an easy task. Opening new possibilities in education, teacher educators can vocalize the following epistemological questions in their daily practices: Why should we follow a certain method, approach, or procedure? In what sense can self-education help us transcend the limitations of such procedural learnings? In what way can we let go of a formulaic understanding of teaching practice? Is it possible to achieve a critical, generative, and transformative understanding of teacher knowledge without using a procedural method? These questions can encourage teachers and teacher educators who have experienced traditional schooling systems to articulate their powerful voice using phenomenological and epistemological understanding of being, knowledge, and learning ingrained in their biographic situation.

Later, in *Curriculum Theorizing and Teacher Education*, Phelan (2015) acknowledges her book as a collection of voices, stories, and lives of students and teachers, and characterizes these voices as a means of self-expression and self-representation during dialogic encounters. She asserts that teacher candidates should have freedom to express their voice in the online wiki environment designed for teacher candidates as a *community web* to practice plurality:

> Finally, participants require enough freedom to argue, debate, and negate ideas without feeling "edited" or, even more significantly, without feeling that their voices can be "deleted" from the wiki. The difficulty, of course, is that the achievement of a shared professional purpose is both a prerequisite AND an ongoing accomplishment of democratic engagement within the profession. (Phelan, 2015, p. 129)

The freedom to express themselves in the online wiki environment anonymously can encourage teacher candidates to risk self-disclosure, potentially enabling understandings of teacher biographic situation even more openly than in face-to-face classroom dialogues. I can relate to Phelan's sense of freedom by which teachers can express their feelings, understandings, and arguments with no restrictions and am wondering if educators can facilitate this non-coercive space for teacher candidates and students in other environments as well.

Voice and Empowerment. To empower students and teachers in education, we can work to strengthen their voices. Recognizing students and teachers' voice in the curriculum is key, Maxine Greene (1971) argues, and in the official curriculum the subjectivity of the student is often excluded. For visualizing how estranged from self the student might be, Greene refers to Schutz's allegoric description of a stranger in the town looking for the map (pre-structured curriculum) asking an expert (teacher) how to get from A to B. Students might sound like strangers to the subjects of study, however, despite such estrangement they can be encouraged to keep in touch with themselves, to search for subjective meaning, and individual understanding despite their circumstances. Understanding self and individuality using continuous dialogue with teachers can be the main dynamic of a progressive curriculum that positions students as central. If education is not centered upon thriving and developing students and teachers, what other objectives can be considered as important and why?

In my high school experience, I recall the occasions when teachers valued students' voice and dialogue. Some of our teachers set certain time for each educational session to open a dialogue during which students could express their opinions freely. My English teacher in grade 11 provided us opportunities to raise questions regarding social and political issues. He never stopped us from questioning our circumstances and he listened to our concerns inquiringly. The peace and tranquility we could experience in our dialogue encouraged us to voice our questions and value our subjective point of views. Teachers can empower students' voice once they are curious about understanding their subjective meanings of what they experience. I also remember those teachers who were authoritarian, who did not encourage student voice. With such teachers, I can hardly recall my voice as there was mostly monologue during which we students were solely listeners. Evidently these teachers did not believe in dialogic encounters as they considered students' voice as interruptions to their lessons or a threat to their authoritarian control of the class.

In my IELTS preparation courses, I encourage my students to understand the potential power of their voice. Being exposed to a prescriptive curriculum in which memorization is considered central, many have lost the quality of their voice. It takes time for them to appreciate their powerful inner voice and understand that their voice and subjectivity are keenly knitted together. The prescriptive as well as collective curriculum they have experienced has silenced their individual voices, and in interview situations this fact disables them, as their anxieties causes their voices to lose its strength, power, and transparency.

When they understand the power of their voice, they can connect to their powerful inner voice and attempt to develop it more fully. Some of them understand how a *grip* can disable their transparent and clear voice and require my understanding of the sources of their grip to empower their voice and develop their subjectivity. I usually ask them to regress to their educational experience and observe the source of tensions in their school memories.

In *Teacher as Stranger*, Greene (1973) encourages teachers to become self-conscious about their sociopolitical, cultural, historical, and personal influences on the development of teacher self-awareness and their pedagogical practices. By self-consciously taking a stranger's vantage point on daily life, teachers can look "inquiringly and wonderingly on the (varying) world in which our students and we live" (Greene, cited in Miller, 2010a, p. 136). Through this lens, Greene positions teachers positively in a space of doubt, fragility, and wonder searching for subjective meaning, enabling them to contribute to an innovative and creative curriculum. Greene's point of view resonates with me deeply as my autobiographical explorations strengthen the power of my psyche as a teacher. To understand my students' positionality (and fragility) during my tutoring sessions in my language school, I suspend my judgment to inquire wonderingly on their lifeworld so that I understand their inner barriers to learning; the result is many become comfortable in revealing their anxieties through previously untold stories of their educational experience. Such caring intervention can position me as a counsellor, psychologist, consultant, and mentor whose knowledge of *currere* can invariably support students to find their mutual and individual space in education. Students and teachers can both assume the role of a stranger, engaging in exploring new dimensions of themselves and their educational experience. Who is not a stranger to self? Who knows the dimensions of their subjectivity and personhood thoroughly? Being a stranger turns out to be even more significant to teachers alienated from their lived experience due to going through behavioristic schooling, traditional curriculum, and procedural education.

Oakeshott (1959, p. 11) asserts that education is an invitation to a conversation in which we "learn to recognize the voices, the proper occasions of utterance, and in which we acquire the intellectual and moral habits appropriate to conversation." He considers the outcome of intellectual achievement in terms of its contribution to the conversation. Teachers can invite students to contribute to this dialogue by understanding their shared space and acknowledging their positionality in education. I understand how providing this supportive space has motivated my teacher candidates and students to understand the power of their subjective thought system and intellectual capacity. Such educational conversations can improve the intellectual, emotional, and social well-being of ourselves, students, and other teachers. In the process of thriving, autobiographical voice can reveal the identity, gender, and individuality of the recounter which I regard as the prominence of autobiography.

Grumet (1990) elaborates on autobiographical voice as a medium for cultural, political and social processes for teachers and asserts that her use of voice as a *feminine* marker distinguishes her autobiographical work. She theorizes a more complex notion of voice categorizing three parts in academic voice: situation, narrative, and interpretation:

> The first, situation, acknowledges that we tell our story as a speech event that involves the social, cultural, and political relations in and to which we speak. Narrative ... invites all the specificity, presence, and power that the symbolic and semiotic registers of our speaking can provide. And interpretation provides another voice, a reflexive and more distant one .... This trio may save us from the objectification of identity politics by recognizing the dynamic process through which identity is grounded in history, and desire, subjected to description and reflection and constantly presented to and negotiated with other people. (Grumet, 1990, pp. 281–82)

Understanding that teacher voice indicates sociocultural, political, and historical meanings can inform and empower teachers and teacher educators to reclaim their identity and subjectivity.

By telling their stories, educators can vocalize their gendered and individualized understanding of their biographic situations with other teachers to help them understand the meaning of different teaching orientations through reflection, contemplation, and constant questioning of their pedagogical understanding. As Grumet (1990) asserts, autobiography is a space to reflect the specific experiences of teachers and students. Teachers can freely assert their gender orientation, family history, sociopolitical influences, and other personal and private aspects that are normally neglected in quantitative research. Acknowledging situation, narrative, and interpretation is surely a preliminary stage in an experience-based learning process through which teacher subjectivity and personhood are regarded as pivotal to educational experience. Rooted in teacher subjectivity, voice and place are intermingled and interconnected in understanding teacher autobiographical stories and lived experiences. They are so interconnected that understanding one demands knowing the other. I will inquire into the concept of place in autobiographical inquiry to achieve a deeper understanding of this concept in the teacher biographic situation.

Place

My former and current places of residence are embedded in my autobiographical narrative of educational experience. Autobiographical experience occurs in place as well as time, and it registers influences from social, cultural, and political events which construct one's lived experience. At the University of Tehran in the capital city of Iran, I conducted my undergraduate studies in English Language and Literature between 1994 and 1998 during which I acquired the foundations of teaching methodology and English Literature. I recall in the first years of bachelor program; my English language proficiency was somewhat below standards. I had to improve my accuracy and fluency as I was learning. The inner struggle was intense; however, I was deeply determined to succeed in my program in both language skills (micro) and language content (macro) as that was the only way I could master English language and literature. As a student, my teachers' comments on my progress meant a lot to me. Adhering to the myth of acquiring a native speaker's accent, I concentrated on my own accent training using English dictionaries and radio programs from the onset of my program. Toward the end of my program as a senior student, I remember the time when I was standing next to the corridor on the second floor of English language department with a close friend of mine, Deldari, who was a genius in languages. To improve my spoken English and to learn some new words from him, I was speaking in English with him when one of my professors, Dr. Kasraeyan, approached us. Engaged in our conversation, we did not notice him approaching. However, he was overhearing our dialogue as he drew closer and closer. He turned to me and commented; "Your accent is beautiful!" I was delighted to hear his generous comment as I had studied for 4 years to improve my English language proficiency and his remark confirmed my achievement.

At Shiraz University—Shiraz is a major city in Fars province in Iran—I completed my graduate studies in Teaching English as an Additional Language, studying there from 2001 to 2003. My English language teaching career in language schools started during my master's program when I studied the methodological, linguistic, psychological, and social aspects of language teaching. I collaborated with several English language professors at

Shiraz University, among them Dr. Sadighi who supervised my master thesis, Dr. Bagheri who helped me secure a part-time teaching position in Shiraz University Language Center in Qomabad and Dr. Parhizgar who supported me to secure a tenured teaching position in Arsanjan University following my graduation in June 2003.

Before moving to Canada as a skilled worker, for six years I worked as a full-time English language lecturer in Arsanjan University; that provided me a strong academic work experience. My teaching experience and overall command of English language contributed to my application as a skilled-worker immigrant to Vancouver where I literally started from scratch in June 2009. Upon my arrival, I stayed at my friend's apartment with my family for two weeks. I will never forget the beauty of the place underneath as our long-haul Lufthansa flight was landing. My friend, Hossein, gave us a ride to his place on the Northshore. I could hardly believe my eyes when he was driving on Lions Gate Bridge: sunny with seagulls flying by, the Grouse Mountain view upfront, Stanley Park's breathtaking scenery, and the gorgeous seawall sight on both sides of the ocean with people walking, jogging, skating, and cycling. Exhausted from search, finally I found a one-bedroom flat to rent in West Vancouver where we stayed for a year. After my spouse was admitted to doctoral studies in the UBC Department of Language and Literacy Education in February 2010, we moved to student housing. Once we moved to campus in August, I found spare time to explore my life trajectory and to examine my past educational experience.

I was not quite satisfied with myself—the meaning of my life—so I could not initially attach to my place of residence. To understand the source of my psychological anxiety, I discussed the matter with friends on campus who shared dissatisfaction with their integration and assimilation into their residence. To explore my questions academically, I studied several articles on immigrant's settlement issues and presented the findings of my research in conferences and seminars at UBC Liu Institute for Global Issues and BC Teaching English as an Additional Language (BC TEAL) between 2012 and 2013. The more I explored my questions academically, the less I became satisfied with my findings. There was a lack of data—deep understanding—in my findings. After a while, I could easily predict the outcome of the papers I was reading and I did not experience any transformation—transformative understanding. My inner self was not well content with the journey I was pursuing. I could feel a hole in my psyche which was the main reason why my connection with UBC was superficial.

Starting in August 2010 and ending up in July 2019, I lived for nine years on campus during the period when my spouse and I conducted our doctoral studies and graduated from UBC. As noted earlier, upon graduation I returned to Shiraz to open my language school—a dream that turned into actuality due to understanding my subjectivity and the power within—an outcome of my practice of the autobiographical method of *currere*. Prior to completing my doctoral studies, I had been procrastinating when it came to decision-making. *Currere* empowered me and connected me to my resources within.

As a resourceful individual, I embark on the possibilities, dreams, and fantasies my subjectivity discloses in my new place. Being and place are so close that our existential experience invariably occurs in place. I employ this understanding of place in my teaching courses to provide students to convey a grounded understanding of their learning experience. In my IELTS preparation courses, sometimes students do not have convincing ideas to discuss general topics in part 3 of their interview. To overcome this issue, I invite them to relocate themselves, suggesting they visit the place that could give them the required information to develop discussion topics. For instance, I asked Sharareh, who had trouble speaking on children's literature, to visit a bookstore, find children's literature, read the books, and understand what the examiners mean when they refer to children's literature. She visited a bookstore and followed my instructions closely. Locating herself in a new place where she could physically be in touch with the books, she felt more confident discussing topics related to children's literature. This is one example of how place in autobiographical writing can set the scene for exploring self as our existential experience unfolds in the boundaries of time and place. There is an interplay between self and place as place can provide the scene for our being to present itself.

Our existential and educational experience takes place in specific locations. The regressive phase of *currere* can revitalize our existential memory and connect us to being and lifeworld in place. In my autobiographical writing, I typically use my place of residence as a point of entry into my educational experience as it is a concrete aspect of lived experience which connects me to past, present and future memories in four dimensions of *currere*. When writing my autobiography, place can tie me to my learning and teaching experiences. As place is embedded in teacher educational experience and lived memories, deeper layers of place can unfold their meaning within the contextualized stories of teachers (Barane, Hugo, & Clemetsen, 2018). Regarding the deep meaning of place, Elbaz-Luwisch (2014) describes her chapter on memory as "resemb[ling] a meandering stream that curves back on itself at times, but still arrives, eventually at a wider and deeper place, a fuller understanding of memory in its connections to teaching and pedagogy" (2014, p. 2). This paradoxical understanding of place in autobiography reveals its deeper layers of memory as one *curves back* on self. As a stream meanders on its bed, teacher subjectivity (being) is contextualized and localized by its place. The interaction between teacher subjectivity and context provides new meanings as in my case—being an Iranian-Canadian educator—my teaching experience is shaped by both contexts.

I could hardly imagine starting an autobiographical research in Iran, probably because of the prevalent quantitative research methods or due to my experience of displacement in Vancouver that contributed to an emerging of an autobiographer in me. The interaction between teachers and place opens a constant dialogue between them as the stream is not confined to its bed and can expand its bank. The interactive dialogue between teachers and place can provide new understanding and meaning for students, teachers, and place.

Place and Social Space. Autobiography is composed in a constant dialogue between local place and subjectivity of teachers. There is a deeper relationship between self and place understanding which gives us a sense of the psychological and social forces directed towards self. Place shapes self and accords identity and structure to teacher subjectivity. My pedagogy, methodology, and practice communicate with my place and are informed by place. Without place, our understanding of these aspects of teaching becomes decontextualized, delocalized, and unsophisticated. Autobiographical understanding of place and social space is closely linked with sociopolitical influences and events in my places of residence. When I compare my teaching experience in Vancouver and Shiraz, I understand both places and social spaces as containing their unique features. My subjectivity communicates differently in the two places of residence as the sociopolitical, cultural, historical, and racial forces vary in both. Edgerton (1991) confirms that autobiography does not exist in solitude as it connects self to place, history, culture, and race:

> Autobiographical writing enables students to study themselves. Such study links self to place, and place is simultaneously historical, cultural, and racial. The autobiography of the "other" - indeed an "other" who shares a geographical place can provide, in a sense, a foil to one's own history. Via another's life one understands more fully one's own, as well as social and historical ties that link both lives to a particular place .... (cited in Kincheloe & Pinar, 1991, p. 78)

Geographical places experienced either as the context of residence in autobiographer's first-hand experience or as narrated in other autobiographical accounts can link the audience to their individual, historical, and cultural circumstances.

Being and place have a cordial reciprocal relationship; being subjectively present is manifested in place and takes the characteristics of its place. Edgerton (1991) writes that to understand place in curriculum studies, one should be familiar with the concept of "other", "difference", and "them and us." She invites teachers and other curriculum workers to teach in ways that "reincorporate the excluded" and avoid "othering" people (Edgerton, p. 78). She refers to an allegorical understanding of home as place and notes that othering people in their home can reinforce the concept of Greene's *estrangement* (1973) in teacher education. Through facilitating teacher connection with place and understanding teacher social, political, and historical space, curriculum can become an interactive medium of inclusion and mutual understanding. Teachers' connection to place and interaction with place can construct their vibrant social space. Thinking autobiographically links teachers to place and makes them conscious about their social and political space. Teacher autobiography without acknowledging its place and social space sounds like a river without its bed stream and bank. By connecting to social and historical space, teachers will include *others* in their own (auto)biography to prevent the process of self/other alienation in educational experience. Others are an integral part of teacher social space and understanding self and other in such social space is mutually inclusive.

In my school, I understand some students do not feel connected to their social, political, cultural, and racial space and are not well grounded. In my psychoanalytical counselling sessions, I invite them to observe the place where their primary schooling experience has occurred. They regress to their early schooling experience and retrieve the memories. Once telling their stories, they typically encounter certain gripping moments understanding the sources of which takes my ontological, psychoanalytical, and hermeneutic knowledge. I share my understanding of the tensions in their subjectivity and invite them to regress to their educational experience and excavate their memories so that they will independently understand their schooling experience fully. As understanding the sources of unease within takes academic research and erudition, most of them prefer to postpone exploring self and the world within. Teachers can examine their own educational experience and emerging social space prior to transferring their transformative learning experience to their students. Upon understanding their own social space, they can transfer this knowledge to their teacher candidates and students as teacher knowledge of self can transcend its boundaries and immediate space of emergence to be transferred to others in school. Teacher autobiographical knowledge enables this transcendence as self—once well developed—spontaneously communicates with its sociopolitical, cultural, racial, and educational space to transfer this useful understanding to other teachers.

Place and Emergence. In an emerging understanding of subjectivity, place signifies different meanings for curriculum theorists and practitioners. For instance, Pinar (1991) discusses that studying place is a form of "social psychoanalysis" that enables the students to "emerge as figure" (Kincheloe & Pinar, 1991, p. 165), and participate critically in their historical present. Regarding Pinar's understanding of place, students are social and historical beings actively engaged in their self/other creation. So, place is an emerging space of active participation in creating one's historical being and social identity. In her chapter in *Curriculum Intertext*, Lynn Fels (2003) refers to an aesthetic aspect of curricular places of possibility. Fels understands curriculum as a narrative that connects us to imaginative spaces:

> My work investigates curricular places of possibility, absence, and disruption realized through performance. Performance not as process nor as product, but as breath, intermingling, unexpected journey landscapes reeling against the sky in a sudden moment of recognition. I am curious about the spaces that we breathe into being through imaginative play and exploration, curricular spaces that open to us with invitation. (Fels, 2003, p. 173 cited in Hasebe-Ludt & Hurren, 2003)

As confirmed, the spaces that we breathe into construct our social and political spheres informed by being. Teachers' being as the source of imagination, creativity and aspiration breathes transformative meaning into curriculum development. Student subjectivity becomes intermingled with this transformative space as self is in touch with social and historical spheres. The possibilities that teachers and students can imagine for themselves are shaped by their understanding of subjectivity. Without imagination, could teachers envision future possibilities within and exceeding the boundaries of their emplacement? Fels' conception of performance is helpful here, as it encompasses lived memories and future opportunities of self-education as breaths going in and out every second—a moment of consciousness within. As our breathing, the emerging experience of place can occur constantly. In regressive phase of *currere*, autobiographers start with conscious breathing in and out once they get ready to retrieve their educational stories. Our understanding of place can be perceived as an emerging experience of self as it communicates with others.

Engaged with their autobiography, teachers can understand the conscious power of curriculum within to connect with the breathing space of themselves, learners, and sociopolitical sphere. Teachers who delve into their personal space using autobiographical research can create a caring and empathetic place of emergence for themselves and their students so that they experience transformative education.

Understanding place will encourage teachers to facilitate students' progressive movement in curriculum studies. Renee Norman (2003) describes Aoki's autobiographical conception of places in-between in curriculum:

> Ted spoke of place, and he dis/placed us in many different spaces and locations and in-betweennesses of curriculum. All these whispers, all these places, the movement between where we are, where we've been, where we're going, and all the many places in-between. (Norman, 2003, p. 256 cited in Hasebe-Ludt & Hurren, 2003)

Teacher subjectivity is thus constantly constructed in a dialogue with past, present, and future. Teachers and educators are continuously in movement as their autobiographical being is informed by their memories and possibilities. Norman understands Aoki's conception of place as an imaginative, creative, and imminent space of possibilities.

The place of in-betweenness in Aoki's term can refer to teachers' cross-contextual and cross-curricular lived experience—the conscious transformational experience within from one place of emergence to another—or the shared space between the teachers and students in curriculum. More particularly, teachers are invariably emerging into new possibilities in their transformative journey within time-space and the possibilities arising from their time-space travel. Autobiography is intermingled with place and autobiographers assume self, informed by place—either as physical, psychological, or psychoanalytical. As human beings, we are situated in place and our autobiographical being responds to the conditions and boundaries of place. Our memories are bound to place. For example, reflecting on my past in a high-rise student study center on UBC campus, I was reminded of my graduate studies in Shiraz University. During my graduate studies, I stayed on the 11th floor of a high-rise dormitory [*Mofatteh*] and studied in its penthouse on the 13th floor. As I recall my memories as a graduate student in Shiraz University, I advanced to my present as a doctoral student, and visualized my future in teacher education in academe, finding my place of emergence in-between past and present. The imaginative understanding of place and emergence in Fels, Aoki, and Norman's idealization can hardly fit into a procedural curriculum as memory travels beyond imposed structures of curriculum and constructs its own meaning of curriculum. Without an overview of curriculum movement, an innovative understanding of concepts such as voice and place and how memory constructs our reality informed by these notions seems to be impossible. What follows is a brief overview of a specific curriculum movement, recapitulating the origin of autobiographical understanding of curriculum.

The Curriculum Reconceptualization Movement

Over the past fifty years, a movement from behaviorism to cognitivism has occurred in understanding curriculum that focuses on mental process to understand cognition which emerged in the 1960s and 1970s in the United States. The cognitivist paradigm specifically argued that the "black box" of the human mind can be opened, and its content can be analyzed to be understood. While behaviorism studied human behavior in a series of stimulus-response reflexes as in animals followed by reinforcement and punishment to control the behavior, cognitivism [in response to behaviorism] inquired into human intellect. That move represented an effort to move scholarly attention from externals—behavior—to internals, teachers and students' minds. A parallel move—located not in educational psychology but in curriculum studies started in the 1970s, inaugurated at the historic 1973 University of Rochester (New York, USA) Curriculum Theory Conference.

From that conference, the movement known as the reconceptualization was underway. Inspired by existential, phenomenology, and neo-Marxism, a series of scholars devoted themselves to replace the sequential curriculum with the critical curriculum, one skeptical of taken-for-granted assumptions and determined to understand curriculum as an ongoing (if complicated) conversation enabling students to understand themselves, the worlds they inhabit, while working for the worlds they want for future generations. The conception of curriculum that emerged accented the entwined relations between students and teachers' subjectivity and the larger society. The movement introduced a progressive understanding of learning which concentrated on the teachers and students experience of the subject material. Before the reconceptualization, conventional notions of curriculum had centered upon designing and planning the subject materials covered as the course books at schools that overlooked the main participants of the courses—the students and their teachers.

As noted, elements of the movement were political; for instance, Apple, Giroux, Kincheloe, and McLaren saw students and teachers not as agents but as victims of political oppression. As Zhang Hua writes, instead of following a top-down system in which the teachers were the sole transmitters of knowledge and their students as the products shaped by that premade knowledge, the reconceptualized movement introduced an innovative bottom-up understanding of curriculum (Zhang & Pinar, 2015) which considered the subjectivity of each individual teacher and student as the pivotal point of curriculum. These political scholars shared the "bottom-up" idea concentrating on subjectivity and emphasized stories of individual teachers and students reflecting on their educational experience. Interest in the scholarly study of subjectivity from ontological [relating to the nature of being] and phenomenological [philosophical study of existential experience] perspectives increased. Learning from students and teachers' narrative inquiries through lifewriting, biography, autobiography, ethnography, and autoethnography increased (Clarke, 2012; Cohen & Porath, 2013; Leggo, 2012). Inquiries into educational experiences of each individual student and teacher opened a new space to learn about their personal stories, including social determinants and aspirations. These lived narratives provided a unique opportunity for the researchers and authors to share their unique stories within their academic communities and for the readers to learn about and from the lived experience of each author. Prior to the movement, the prescribed curriculum was largely founded on subject materials and marketing understanding of education discussed in the following.

The Movement and Tylerian Proceduralism Standardization

Tero Autio (2003) argues that the reconceptualization took place on two levels. On the school and teacher level, the movement rejected marketing concepts of "accountability, competitiveness, and performativity" (p. 302) while valuing the importance of the students and teachers, their needs, values, emotions, and learning experiences. The reconceptualization represented a repudiation of the marketization of education which embraced the Tylerian model connected to standardized tests. Instead of focusing on standardized assessment, reconceptualist scholars helped educators and their students perceive and value their individual meaning and subjectivity at the center of education and content materials.

The key thinkers were William Pinar, Maxine Greene, Madeleine Grumet, Ted Aoki, Dwayne Huebner, James B. Macdonald, Max van Manen, Janet L. Miller, David Jardine, and Donald Vandenberg (Magrini, 2015). These theorists and scholars all focused on the subjective meaning of teachers and students' experience of the official curriculum, committed to teachers and students' well-being, thriving, and transformation. It was William Pinar who invoked the Latin infinitive form of curriculum—*currere*—to denote students' and teachers' lived experience of curriculum. Pinar developed the autobiographical method of *currere* in 1975—that allowed the educators and their students to practice learning about their subjectivity, including its social and political aspects. I will elaborate on Pinar's autobiographical method and its social dimensions in self-development in more detail later, both as the point of entry to understand my own educational experience and prior to opening a dialogue for teacher personal and professional development in the following chapters. Without a conscious understanding of my own capabilities, possibilities, and fantasies using *currere*, opening a dialogue with my professional and academic communities seems futile.

The Autobiographical Method of *Currere*

Autobiographical theories of curriculum were pioneered by Pinar's (1975a) autobiographical method of *currere* that challenged the traditional understandings of curriculum by drawing on phenomenological and existential traditions of thought. To supply the field of education with a substantive theoretical framework through which we understand human educational experience, Pinar introduced *currere* (Pinar & Grumet, 1976). From the Latin infinitive form of curriculum, *currere* means "to run the course" or "the running of the course" (p. 18). It is a journey in the course of one's educational experience; this conception provides an alternative to the dominant understanding of curriculum development and assessment of materials and strategies. Rather than seeking to formulate objectives and outcomes, the method is, in my view, an approach to life. *Currere* draws upon the phenomenological, psychoanalytic, existential, and hermeneutic meaning of thought to challenge hegemonic understandings of curriculum development as exclusively procedural.

The earliest interest in *currere* is traceable to Pinar's 1972 article titled *Working from Within* (Pinar, 1994a) in which he suggests that teachers start from the prefigurative or preconceptual sources of inspiration and imagination within them. Inspired by the abstract expressionist painter Jackson Pollock (Szafran, et al., 2014), Pinar notes: "Like some modern painters, my students and I have come to feel that we rarely need to refer to subject matter outside ourselves. We work from a different source. We work from within" (Pinar, 1972, p. 10). Later, Pinar (1975a) outlined twelve features of traditional schooling which self-alienated children by distracting them from self-love and autonomy, and an atrophy of fantasy life and esthetical perception. In authoritarian schools, he concluded "we graduate, credentialized but crazed, erudite but fragmented shells of the human possibility" (p. 381). He sets the stage for the development of an autobiographical method for curriculum inquiry in his finalizing paragraph: "What configurations this loyalty to one's subjectivity must take, and what such configurations mean for theorists of the process of education are not yet clear. To these questions, we must proceed next" (Pinar, 1975a, p. 382).

Pinar's portrait of education reminds me of my high school educational experience during which the students were crazed to compete for achieving higher scores overlooking their personhood and subjective well-being in the process of learning experience. In Iran, the educational system is founded on credentialization during which students compete for achieving higher scores. I recall the time when I was imploring my biology teacher in grade 10 in high school to give me a higher mark so that I could get a higher grade-point average and rank first in our class. My educational system could be based on individual learning and achievement than competition by which students were divided into successful (high score achievers) and unsuccessful (low score achievers). Years later, when I got a full-time lecturer position in Arsanjan University, I was careful not to judge my students' personality based on the scores they achieved and respect their humanity apart from the scores they attained. Now, I understand due to credentialism, many graduate students with high scores are looking for a job. Of note, most of these high-achiever applicants can be said to have been crazed by the educational system and they are threatened with the loss of their creativity, critical thinking, and analytical reasoning. What they gain is test anxiety.

Once teaching IELTS preparation courses in my language school, I use psychoanalytic and hermeneutic understandings in my doctoral studies at UBC to consider the sources of tensions and remove the psychological obstacles prior to the actual teaching process. Most of my students are obtaining their IELTS score to immigrate to Canada and I am wondering if their subconscious mind considers immigration as an escape from the tensions within? Are they satisfied with their being and becoming? Did their educational experience provide a joyful understanding of self? How can moving to another country release the tensions in these anxious students?

To reverse this undermining experience of education, teachers and students can work from within to re-educate themselves using the autobiographical method of *currere*. As Miller asserts, *currere*—both a concept of curriculum and a form of inquiry—interrogates the students and teachers' "inner experiences and perceptions" rather than external learning objectives and school-subject content (2010b, p. 62). Once connected to their inner world, this transformational experience can provide a conscious meaning of their subjectivity as a point of entry to self-education. This transformative experience for me started with understanding how my subjectivity was shattered due to my educational experience. Once anxiety penetrates self and divides self into small pieces, the power of self is reduced as it is not a complete whole. Fragmented self is weak. Educational experience might deliberately or undesirably produce fragmented individuals that are easy to control and rule over. My tensions inside were due to undesired pieces in my subjectivity that made me uncomfortable, incompetent, and incomplete. In test situations like interviews, for instance, I was unable to demonstrate my actual competence and depth of knowledge. I became frustrated once I failed in major job interviews or when my performance fluctuated in professional and academic video conferences. I could see some pieces in me were working against me to make my subjectivity weak and inefficient, specifically in tense situations where I felt literally helpless, nervous, and fragile. The autobiographical method of *currere*, however, contributed to my reconstruction of self—a self that I can live with peacefully and confidently with a caring support for self and others. Now, my self does not work against me as I experience coherence, connection, and equilibrium in all my attempts. This is the power of subjectivity revealed using *currere*. I am happily, joyfully, and non-judgmentally engaged with my social and political spheres and in love with the meaning of life. From within, I spread pure joy and happiness to my surroundings as I am connected to my coherent ego—solid understanding of consciousness. Once I keep silent, there are no mental distraction and noise to take away or decrease my peaceful reflection and contemplation. I can feel my breath coming in and out and the constant rebirth of my ego. I am in touch with my moments. I bracket now moments to understand their individuality and meaning.

Grumet considers *currere* as almost parental in its potential: "As *currere* simultaneously acknowledges the students' experience and encourages them to distance themselves from it, *currere* is repeating the patterns of ego development initiated in the infant's early object relations" (1976, p. 128). Acknowledging one's educational experience which takes a great deal of autobiographical work precedes distancing self from the experience. Teachers understand the capacity of ego through these processes and can then push the boundaries prescribed by their educational experience. In my autobiographical experience, *currere* detached me from undesired aspects of ego such as test anxiety when I reflected on my educational experience and discovered how my subjectivity was entangled with anxiousness rather than consciousness. Once your subjectivity is occluded by tensions within, mind is controlled by rushed [typically false] decisions and judgments as the engagement prevents the brain from ordinary processing consciously.

Currere distances the autobiographer from the non-ego—the curriculum—to facilitate an entry into one's false self, constructed due to one's educational experience to release ego from non-ego. Once ego is rescued from the tensions caused by curriculum using the reflective study, subjectivity arises from its bed to explore its new meanings, possibilities, and fantasies. This is when the autobiographer experiences a rebirth—an utter feeling of joy and connectivity within. The autobiographical method facilitates one's engagement with political, public and intersubjective domains. Pinar (2011) proposes that by inquiring into the lived experience through the autobiographical method of *currere*, teachers can seek a new meaning of self and reconstruct their educational experience. Through *currere*, teachers can observe, understand, and reconstruct their subjectivity that has been constructed through educational experience and apply this innovative understanding to their teaching context. This emancipatory journey opens teachers to untapped layers of meaning and consciousness within as in my case I experience no anxiety following my explorative journey with the method. Pinar's concept of *currere* (cited in Norris, Sawyer, & Lund, 2012), views "a person's life as curriculum" (p. 12) and involves "an act of self-interrogation in which one reclaims one's self from one's self" (p. 13) once one analyses and synthesizes the meanings of life that one carries. The method seeks "an architecture of self, a self we create and embody as we read, write, speak and listen" (Pinar, 1994c, p. 220), and through which one can "reconnect the minimalized, psychological self to the public, political sphere" (p. 219).

Interestingly, this explorative journey within is an unsolicited adventure through which the explorer will experience tense moments of energy release.

I recall times when I burst into tears as I curved back to my memory to review early schooling experience. I could observe myself as a helpless child oppressed by curriculum with no care to rescue me. I was so fragile and innocent once I was penalized, tortured, and tormented in my primary school. I recall the time when my math teacher in grade three imprisoned me in the classroom as I was not listening attentively or the time when I clean forgot to complete my assignments. She allowed all students leave and shut the door at me when I was only nine years old. I was crying hysterically when no one opened the door. For about five to ten minutes, I was left alone in a four by four-meter cream room with desks in five rows and an old blackboard. Once released by the principle of the school after my math teacher had already left, I dashed home so that my parents would not notice my late arrival as that could make a new problem. And I am wondering why some of my primary school teachers could torture and torment students who were not attentive for certain psychologically-rooted reasons such as hyperactivity, fidgeting, attention deficit disorder, or simply lack of motivation?

Currere has contributed to my well-being by studying my school experience including dramatic memories and has furnished an understanding of my subjectivity vis-à-vis the tensions within to create my reality. Discovering a non-ego constituent in my subjectivity and more significantly eliminating this undesired twist from my psyche took an unassisted penetration into educational and existential experience—a rewarding yet arduous journey.

Overcoming psychological barriers such as resistance, understanding ontological and phenomenological meanings of the lifeworld, connecting to the existential realities of other autobiographers, reconstructing fragmented minds constructed by banking education, and understanding the hermeneutic meaning of existence all contributed to reconstructing my subjectivity and connecting to the world within. Once reality is reconstructed, students, teachers, teacher educators, activists, and scholars can make problematic the status quo in schools and provide directions in a dialectic sphere of curriculum as indicated in the aspirations of the *Currere Exchange* conference and journal (http://currereexchange.weebly.com).

Pinar (2004) argues that academic [intellectual] freedom—achieved through *currere*—is the necessary condition of education:

> What can we do? First, we must understand our situations, both as individuals and as a group. For the sake of such understanding, I employ the concept of *currere* - the Latin infinitive of curriculum - to denote the running (or lived experience) of the course, in this instance, the present historical situation. This autobiographical

method provides a strategy for self-study, one phase of which seeks synthetical moments of "mobilization" when, as individuals and as teachers, we enter "the arena" to educate the ... public. That arena (the public sphere) - now a "shopping mall" in which citizens (and students) have been reduced to consumers - can be reconstructed in our classrooms by connecting academic knowledge to our students' (and our own) subjectivities, to society, and to the historical moment. (Pinar, 2004, pp. xiii–xiv)

Understanding self begins from within. *Currere* introduces self to self—an understanding that is taken for granted in school curriculum. Through autobiography, one can observe the distance within and start to know the meaning and lifeworld overlooked. In regressive moments, the autobiographer retrieves the memory to identify the pieces of puzzle. Future dreams and fantasies comprise other pieces of riddle once the autobiographer progress to explore more unraveled meaning. Analyzing such memory takes the autobiographer to deeper understanding of being—one's lifeworld. *Currere* reconstructs subjectivity following its synthetical dimension once the autobiographer creates the meaning of lifeworld, education, and educational experience.

When synthesizing my memories and dreams, I could realize myself free from the tensions of non-ego in my subjectivity. In my rebirth, I am in full control of my reality as I create the meaning of life. In my outer circle once connecting to my graduate students, I am invariably confident in understanding their reality and analyzing their meaning of life to contribute to their feeling and being in the world. My non-judgmental analysis of their reality is due to my freedom from non-ego that could distort the perceived meaning. In my thinking process, I am engaged in a hermeneutic understanding of lifeworld which let the meaning unfold itself—a moment of creation. Teachers can employ the autobiographical method of *currere* composed of four existential phases; regressive, progressive, analytic and synthetic during which one's educational experience is respectively recollected, envisioned, analyzed for the present reality, and synthesized for a deeper understanding of self (Pinar, 2012) to transform self. Once educators mobilize themselves during synthetical dimension of *currere* following self-examination and self-study, they can transform their understanding of education and reconnect to their social and political spheres.

The temporality of *currere* arises out of human being's existential reality. Humans are temporal beings and autobiography can study such temporal reality as lived experience. In their temporality, human beings can seize now moments—present time. Their past is lived experience of the world and the future is an envisioned possibility that will unfold in time. Regressing to the lived experience and progressing to the future fantasies provides an in-depth understanding of the present understanding which helps the autobiographer to look into the world wonderingly and inquiringly.

The Significance of Subjectivity in Curriculum Studies

In curriculum studies, if we consider only one single aspiration for educational experience, it can be self-education as the foundation of a healthy society. Without self-fulfilled individuals who can understand the strength of their voice and contribute to their public sphere, democracy loses its power. I will discuss the dialogic aspects of subjectivity and self-development in curriculum studies in detail in Chapters 3 to 5. Dewey (1916) considered educational experience as a bridge that connects self to society. Once individuals realize the significance of their subjectivity through studying their educational experience, they can contribute to building a dynamic society as private and public intellectuals.

In my IELTS preparation courses, I encourage graduate students to connect to their social space following their understanding of self—such conscious [anxious] understanding of self typically emerges in tense situations such as in IELTS exam. Being exposed to test-centered curriculum and banking education, my students all show the symptoms of test anxiety before or in IELTS exam. Teaching in my language school in the 7th floor of a building with a spectacular view in Maliabad neighborhood in Shiraz, I open the window and invite my students to have an overview of the place they reside. Those students in my class with test anxiety usually might not be well-connected to their surroundings, context, and society as their anxiety has disconnected them with their place of residence. When I encourage them to reconnect to their physical context and feel the beauty of their ambience, they find my approach to life engaging and refreshing. Being conscious of test anxiety inculcated due to banking education, I understand how self-reflective study of educational experience can transform their understanding of being and their social engagement. To facilitate self-education, I introduce some books on psychology and psychoanalysis apart from IELTS so that they understand the power of subconscious mind which can help them connect with their subconscious mind and present moments.

Before my doctoral studies, I could hardly have imagined opening my own language school independently. *Currere* empowered me to become an independent thinker, creator, and educator who could transform his individuality and is committed to helping students to develop their subjectivity by broadening their lifeworld experience. This rich and rewarding experience is my main motivation as I can empower my students to improve their self-reflective and meaningful learning experience in their context of residence and observe the joy of their transformative learning experience. Curriculum in this sense becomes a personal, individual, social, and political process. Pinar emphasizes that subjectivity is significant to study and teaching, and it is not separable from the social and political:

> The significance of subjectivity is that it is inseparable from the social; it is only when we—together and in solitude—reconstruct the relation between the two can we begin to restore our "shattered faith in the regeneration of life" (Lasch 1978, 207) and cultivate the "moral discipline ... indispensable to the task of building a new order" (Lasch 1978, 235–36). Our pedagogical work is simultaneously autobiographical and political. (Pinar, 2004, p. 6)

As Pinar notes, subjectivity is not restricted to an autobiographical understanding of self, and encompasses our social and political experience. Understanding and reconnecting to our self is an introduction into understanding the nature of institutionalized knowledge we have experienced which can prepare us for sociopolitical enactment. Self and the context where self builds a connection with its community or society are in a closely-knit relationship. In my dialogue with students, teachers, and friends, my autobiographical knowledge of curriculum achieved during doctoral studies contributes to transformative conversations on self and the tensions they might feel within such as test anxiety inculcated due to banking education in Iran. When self thrives as a result of self-reflective learning experience, the interactions with social and political spheres become inevitable. Self does not exist in vacuum so the knowledge gained relates to social and political domains.

Michael W. Apple (2004) underscores an understanding of this aspect of knowledge for economic, social and political transformation:

> It is important to realize that while our educational institutions do function to distribute ideological values and knowledge, this is not all they do. As a system of institutions, they also ultimately help produce the type of knowledge (as a kind of commodity) that is needed to maintain the dominant *economic, political, and cultural* arrangements that now exist. I call this "technical knowledge" here. It is the

> tension between distribution and production that partly accounts for some of the ways schools act to *legitimate* [emphases are mine] the existing distribution of economic and cultural power. (Apple, 2004, p. xxii)

In what way is it possible to understand one's subjectivity without studying the legitimate knowledge one has acquired in educational experience? Understanding our true self is only possible by a reconstruction of the legitimate knowledge acquired in our curriculum. That is the reason why understanding one's subjectivity through an introspective journey is significant in curriculum.

Maintaining the existing economic, political, and cultural arrangements take its toll on subjectivity meaning that once curriculum is targeted at inculcating its ideological values and producing legitimate knowledge, individual differences are taken for granted. Legitimized knowledge as the main objective of curriculum can be produced once individual differences are sacrificed as individuation means understanding each student and designing curriculum based on their personal, emotional, psychological, and spiritual values which is possible in small class sizes where teachers favor one on one quality time for individual student prosperity and well-being. Curriculum, however, induces legitimized knowledge to produce like-minded students who follow the existing ideological values and knowledge. Curriculum in this sense is the main agent responsible for introducing the non-ego constituent to students' subjectivity to craze them. Using the self-reflective method of *currere*, teachers and students can regress to their educational experience to understand the non-ego constituent as the main source of unease within. Without an introspective study analyzing self-meaning and releasing from the psychoanalytical tensions inculcated by curriculum, ego will not be freed from non-ego to understand lifeworld. The outcome of autobiographical study is reconstructing the autobiographer's subjectivity and understanding personal, social, and political spheres. That is how autobiographers experience a rebirth by the end of their introspective study.

As curriculum endeavors to legitimize technical knowledge, from my experience with graduate students teaching IELTS preparation courses following my engagement with *currere* and hermeneutic understanding of lifeworld, I understand how my schooling experience has legitimized illegitimate knowledge in myself and my students. My students have their master or doctoral degrees with a high-grade point average from distinguished universities in Iran. Their legitimized knowledge acquired in banking education, however, has largely produced anxious students who are used to memorizing chunks of language. Their critical thinking and reasoning ability is minimal which is noticeable when I take them out of their comfort zone to discuss and develop new topics. I encourage them to improve their argumentation power which they usually find the most difficult in their challenge with IELTS. One major issue I encounter with the self-development of my students prior to taking the test is their attitude which is related to the subconscious mind. Subconscious mind as the source of power can communicate constructive meaning once it is well developed through a personalized curriculum. Subconscious mind is the engine of our psyche empowering subjectivity. Legitimized knowledge can produce distorted subconscious mind in students and teachers so that their self-concept and self-image become shattered. Once self-understanding is smashed, the inner voice of students submits gloomy images and disapproving signals as ego has lost its strength.

Using autobiographical studies, teachers and students can connect to themselves and to their social and political arenas once they understand how legitimized knowledge has alienated them and inculcated a false understanding of self instead. *Currere* provides this innovative understanding of our subjectivity in relation to others as Morris (2015, p. 106) asserts; "Autobiography can change our relationship with each other because we understand relations differently." This transformation is because of a new understanding of self which relates to our social and political domains to transfer subjective understanding of our lifeworld. Without examining self, students and teachers will not be able to identify their true self. Subjective reconstruction entails a transformative understanding of self by the autobiographer to create new meaning of educational experience which is achievable using self-reflective study.

Subjectivity and Evaporation of False Ego (Superficial Self)

Inquiring into our educational experience can provide an understanding of our subjectivity—"the lived sense of self"—that is taken for granted in "circumstances of everyday life" (Pinar, 2006, p. 3) and can begin a self-reflective and hermeneutic approach to lifeworld. Understanding an allegorical sense of self-actualization as a journey, Wang (2004) proposes that a physical journey might give rise to a third space "a space of creating one's own subjectivity among and through the multiple layers of the self" (p. 9). This inner journey to a third space is enabled through studying our educational experience and nurturing our subjectivity through a "complicated conversation" (Pinar, 2004, p. 188) with ourselves and others. The foundation of a complicated conversation is based on a complicated self that can be understood using *currere* to synthesize the meanings of lifeworld. After the evaporation or shattering of false ego—the superficial self the psychoanalyst Winnicott saw as a defensive facade (see Abram, 2012)—which follows regression to educational memories, progression to future possibilities, and analysis of the accounts, it is proper time to mobilize self through synthesis to understand one's latent meaning in the present. Here the autobiographer involves in a hermeneutic understanding of lived experience to connect with ego freed from undesired attachments and legitimized knowledge to experience self-mobilization that is a prerequisite for social and political mobility for teachers as Pinar (2004) confirms:

> Public education structures self-formation and social reconstruction while, in many of its present forms, it blocks both. Teachers ought not be only school-subject specialists; I suggest that they become private-and-public intellectuals who understand that self-reflexivity, intellectuality, inter-disciplinarity, and erudition are as inseparable as are the subjective and the social spheres themselves. (p. 10)

As Pinar writes self-formation is taken for granted by public education which is the main source of discomfort and unease in the subjectivity of students and their teachers.

Without subjective reconstruction, how can teachers whose subjectivity is constructed by public schooling contribute to their own and their students' well-being? Construction of our subjectivity using autobiography is the preliminary step required for social reconstruction as superficial ego does not own the integrity and power for social and political reformation. To accomplish self-formation using self-education, educators can unlock the blocks engineered by curriculum prior to connecting with social and political spheres. Teachers and teacher educators as facilitators of self-education themselves and for the students in the educational system can understand the strength of self-erudition and include this self-awakening knowledge in their daily teaching practice. Working from within as an intellectual pedagogy and practice can equip teachers and teacher educators with a fuller understanding of their true ego disguised by legitimate knowledge. This ongoing engagement with subjectivity in curriculum studies can open fresh pathways to self-understanding and evaporation of distorted ego for teachers, educators, and students. Using self-reflexivity, teachers will understand the unexamined possibilities of education once they let go of their false ego which can prevent self-connection.

I recall the time when I was invited to parties by my colleagues and university professors at Arsanjan Azad University. As I was enjoying their company, I experienced a feeling of lack—a hollow place—within. As an extrovert who was the joy of the gatherings and get-togethers, I showed to be joyous outside with a sense of disconnection inside. The path to my ego was blocked by tensions within—the unease manufactured by public-school curriculum. I tended to tell my personal stories in parties to friends but as I turned to the deeper layers of educational experience, I could see lack within which made me uncomfortable. Those colleagues around me thought I was always satisfied with my life, however, that accounts they received were superficial as deep inside I felt deeply anxious, nervous, and incompetent. When telling my educational stories, I paused and preferred not to go any deeper. Part of my ego was silenced and quietened. I could feel without understanding my early schooling experience and reconstructing my educational experience, I was unable to understand myself. There was a disconnection in my psyche—a gap. I was into philosophy, deep thinking, and keeping my daily journal. Learning about philosophy provided a meaningful understanding of life, however, I was looking for a hermeneutic and interpretive understanding of life where I could understand the holistic meaning of life vis-à-vis my subjectivity. I needed to attune my subjectivity into lifeworld, to readjust my traditional learning lens, and to reconstruct my subjectivity. However, anxiety controlled my mood, decision-making, and thought system. I easily became angry, upset, and irritated. I failed in many major interviews, I recall. In tense situations such as a presentations, performances, exams, or interviews, an integral part of me did not collaborate well and worked against me so that I experienced failure and dissatisfaction.

Through my autobiographical research in doctoral studies, I could reclaim my peaceful and tranquil self, reconstructing what Pinar terms "an architecture of self" (1994b, p. 219). Understanding my coherent and integrated self and connecting to my subjectivity could give me a strong sense of lived experience and a deep feeling of joy within. Every morning, I wake up with a hermeneutic understanding of self and lifeworld. I am looking forward to hearing good news, meeting great people, and experiencing exciting moments. My autobiographical time and place give me a deep understanding of lifeworld as I can observe my subjectivity connected to the universe. Life to me starts from within as outside world reflects my feelings, emotions, and thoughts. Now, I am curriculum the same as *currere* is understanding and running the course of lifeworld. Who is the runner of the course if not me? Following an excavation of self and understanding my subjectivity using the hermeneutic phases of *currere* once analyzing and synthesizing my educational experience, my ego becomes released. Following an evaporation of false ego—anxious self—I can understand "integrity", a complete sense of wholeness and coherence. Owing to my coherent subjectivity, I can contribute to the well-being of my graduate students in my language school using my psychoanalytic, hermeneutic, and autobiographical knowledge. This is how my autobiographical understanding of the world has contributed to the construction of my academic community and social sphere. I can vividly recall the time when I was unconfident creating course syllabi, outlining school planners, or mapping course design. As my students were cheerfully engaged with their learning experience in my classes, I was hesitant if I was doing it right. Following my doctoral studies, I am confident I can succeed in running my language school and encouraging my graduate students to start from within to reconstruct their understanding of educational experience. I never doubt my possibilities as my understanding of lived experience and curriculum development originates from within. I shine and let the world shine around me. Once I am with people, I feel connected with my inner time and place. When I am alone, I have rendezvous with self. My lifeworld now is replete with self-satisfaction, creation, connectivity, and erudition. I am the creator of my own joy, time, and subjectivity. The light inside me emits prosperity and happiness to the world. My students express their satisfying experience of learning as I transfer my psychoanalytical and hermeneutic understanding of their personal and social development in our transformative dialogue during IELTS courses. Once they learn about the probable sources of their test anxiety from an educational and developmental point of view, they become more enthusiastic to improve their knowledge of self and reconstruct their educational experience using self-reflection, self-contemplation, and erudition. Apart from the IELTS materials we cover at school, my students read books on subconscious mind, the power of now, personal power, life purpose, self-development, and autobiographical writing.

Felman (1993) indicates that "interpretations [of autobiography are] always incomplete, always interminable" (cited in Miller, 2005, p. 53). Although we can never completely understand self, through autobiographical work we can—to the extent external and internal conditions permit—perceive and reconstruct our subjectivity and our subjective understanding of biographical and educational significance. Autobiographical theories have provided me with a self-reflective method to create a more authentic relationship with self and to be more fully myself. I have noticed that my understanding of teaching pedagogy and practice has been transformed towards an individualistic curriculum and personalized approach to education. My relationship with students is not exclusively centered on subjects or materials, it is, however, oriented towards their individualistic and subjective approaches to learning and being I am enabled to understand their individual and personal learning styles and existing circumstances. Understanding new dimensions of my subjectivity has made me feel grounded in my existing social, cultural, and educational spheres. I participate more in academic and non-academic social activities, have contributed to my Iranian-Canadian diaspora in cultural gatherings and religious rituals, and feel meaningfully connected to my present and past educational experiences.

The sense of belonging to a new place of residence has always been a contentious issue for many immigrants, as their lived experience becomes cross-contextual and trans-cultural, and their educational memories have been engraved across places of residence (see Trigg, 2012). As a global citizen, I am reconstructing my subjective meaning and reality through academic scholarship, erudition, and my trans-cultural lived experience has favored me a conscious understanding of place. My coherent and sustainable understanding of subjectivity has contributed to my critical as well as creative engagement with inner and outer worlds as a human, student, teacher, researcher, and educator. Following my reflective and contemplative thinking and writing, this inclusive understanding has helped me to transcend the boundaries of false self, pre-structured by a procedural understanding of curriculum and pedagogy. Reflective analysis and synthesis of learning experience is perhaps specific to human mental capacity which allows us to reconstruct our learning experience and consequently our subjective understanding of self, inculcated during our educational experience. Autobiographical study excavates such rich experience to unravel its latent meaning and create unexplored understanding of one's being existing in educational experience. Without this self-reflective, self-analytic, self-synthetic, and self-contemplative learning experience, understanding our true self and connecting to deeper layers of meaning, inner, and outer worlds seem impossible.

Free Association and *Currere*

To facilitate a self-exploratory study of educational experience, *currere* invokes the psychoanalytic technique of free association (Freud, 1920). One freely examines one's thoughts, memories, dreams, and fantasies without prompting or intervention. Freud claimed that this technique reveals three obstacles often blocking the process of self-realization and self-actualization: *transference*, *projection*, and *resistance*. Transference is the process of transferring feelings and emotions one has for one person or group to a different person or group. I learned the concept of transference once I received feedback on my first writing assignment in an unclassified course on curriculum issues and theories by Professor Pinar in summer 2014. To explain the meaning of transference, I can give an overview of my early schooling experience. In my primary school, I remember my painful experience of being bullied by classmates because of my Farsi-Turkish accent. To find a well-paid job when they were young, my parents moved from Tabriz—a city in the north-west of Iran where residents speak Azari-Turkish—to the capital city of Tehran where people use the official language of Farsi. They were married in Tehran and all the children were born there. The language spoken at home with parents was mainly Azari-Turkish. Siblings, however, switched to the official language of Farsi once talking to each other or sometimes with parents. Our code switching provided a bilingual comfort zone at home where we could use both languages; nevertheless, at primary school I was bullied due to my accented Farsi pronounced with typical Turkish phonemes (identified as units of sound that distinguish one word from another in a language). Reflecting on my early schooling experience, if I blame the policy makers or curriculum specialists for my experience of being bullied by my classmates, I might be transferring my emotions and feelings triggered by students to policy makers. Transference is largely due to one's anxious mental processing once ego is interfered or blocked by non-ego constituents such as stress and anxiety.

Another obstacle preventing self-actualization is *projection* which is the process of projecting one's own qualities to a different person. This phenomenon is prevalent in those with narcissistic personality disorder. To conceal their personality disorder and darkness within, narcissists might project their own personal characteristics to others such as their partners or friends. For instance, once they feel down and depressed they will project this feeling to others and blame their partners or friends for being depressed. For narcissists, projection is used as a strategy to protect the false self as their connection with self is lost during their development.

Finally, *resistance* is the process of blocking out specific feelings, emotions, or memories. This obstacle prevents the patients from being able to analyze and synthesize certain feelings and memories of lived experience. Their mental analysis is blocked to transformative understanding of self and lifeworld when encountering certain emotions or memories as they are not able to analyze new circumstances and prefer to protect their own understanding. Transference, projection, and resistance obstacles can be removed using free association in autobiographical studies once the researcher curves back to analyze and synthesize lived experience. Once these psychoanalytically-identified obstacles are released, autobiographers can make sound judgments and decisions as such non-ego constituents will not interfere in their analysis and synthesis of lived experience to make appropriate making of life.

Currere employs a modified version of free association whereby teachers explore their own educational experience in four phases. There is freedom in the autobiographical method of *currere* that provides an unassisted technique for the teachers to explore their untapped memories of their educational experience and unravel new meanings following the analysis and synthesis of their memories. Pinar (1975b) considers free association as a non-judgmental or non-evaluative focus on one's lived experience, enabling one to excavate latent emotions, feelings, and memories and make the preconceptual lifeworld—"*lebenswelt*"—more accessible (p. 389). Free association encourages the surfacing of repressed emotions or forgotten memories that can be concealed underneath our consciousness yet present, in our unconsciousness. Bringing the concealed memories to consciousness will reveal latent meaning and create greater awareness of the present for students of themselves. Pinar contends that this consciousness—subjective presence—through free associating can make the researcher a more "existential" being (1975b, p. 390) in a sense that it empowers the researcher to more readily acknowledge existing emotions and feelings, and to reflect on their sources and origins to achieve a deeper understanding of current lived experience.

Free association has facilitated an unassisted access to my educational experience and provided a deeper penetration into forgotten experience, intensifying my sense of being alive, present in the world. By removing the psychological obstacles using free association in *currere*, I understand truer meanings of being, reality, and my lifeworld.

Bracketing

During the entire autobiographical process of *currere*, the participants practice suspending their judgment and distancing themselves from everyday phenomena through a process called bracketing (as it is referred to *in the phenomenological literature*: Chan, Fung, & Chien, 2013; van Manen, 1984). Bracketing enables greater awareness and an expansion of our lifeworlds (Pinar et al., 1995, p. 406). Distancing self from lived experience is crucial, as without taking this measure, self and experience can be so closely entangled that studying experience becomes impossible. To understand lived experience, Husserl (1931) considered direct seeing as looking beyond preconceptions which transcends common sensory experience. To Husserl, bracketing or "disconnecting" (1969, p. 58) as a process of phenomenological reduction provides a non-judgmental and non-interpretive understanding of images one recollects when analyzing one's existential experience. Judgment and interpretation of lived experience can distort our understanding of existential reality; that is why bracketing provides a pause, a moment allowing us to observe our lifeworld non-judgmentally, to see what's actually there. Once teachers' educational experience unfolds itself during regressive and progressive phases of *currere*, teachers can analyze and synthesize the autobiographical accounts to understand their existential reality and interpret new meanings of lifeworld.

Unlike other educational studies that mainly concentrate on the end-products—such as the findings, conclusions, abstractions, and generalizations confidently claimed as "knowledge"—*currere* slides underneath these end-products to "pre-conceptual experience that is their foundation" by making use of the phenomenological process of bracketing (Pinar & Grumet, 1976, p. 41). Through ongoing engagement with existential reality using the method of *currere*, the autobiographer discloses deeper layers of lifeworld as autobiography considers no findings and conclusions final, insights on a path of self-understanding. In such self-study, there exists no final product as the process of increasingly deeper understanding is the main motive. By alleviating the "potential deleterious effects of unacknowledged preconceptions," teachers can suspend both internal and contextualized thoughts [their so-called natural attitude] so that they will be able to reveal their educational narratives (Tufford & Newman, 2012, p. 81). I understand this process as suspending my negative feelings and attitudes regarding educational experience and observing how my knotted reality unravels itself in a non-judgmental mode of being. As preconceptions can structure (and thereby distort) the meaning-making process of *currere*, I employ bracketing to disconnect from my unconscious presuppositions to explore latent meanings.

Aoki notes that in reflecting on their everyday routines, teachers are advised to place their attitude "in brackets" (2004, p. 121), clarifying their feelings, emotions, and actions to "go beyond the immediate level of interpretation of curriculum X." Bracketing provides teachers with a reflective space to freely explore their own meanings and interpretations of everyday educational labor and expand the boundaries of what's possible in their teaching. The method of *currere* encourages new meanings and understandings, enriching teacher narratives as non-judgmental study of educational experience can unfold transform meanings and one's reality within. Teachers' non-judgmental understanding of existential experience can empower them to transcend their routinized practices as they connect them to their conscious mind. Aoki (2004) worries that "often actions are without thoughts," as teachers are submerged in their day-to-day routine, attempting to implement the official and planned curriculum; he invites teachers to go beyond the "immediate exigencies" of their school day to make a "conscious effort to examine the intentions and assumptions underlying their acts" (p. 131). Without a conscious and non-judgmental understanding of educational experience using bracketing, it may be impossible to excavate dormant meaning of education, being, and self. Bracketing can provide a contemplative space for teachers to reflect on their attitudes and practices so that they will include "lived curriculum" in their routine planned curriculum (p. 420). Such reflective process using bracketing can improve the thoughtfulness of teachers, leading to more self-conscious, nuanced and attuned practices in their teaching practices.

It is important to employ bracketing when teaching and counselling so that students feel connected to their caring teachers, so they may confide their personal stories. In my counselling sessions with some of my students, I use bracketing to understand the conveyed meaning precisely. One of my students, Niloofar, opened a dialogue with me regarding her father's narcissistic relationship with her. Taught to be a dependent individual, she now understands that she sought her self-image and self-concept in her father's approval. When listening to her personal stories, I attempted to bracket my judgment and preconceptions so that the reality of her lifeworld could convey itself clearly. Once talking about her father's attitude regarding her educational achievements, she burst into tears. Because I can distance myself from her experience, I can achieve a non-judgmental understanding of her accounts, I listen attentively and empathetically so that she can express her emotions and deep feelings freely. Using my understanding of her lived experience, I offer my psychoanalytical and hermeneutic interpretations of the sources of her codependency.

When I provide some of my analyses and syntheses of her educational experience, she agrees, taking some notes, including formulating strategies to overcome her codependency and develop her personality more multidimensionally. My self-conscious and non-judgmental understanding of her existential experience using bracketing provided her with a kind of comfort zone enabling her to reveal her personal stories and trust me as an empathetic teacher who is there to help.

Temporality of *Currere*

Wang (2010) emphasizes the inner workings of temporality in *currere* as she considers the "inner time, external time, and pedagogical time" (p. 275), studying her students' writings and interviews to understand the process of transformative learning experience for her students. In her in-depth study, she focused on different dimensions of temporality in the method of *currere* to understand the way transformation is effected. She appreciates that in regressive moments of self-inquiry, students who keep silent might not be able to express their feelings and emotions due to the "grip" (p. 279) of those past experiences that can be loosened by attentive teachers who understand temporality of *currere* and its deep knowledge of psychoanalysis. I understand how the grip of the past can disable students and teachers to act freely in the present. In my IELTS preparation courses—to reduce test anxiety—I invite those students who cannot express their feelings and emotions to regress to their past educational experience. One of my students confessed that she was not able to regress as she could not find anything but darkness inside. She was horrified to know of this seemingly pervasive darkness within herself. Suggesting that she could have lost her connection with her true self due to her past educational experience, I encouraged her to excavate the darkness using the regressive phase of *currere*. I understand expressing the fact that she could find nothing but darkness inside could also be an entry to light and a transformative understanding of self. During my doctoral studies, it took me almost three years to free myself from the grip of the past, and come to a transformative understanding of educational experience, from which I created new meanings of my lifeworld. As I was transformed, I recognized the power of my subjectivity and being. Teachers can support students to overcome the grip of the past as they can consciously discern their inner obstacles. Probably it might take time for students to become ready to accept, understand, and overcome their blocks through autobiographical knowledge and academic erudition.

Using free association, my students can examine the temporality of their being-in-the-world as they curve back to their repressed memories to understand the sources of disconnection and unease, thereby release their true self from tensions of the past, including test anxiety. Pinar asserts that release from tensions of the past is indeed possible: "Work with the past, release from it, allows loosened identification with fear of the future, and allows heightened intuitive sense of where one may go" (1994b, p. 59).

Although release from the tensions is possible, in my experience this stage is the most painful and agonizing phase of autobiographical study, as subjective reconstruction starts from acknowledging—even re-experiencing—the tensions of the past during the regressive moments of *currere*. During my autobiographical research prior to writing this book, the grip of the past on me manifested itself as resistance to new meanings and understandings of my lifeworld. I had been aware of the tensions within; however, overcoming the obstacles and tensions within takes courage and persistent self-work. After all, subjectivity is constructed throughout our existing experience and reconstructing subjectivity starts with its deconstruction during which one's educational memories can be retrieved, reviewed, analyzed, and synthesized. There is no easy way out. This psychoanalytical and hermeneutic penetration of the past can be intensely educational, even therapeutic; however, the autobiographer must acknowledge the existence of the grip prior to removing it.

What if the researcher believes there is no grip? Perhaps there is none. But if there are learning difficulties, there is a hidden history whose revelation and analysis can alleviate those difficulties. One's inner voice, or intuition, or even subconscious mind may be the main source of inspiration that can support self-study, academic learning and erudition. The autobiographer's subconscious mind needs empathetic support and care from the conscious mind to release from the tensions within. The self-self relationship is key. Our conscious mind can provide caring support once it becomes strong enough using autobiographical research, psychoanalytical knowledge, hermeneutic understanding, and erudition. Understanding one's autobiographical being across time in regressive and progressive moments of *currere* can empower the autobiographer to understand self and temporality of existence. Huebner (1999) emphasized the temporality of education; being-in-time leaves one open new possibilities in education.

He referenced Heidegger's *Being and Time* (1962) as the most helpful source in his groundbreaking elaboration of the concept of temporality in education:

> I do not intend or presume to provide either a presentation or an interpretation of this phenomenological ontology as he [Heidegger] develops Dasein's temporality . . .. "Dasein's totality of being as care means: ahead-of-itself-already-being-in (a world) as being-alongside (entities encountered within-the-world) . . .. The 'ahead-of-itself' is grounded in the future. In the 'Being-already-in . . .' the character of 'having been' is made known. 'Being-alongside' becomes possible in making present". (Heidegger, 1962, p. 375, cited in Huebner, 1999, p. 136)

This understanding of human being as a time-bound creature is practiced in my engagement with *currere* as the method starts with Dasein's [human being] already-being-in-the-world and progresses to Dasein's ahead-of-itself-in-the-world prior to analysis and synthesis of the autobiographical accounts to understand one's existential and educational experience.

Currere as an autobiographical method deals with temporality of being as it studies subjective experience within time. Our temporality can be appreciated as memories of the past or as fantasies of the future, book-ending our present. By valorizing regressive moments, visualizing future fantasies, analyzing [understanding], and synthesizing [re-integration] the themes that are revealed, release from the past and increased awareness of the present will occur for students of *currere*. Regarding our understanding of being [*Dasein*] and time, Huebner (1999) writes:

> [Dasein] does not simply await a future and look back upon a past. The very notion of time arises out of man's existence, which is an emergent. The future is man facing himself in anticipation of his own potentiality for being. The past is finding himself already thrown into a world. It is the having-been which makes possible the projection of his potentiality. The present is the moment of vision when Dasein, finding himself thrown into a situation (the past), projects his own potentiality for being. Human life is not futural; nor is it past, but, rather, a present made up of a past and future brought into the moment . . .. Education recognizes, assumes responsibility for, and maximizes the consequences of this awareness of man's temporality. (Huebner, 1999, p. 137)

Being-already-thrown into a situation, and envisioning ahead-of-time in the situation makes human being a temporal reality. The present moment is an expression of past lived experience, restructured by future fantasies, each swirling in a fleeting moment of now. An ongoing engagement with the temporality of educational experience can provide a conscious understanding of *their* time and being.

Concluding Notes

As the notion of time arises out of human being's existence, the autobiographical method of *currere* enables us to grapple with temporality of being in the world. Immersing myself in the progressive dimension of *currere*, I can visualize my academic prospects as an emerging scholar and committed teacher. Involved in teaching, co-teaching, presenting, publishing, and researching, I am observing, envisioning, planning, and enacting moments of possibility in my academic profession and future accomplishment. Recalling my past educational experience as an English language educator, I recall a traditional curriculum marked by pre-structured learning to understand the way those dialogic moments with a few of my teachers created a supportive space to vocalize my voice. My present situation—informed by past and present educational experience and animated by fantasies of the future—informs me as an individual, a student, a teacher, an educator, and a researcher to enter "the public sphere" to connect "academic knowledge to our students' (and our own) subjectivities, to society, and to the historical moment" (Pinar, 2004, p. xiv). Freed from the constraints of a traditional schooling [test and stage anxiety] I experience as an emancipatory movement in curriculum research. Releasing self as a transformative academic experience using the autobiographical method of *currere* becomes the point of entry to the question of teacher development. In the following chapter, I connect autobiographical research with teacher development to understand the way this emancipatory field of research can transform our traditional understandings of curriculum.

References

Abram, J. (2012). *Donald Winnicott today*. New York; London: Routledge.
Aoki, T. T., Pinar, W. F., & Irwin, R. L. (2004). *Curriculum in a new key: The collected works of Ted T. Aoki*. Mahwah, NJ: Lawrence Erlbaum Associates, Publishers.
Apple, M. W. (2004). *Ideology and curriculum*. Routledge. Retrieved June 10, 2018, from https://doi.org/10.4324/9780203487563.
Autio, T. (2003). Postmodern paradoxes in Finland: The confinements of rationality in curriculum studies. In W. F. Pinar (Ed.), *International handbook of curriculum research* (pp. 301–328). Mahwah, NJ: Lawrence Erlbaum Associates.
Barane, J., Hugo, A., & Clemetsen, M. (2018). *Creative place-based environmental education: Children and schools as ecopreneurs for change* (English ed.). Stroud, Gloucestershire: Hawthorn Press.

Chan, Z. C. Y., Fung, Y. L., & Chien, W. T. (2013). Bracketing in phenomenology: Only undertaken in the data collection and analysis process? *The Qualitative Report, 18*(59), 1–9.

Clarke, A. (2012). Burgeo and back: Catching oneself in the act of being attentive to pedagogy. In A. Cohen, & M. Porath (Eds.), *Speaking of teaching: Inclinations, inspirations, and innerworkings* (pp. 55–62). New York: Sense Publishers.

Cohen, A., Porath, M., Clarke, A., Bai, H., Leggo, C., & Meyer, K. (2012; 2013). *Speaking of teaching: Inclinations, inspirations, and innerworkings*. Papendrecht: Sense Publishers.

Dewey, J. (1916). *Democracy and education*. New York: Macmillan.

Edgerton, S. (1991). Particularities of otherness: Autobiography, Maya Angelou, and me. In J. Kincheloe & W. Pinar (Eds.), *Curriculum as social psychoanalysis: The significance of place* (pp. 77–79). Albany, NY: State University of New York Press.

Elbaz, F. (2014). *Auto/biography and pedagogy: Memory, and place in teaching*. New York: Peter Lang.

Freud, S. (1920). *A general introduction to psychoanalysis, by Sigmund Freud, LL. D. authorized translation, with a preface by G. Stanley Hall*.

Greene, M. (1971). Curriculum and consciousness. *Teachers College Record, 73*(2), 253–269.

Greene, M. (1973). *Teacher as stranger: Educational philosophy for the modern age*. Belmont, CA: Wadsworth Publishing Co.

Grumet, M. R. (1976). Psychoanalytic foundations. In W. Pinar & M. Grumet, (Eds.), *Toward a poor curriculum* (pp. 111–146). Dubuque, Iowa: Kendall/Hunt Publications.

Grumet, M. R. (1988). *Bitter milk: Women and teaching*. Amherst: University of Massachusetts Press.

Grumet, M. R. (1990). Voice: The search for a feminist rhetoric for educational studies. *Cambridge Journal of Education, 20*(3), 277–282.

Hasebe-Ludt, E., & Hurren, W. (2003). *Curriculum intertext: Place, language, pedagogy*. New York: Peter Lang.

Heidegger, M. (1962). *Being and time: A translation of sein und zeit*. New York: Harper & Row.

Huebner, D. E. (1999). *The lure of the transcendent: Collected essays by Dwayne E. Huebner*. Mahwah, NJ: Lawrence Erlbaum Associates.

Husserl, E. (1931). *Ideas: General introduction to pure phenomenology*. New York; London: Allen & Unwin.

Husserl, E. (1969). *Ideas: General introduction to pure phenomenology*. New York; London: Allen & Unwin.

Kincheloe, J. L., & Pinar, W. F. (1991). *Curriculum as social psychoanalysis: The significance of place*. Albany: State University of New York Press.

Leggo, C. (2012). Poetic inquiry. In A. Cohen, M. Porath, A. Clarke, H. Bai, C. Leggo, & K. Meyer (Eds.), *Speaking of teaching: Inclinations, inspirations, and innerworkings* (pp. 83–108). Sense Publishers: New York.

Magrini, J. M. (2015). *New approaches to curriculum as phenomenological text: Continental philosophy and ontological inquiry*. Palgrave Macmillan.

Miller, J. L. (1990). *Creating spaces and finding voices: Teachers collaborating for empowerment*. Albany, NY: State University of New York Press.

Miller, J. L. (2005). *Sounds of silence breaking: Women, autobiography, curriculum* (Vol. 1). New York: Peter Lang.

Miller, J. L. (2010a). Curriculum as a consciousness of possibilities. *Curriculum Inquiry*, 40(1), 125–141.
Miller, J. L. (2010b). Autobiographical theory. In C. Kridel (Ed.), *Encyclopedia of curriculum studies* (pp. 61–65). Thousand Oaks: Sage Publications.
Morris, M. (2015). Currere as subject matter. In Ming Fang He, Brian Schultz William Schubert (Eds.), *The sage guide to curriculum in education* (pp. 103–122). New York: Sage Publication.
Ng-a-fook, N. (2005). A curriculum of mother-son plots on education's center stage. *Journal of Curriculum Theorizing*, 21(4), 43–59.
Norman, R. (2003). Whispers among places in curriculum intertext. In E. Hasebe-Ludt & W. Hurren (Eds.), *Curriculum intertext: Place, language, pedagogy* (pp. 243–258). New York: Peter Lang.
Norris, J., Sawyer, R., & Lund, D. (2012; 2016). *Duoethnography: Dialogic methods for social, health, and educational research*. Walnut Creek; Chicago: Left Coast Press, Incorporated. doi: 10.4324/9781315430058.
Oakeshott, M. (1959). *The voice of poetry in the conversation of mankind*. London: Bowes & Bowes.
Pinar, W. F. (1975a). Sanity, madness, and the school. In W. Pinar (Ed.), *Curriculum theorizing: The reconceptualists* (pp. 359–383). Berkeley, CA: McCutchan.
Pinar, W. F. (1975b). *Curriculum theorizing: The reconceptualists*. Berkeley, CA: McCutchan Publications.
Pinar, W. F. (1994a). Working from within (1972). *Counterpoints*, 2, 7–11. Retrieved from http://www.jstor.org/stable/42975618.
Pinar, W. F. (1994b). *Autobiography, politics and sexuality: Essays in curriculum theory 1972–1992*. New York: Peter Lang.
Pinar, W. F. (1994c). Autobiography and an architecture of self (1985). *Counterpoints*, 2, 201–222.
Pinar, W. F. (2004). *What is curriculum theory?* Mahwah, NJ: Lawrence Erlbaum Associates.
Pinar, W. F. (2006). *The synoptic text today and other essays: Curriculum development after the reconceptualization*. New York: Peter Lang.
Pinar, W. F. (2011). *The character of curriculum studies*. New York: Palgrave Macmillan.
Pinar, W. F. (2012). *What is curriculum theory?* New York, NY: Routledge.
Pinar, W. F., & Grumet, M. R. (1976). *Toward a poor curriculum*. Dubuque, Iowa: Kendall/Hunt Publications.
Pinar, W., Reynolds, W. M., Slattery, P., & Taubman, P. M. (1995). *Understanding curriculum: An introduction to the study of historical and contemporary curriculum discourses*. New York: Peter Lang.
Phelan, A. M. (2005). A fall from (someone else's) certainty: Recovering practical wisdom in teacher education. *Canadian Journal of Education*, 28(3), 339–358.
Phelan, A. M. (2015). *Curriculum theorizing and teacher education: Complicating conjunctions*. London; New York: Routledge. doi: 10.4324/9780203387078.
Szafran, Y., Pollock, J., Martin, S., & J. Paul Getty Museum. (2014). *Jackson Pollock's mural: The transitional moment*. Los Angeles: J. Paul Getty Museum.

Trigg, D. (2012). *The memory of place: A phenomenology of the uncanny*. Athens: Ohio University Press.

Tufford, L., & Newman, P. (2012). Bracketing in qualitative research. *Qualitative Social Work, 11*(1), 80–96. doi: 10.1177/1473325010368316.

van Manen, M. (1984). Practicing phenomenological writing. *Phenomenology + Pedagogy, 2*(1), 36–69.

Wang, H. (2004). *The call from the stranger on a journey home*. New York: Peter Lang.

Wang, H. (2010). The temporality of *currere*, change, and teacher education. *Pedagogies: An International Journal, 5*(4), 275.

Zhang, H., & Pinar, W. F. (2015). *Autobiography and teacher development in China: Subjectivity and culture in curriculum reform*. New York, NY: Palgrave Macmillan.

2

AUTOBIOGRAPHY AND TEACHER DEVELOPMENT

> To understand the knowledge that teachers possess, we need to know it in the way that the *individual teacher* does. More importantly, as outsiders and researchers, we need to understand how teachers evolve, develop, and change their practical knowledge, and how they perceive this experience. These arguments imply an interest in the teacher as a unique *person*, and as a *learner* who possesses and develops a special type of knowledge, which is significantly influenced and shaped by experiences in various contexts.
>
> (Richard Butt & Danielle Raymond, 1989, pp. 405–06)

Introduction

In my first chapter, I inquired into my own educational experience using the autobiographical method of *currere*. Starting with an abbreviated account of my educational experience, I drew upon the related literature and discussed the ways I achieved deeper understandings of my learning journey. I inquired into the notions of voice and place as key conceptions in biographical and autobiographical research; I provided an overview of the curriculum reconceptualist movement and the emergence of the method of *currere*, emphasizing the significance of subjectivity. I explained free association and bracketing as phenomenological processes and I discussed the temporality of *currere*. I concluded that my inner work mobilized me to enter public and political domains through connecting pedagogical knowledge to my students' [and my own] subjectivity, paving the way for teacher development. With the self-knowledge achieved through reflecting on my educational experience as an English language educator and researcher, I expanded on my understanding of autobiographical research in teacher development. I critique the "rigidity of a top-down centralized system" (Zhang, 2015, p. 49) that so often has characterized traditional systems of schooling; I explored autobiographical self-study as a bottom-up process in educational experience. Elusive questions such as "Who am I as a teacher?" and "In what way will this learning help me to better understand and learn about myself as a teacher?" and "In what sense will this conscious self-knowledge contribute to an understanding of the field of teacher development?" animate my self-reflective research, this autobiographical study. The question I am posing in this chapter is: How can autobiographical research contribute to teacher development?

Problematizing Education

Noddings (2006) reminds us that Socrates advocated self-understanding and insisted that "unexamined life is not worth living" (p. 10). She suggested that an education that does not invite such exploration and self-reflective learning should not be labeled *"education."* In problematizing the nature of education, Britzman (2009, p. 28) puts forward a phenomenological issue:

> We have grown up in schools, have spent our childhood and adolescence observing teachers and our peers, and when we enter the field of teacher education, this avalanche of experience we have undergone, made from schooling, confirms itself (Britzman, 2003b, 2006). Growing up in education permeates our meanings of education and learning; it lends commotions to our anticipations for and judgements towards the self and our relations with others.

As Britzman appreciates, our educational experience *permeates* our meaning of education which in turn structures our judgment towards self and other. Why is it critical for teachers to study their own educational experience? In what way would one know what educational experience one has undergone without a self-inquiry into that experience? To what extent can one's grades or descriptive semi-annual reports reflect the education one has experienced and, more importantly, the inner journey one has undergone? Self-understanding in teacher development invites teachers and their students to inquire into their educational experience to examine their lifeworld and permeated meaning which is the only approach to understanding their concealed meanings. This self-exploratory learning journey commits teachers to understand their educational experience by writing their autobiographical account of education and reflecting on the related literature. Through reading teacher autobiographical research, teachers and teacher educators are encouraged to reveal their own lived stories and examine the way their educational experience has permeated their understanding of education and teaching practice. By revealing autobiographical accounts of their educational experience, teachers can understand their meanings of learning, teaching, education, schooling, and curriculum and can understand their educational experience more fully. Untold stories such as first-hand educational experiences can open new pathways to teacher understanding and can problematize traditional understandings of education once they are shared.

Prior to my autobiographical research in my doctoral program, I suffered from acute test anxiety. I recall the times that I failed crucial exams and interviews due to test anxiety. These were disappointing and disabling experiences, especially considering the test-based curriculum dominating the competitive world of education. I lacked the desire to compete that the curriculum required me to possess. Being a father of two, my failure affected the socioeconomic status of my family. During my journey of self-study during my doctoral program, however, I overcame my anxiety. I recall the time when I was being trained to work as an IELTS examiner in Vancouver. In my first exam, I was so anxious that my coordinator noticed. When I finished my doctoral program, I was totally in control of my mood and I could understand my students' own anxious feelings during interviews. After finishing my doctoral program, I moved to Shiraz and transferred my IELTS examining certificate and career. As all candidates in Iran have been exposed to test-centered curriculum and banking education, they are often anxious during their interviews with me as an examiner. Now I can understand how much these candidates are anxious. *Currere* (as running the course has) educated me to constantly contribute to my own and other students' well-being.

When candidates enter the interview room and sit on their seat facing me, I ask them to begin with a deep breath reminding me of the regressive moments of *currere*. I show them by example what I mean by taking a deep breath. When they notice my peace and composure in front of them with closed eyes following a deep breath, they are encouraged to follow me.

They give their positive response once asked if they are ready to start the interview. In their follow-up feedback once completing their online forms in their emails or adding comments in the center Telegram, they add inspiring remarks on how my treatment has made them feel comfortable and relaxed in test situation. I can help them overcome or reduce their test anxiety during their interviews as I have studied my educational experience using autobiographical writing to reconstruct my subjectivity, understand the meaning of being, and get rid of test anxiety. I have received reports from other IELTS candidates that their examiners could not facilitate a peaceful and accommodating test situation to eliminate or decrease their test anxiety when taking the test.

The main reason why the examiner's attitude can determine the candidate's relaxed or anxious performance goes back to our educational system and curriculum. Experiencing a top-down educational system in Iran, students are expected to achieve confirmation of their thinking process from a higher position in educational hierarchy. Therefore, the examiner's relaxed or anxious mode of being can be a determining factor in the candidate's performance, specifically for those who are at a lower level of proficiency and self-confidence. Most examiners who have gone through a top-down curriculum in Iran have test anxiety themselves so in IELTS interviews they can hardly contribute to their candidates' smooth and comfortable test performance.

Teacher Knowledge. Maxine Greene (1973) considers the teacher as an incomplete project interacting with others in the process of meaning-making, thriving, and becoming. Without problematizing the existential reality and being open to "a multiplicity of realities" (p. 11), in what way would teachers understand the nature of their own existential and experiential reality? Greene reflects on teaching as philosophy in progress and proposes that teachers can be open to problematizing their philosophy of teaching when they are in dialogue with others. As unfinished articles, teachers undergo a transformative learning experience during both inner dialogue with their own inner world and reality and outer dialogue with other teachers and students in the school (Greene, 2001). Once teachers evaluate their own philosophy of teaching as an unfinished project and reconstruct their own meaning, they are also involved in a dialogic space with their students by inviting them to reconstruct and expand on their own meaning. This transformative learning experience which invites teachers and students as an educational community to problematize their educational experience using experiential inquiry has been discussed by other scholars. Once answering a question on the nature of learning and learner in educational inquiry, Clarke and Erickson (2004) note:

> Our answers, as an educational community, to questions about the nature of the learning process have changed considerably over the past fifty years as we have shifted from a predominantly behaviorist model of learning to more cognitivist and phenomenological models. In fact, there is a much greater diversity of perspectives on learning now than fifty years ago with respect to the preferred ways of thinking about and studying these questions. (p. 43)

Inviting students to inquire into their educational experience is considered as a revolutionary approach to learning by students who have experienced a primarily behavioristic curriculum. In my courses, when I encourage my graduate students to depend on their thinking power rather than memorized chunks once answering my discussion questions in IELTS interviews, they initially find it difficult to value their own critical thinking and reasoning. Once they find their own voice and individual ideas, opinions, and thoughts, they understand how their educational experience has crazed them. Their transformative learning experience starts with overcoming their resistance to understanding phenomenological thinking and being. I share my experience of test anxiety prior to my doctoral degree with them to open a dialogue on their anxiety. Teacher existential, psychoanalytical, phenomenological and hermeneutic knowledge can pave the way for student individual thinking and being. Considering the diversity of learning and teaching, reflective inquiry into teacher educational experience through autobiography reveals the quality of education teachers have experienced. Individual educational stories like pieces of puzzle can unravel new meanings of education and contribute to our specific understanding of such unique educational experiences by teachers and students. Inquiry into the psychological, social, cultural, and political content of each individual teacher will provide a meaningful understanding of education for all teachers and students by encouraging them to understand themselves using self-study, self-education, and autobiographical research.

Remembering and Retelling. Anthony Clarke (2012) attends to pedagogy, noting that his study has emerged from Avraham Cohen's interest in the "inner life of the educator" (p. 58). Following Cohen's curiosity, Clarke wonders if attending to one's inner life as an educator can contribute to one's success in teaching, asking: "If, as Avraham suggests, that inner work has the potential for increasing our consciousness of being in the world, and a greater consciousness enhances the ways in which we relate to the people and contexts in which we live and work, how might catching myself being attentive to pedagogy enhance my teaching practice?" (p. 61). Clarke concludes that it is "the remembering and retelling [of his story] that provides for a rendering of the relationship between teacher and learner" and that "a rendering of self, in whatever shape it might take (in [his] case, catching self being attentive to pedagogy), constitutes inner work" (p. 62). To me, inner work includes my continuous attentiveness to students' experience of learning. The students who attend my English courses would like to improve their proficiency, intending to apply and be admitted to a decent university. Being attentive to my pedagogy using phenomenological knowledge, I can understand their inner obstacles, evident in their mental noise. Some complain about their inability to concentrate and to comprehend when taking the IELTS exam. In my attuned dialogue with them, I examine the sources of their mental noise in their educational experience. Their unconscious mind sends negative messages regarding their competence and proficiency in competitive situations like IELTS exam. When they understand that their mental noise can be quieted through academic study and self-work, they find their confidence in themselves and trust me as their educator. When they are informed about my own mental noise during exams prior to my doctoral study, they trust me and tell me more about their mental processes so that I can contribute to their conscious thinking and emancipatory understanding.

Clarke's notion of "remembering and retelling" reminds me of the autobiographical method of *currere*'s regressive dimension that allows one to recall memories; its conception of "catching self being attentive to pedagogy" resembles Husserl's bracketing or "disconnecting" (1969, p. 58), a moment of watchfulness. The autobiographer remembers repressed educational experiences and starts narrating the stories that thereby surface. Regressing to repressed moments in one's existential experience provides self-contemplative and self-reflective understandings of one's present. During this journey, the autobiographer can bracket time and being in consciousness. Once teachers become attentive to the sources of their present practice, their individual experience of education creates meaningful understandings of the self one is now. Teachers' attentive understanding of history of their pedagogy enables disconnecting from the routine daily practices and reconnecting to self-reflection, triggering transformative educational experience. Autobiography facilitates such transformative experience for teachers; it is the promise of the method of *currere*.

The educational significance of remembering and retelling one's life history is highlighted in other scholars' narratives. For instance, Carl Leggo (2012) asserts his Christian faith and commitment at the onset: "I like Christ—a lot (especially his pedagogical heart, prophetic voice, poetic imagination, and provocative courage)" and states that: "In order to understand the complex and convoluted and conflicted stories that shape my experience of 'inner life,' I need to learn how 'to read again, to go through again' my autobiographical texts as a religious seeker" (p. 85). The only way for educators to bring peace to their students is through being at peace with themselves first. Once autobiographers become attentive to their lived time and place through self-reflective writing, they can experience spiritual moments within themselves and outside, in the world. I respect Leggo's spiritual life as a scholar whose faith in Christ translated into a profoundly welcoming mode of learning and teaching. In my Creative Writing course with Carl Leggo, his love of Christ could present itself as an open, genuine, and deep dialogue with students. Leggo loved all his students equally and taught us all how to listen consciously, attentively, and non-judgmentally.

Leggo's attentive listening reminds me of Husserl's disconnecting—a conscious experience of watchfulness. When educators experience peace and tranquility within, they can bestow feelings of peace and well-being through their teaching. Leggo concludes by citing Palmer's (2004) words on "the traditional binary opposition between light and dark" (p. 85) emphasizing that the only way to bring peace to the world is by being at peace within ourselves. Through remembering meaningful moments in their educational experience and retelling these stories, teachers can bring peace to their students, to themselves, and to the world they inhabit. Remembering can lead to conscious moments of presence. Once teachers travel through their memories and explore their being as it is intertwined in those stories. What we remember and retell structures our present mode of being-in-the-world. Remembering and retelling represent preliminary stages of inner work for teachers and educators to reconstruct their relationships with students and with their lifeworld.

The Seeds of Reverence. In his teacher's credo "Living Poetically," Leggo (2012) delves into his life history in ways that resonated with me. Leggo called his autobiographical story a "tough text full of wonder" and emphasized that educators can restore "reverence" (Woodruff, 2001, p. 38) to its suitable—central—place in education: "To teach reverence", suggested Woodruff, "you must find the seeds of reverence in each person and help them grow" (cited in Leggo, 2012, p. 13). "That is, and has always been, my starting place" (p. 90). Finding seeds of reverence in others is rooted in understanding my own subjectivity as connection with personal sphere facilitates love for others. In my school, I can find the seeds of reverence in each student and show them their best sides of their subjectivity and being-with-others. Anxious students can hardly understand their own subjectivity non-judgmentally. My students typically critique their own personality, agitating their peaceful state of mind constantly. In my dialogue for development, I encourage them to love their own being. Removing the inner obstacle of self-criticism takes rigorous inner work. Once teachers find the seeds of reverence within their own subjectivity and their students, they can teach themselves self-love which begins with understanding self-worth and self-appreciation. In their dialogue with students, teachers and educators are expressing (perhaps indirectly) their self-concept and transferring that self-love to their students. I encourage my students to recreate their self-concept and understand the inestimable value of their subjectivity. I feel deeply committed to psychoanalytical and hermeneutic knowledge in service to their self-development and well-being.

This is one of the main reasons why I returned to Iran upon completing my doctoral degree. My inner voice incessantly reminded me of the urgent need to contribute to the well-being of the students who have suffered banking education in Iran. I could overcome my test anxiety following undergoing the four phases of *currere*, exploring my life history as a student, reconstructing the meaning of my lifeworld, being, and education following release from the tensions within. In my school, I teach students who need my empathetic care to find their self-worth as their educational experience has deprived them of their inner self. It is painful to see students who disown their subjectivity as their self is arrested by inner obstacles due to their educational experience.

My teaching experience in Arsanjan Azad University in Fars Province in Iran—with up to 60 students in General English Language courses—resembled Leggo's first year of teaching in 1976 at R. W. Parsons Collegiate in Robert's Arm, Newfoundland (Canada), with 48 grade-seven students, mostly uninterested. I am wondering why my students were mostly uninterested in being at school and showed a resistance to learning the English language. Was it due to their schooling experience in Iran where English was taught as an additional language with inadequate time—only 2 hours per week? Or was the class size an issue? Could I change their attitude to learning this language? As an educator, in what way could I find and grow the *seeds of reverence* in my students? Without growing these seeds in themselves and in their students, educators can hardly realize full potentials and possibilities of students' educational experience.

The figures and numbers mentioned above remind me of Pinar's critique of educational system when he likens public education to a shopping mall where students are reduced to customers. In the light of Pinar's critique, I can understand the students' feelings about attending school when Carl Leggo recounts:

> Forty-eight grade seven students are a lot of students, and many of them didn't really want to be in school. Many of them didn't know what they were doing in school. The few who wanted to be in school were often upset with everybody else for being noisy nuisances. (Leggo, 2012, p. 91)

In what way can teachers change this attitude in their classrooms towards an understanding of schooling without self-education and-self learning in the first place? It is possible to cultivate the seeds of reverence in the students if teachers have already found, planted, cultivated, and maintained the seeds in themselves properly. Once teachers connect their academic knowledge to their subjectivity, they become capable of transferring this awakening experience to their student, transforming their educational experience. Teachers' self-education is the point of entry to communicating the love of education.

Autobiography in Teacher Education

Pinar et al. (1995) identified three main streams of scholarship linked to autobiographical and biographical research. They indicated that like streams these scholarships occasionally might merge with the themes and methods of one another, however, it is possible to classify these streams as they meander on their own. The first stream they characterize as *autobiographical theory and practice* and it encompasses these major concepts: *currere*, collaboration, voice, dialogue journals, and place. The second stream is characterized as *feminist autobiography* including community and the reclaiming of self. The final stream concentrates on *teachers' biography and autobiography*. This stream, as the focus of my chapter, comprises four categories which I will discuss each scholarship in the following.

Teachers' Biographical and Autobiographical Research

Pinar et al. (1995, p. 553) identified four categories for teachers' biographical and autobiographical research: teachers' collaborative autobiography [Butt and Raymond], narrative inquiry: personal practical knowledge [Clandinin and Connelly], teacher lore [Schubert and Ayers], and studying teachers' lives [Goodson]. Looking at teaching from the inside is noticeable in each of the four categories in autobiographical and biographical research.

In *Research on Teachers' Knowledge: The Evolution of a Discourse*, Freema Elbaz (1991) concentrates on teacher knowledge "from the inside" (p. 2) to understand curriculum as biographical and autobiographical text. Elbaz primarily focused on teacher thinking, the culture of teaching, and the personal practical knowledge of teachers. Schubert used teacher lore to indicate an inner focus on teaching and teacher practice: "We use lore to specifically delineate that knowledge which has guiding power in teachers' lives and work. We are moving beyond viewing knowledge as concepts to include the values, beliefs, [visions], and images that guide everyday work of teachers (a pervasive notion of experiential knowledge)" (Schubert, 1991, p. 224, cited in Pinar et al., 1995).

Elbaz (2005) draws on ideas about teacher knowledge, teacher development and school reform, and focuses on narrative as methodology for understanding the lives of teachers. Elbaz asserts that: "Narrative research makes it possible to pay attention to the wider concerns that shape the work of teaching, looking at the whole lives of teachers and other educational practitioners, and exploring those lives as embedded in multiple contexts" (p. x). Challenging the authoritative discourses of educational policy, theory and research, Elbaz (2014) examines diverse ways of thinking, writing and theorizing from biographical and autobiographical research which is contextualized in teacher practice, and explores the way place-based teaching plays a pivotal role in teacher autobiographical thinking, pedagogical knowledge and practice. Once educators write their autobiography, they can engage in collaborative autobiography to share their personal, educational, social, and political perspectives in dialogue. Sharing ideas, teaching pedagogy, and practice using collaborative autobiography can contribute to educators' self/other education and shared well-being.

Collaborative Autobiography

> The way biography brings together experience, thought, acting, theory, practice, research development and self-education [and wellbeing], and the way it makes

research relationships among insiders and outsiders more collaborative, gives biography, as an epistemology, tremendous integrative, synergistic, and emancipatory potential[s].

(Butt & Raymond, 1987, p. 88)

Richard Butt and Danielle Raymond (1989) emphasized understanding teacher thinking and knowledge through biography and autobiography and claimed that researchers have not paid sufficient attention to this reservoir of untapped knowledge of teachers to understand what knowledge they possess and how they have learned that knowledge. They introduced "life course" research (p. 403) to focus on teachers' perspectives on the changes experienced during their professional practice and what the teachers have learned from such changes.

Life cycle research has been employed in psychology and other applied behavioral sciences like cognitive science and anthropology. Butt and Raymond draw upon this type of research to inquire into the nature of teaching, teacher knowledge and practice and called it "life course" which in reconceptualist research resembles the autobiographical method of *currere* as running the course of life during which teachers explore their lived experience to understand their autobiographical meaning:

> The prime interest of our own work is the nature and development of the knowledge [and understanding] that teachers hold and use. We focus initially on the individual autobiography, looking eventually for commonalities among teachers. We see the process of autobiographical writing as emancipatory and as assisting in teacher development. We see individual case studies, collections of case studies, and the identification of collective commonalities as informing school improvement efforts.
> (Butt & Raymond, 1989, p. 405)

Butt and Raymond (1987) accentuated the strength of biography over phenomenology and claimed that biography highlights the "conscious and unconscious of [lived experience in] the past over the present" and is well suited to understanding teaching experience and the curriculum while phenomenology is obsessed with "the present" (p. 76). Butt and Raymond explored teacher biography and autobiography as educational praxis. Autobiographical and biographical praxis refers to teacher thought, knowledge and experience. Praxeology refers to human action as we are engaged in purposeful behaviors. Butt (1990) asks four fundamental and provocative questions in research on teacher knowledge:

> What is the nature of my working reality? How do I think and act in that context and why? How, through my work life experience and personal history, did I come to

be that way? How do I wish to become in my professional future? (Butt, et al., 1990, p. 257, cited in Pinar, et al., 1995)

Schubert (1991) considers praxis as a combination of theory and practice in teachers' work and focuses on their biographical and autobiographical research to explore the "experiential knowledge that informs their teaching or the revealed stories about their practical experiences" (p. 208). Butt and Raymond identified significant features in teacher autobiographical research such as teachers' personal experience as educational praxis in schools and the necessity of sharing this personal experience in forming teacher community and not only writing their teaching experiences. They believed that collaboration and cooperation is essential in biographical and autobiographical praxis, and considered the teachers as co-researchers in the classroom (Butt & Raymond, 1987, 1988, 1992).

So, collaborative autobiography can open a dialogue among educators and researchers to share their educational experience with each other. Specifically, in critical thinking and reasoning, this method can provide a learning opportunity for the discussants or interlocutors to imagine new possibilities in education. Sharing ideas, thoughts, and educational experiences using the method can strengthen teacher professional knowledge and understanding, and empower teacher community in academic and professional settings.

Narrative Inquiry: Personal Practical Knowledge

> The educational importance of this work [narrative inquiry] is that it brings theoretical ideas about the nature of human life as lived to bear on educational experience as lived.
> (F. Michael Connelly & D. Jean Clandinin, 1990, p. 3)

In teacher development, narrative inquiry follows *currere* as an autobiographical method of inquiry into lived experience of teachers. Narrative inquiry is a process of meaning-making from personal experience mainly through storytelling (Connelly & Clandinin, 1988). Drawing from over twenty years of experience in teacher education in their book on narrative inquiry as a qualitative method, Clandinin and Connelly (2000) discuss teacher experience as lived. They trace the origins of narrative inquiry in the social sciences and offer practical advice for conducting fieldwork and composing field notes. Chambers (2003, p. 230) asserts that Clandinin and Connelly are "undoubtedly Canada's best-known curriculum scholars of narrative inquiry." Chambers indicated that

Clandinin and Connelly (2000, p. 190) discovered that *relationship* is "at the heart of thinking narratively ... key to what it is that narrative inquirers do" (cited in Chambers, 2003, p. 230).

Considering humans as "storytelling organisms" (Connelly & Clandinin, 1990, p. 2), narratives can help teachers to understand their storied lives in classrooms individually and socially and achieve their meaning. Using a variety of methods including journal records, interview transcripts, observations, storytelling, autobiographical and biographical writing, teachers can report and reconstruct their lived experience. Connelly and Clandinin (1988, 1990) propose that teachers enact theories of teaching and learning residing in their heads in their routine practice in the classroom. Personal practical knowledge is a combination of theoretical and practical knowledge rooted in teachers' lived experience. Clandinin (2013) defines personal practical knowledge as: "*Personal practical knowledge* is knowledge which is imbued with all the experiences that make up a person's [biographical] being. Its meaning is derived from, and understood in terms of, a person's experiential history, both professional and personal" (p. 68). Regarding the shared meaning of personal practical knowledge, Clandinin (2013, p. 72) draws upon Dwyer (1979) dialectical and intersubjective understanding of knowledge:

> The research process is, accordingly, an interactive, dialectical one characterized by Dwyer (1979) as "a particular form of social action that creates dialectical confrontations and produces intersubjective meaning". (p. 211)

Teachers negotiate and reconstruct meanings of their teaching experience in class through narrative accounts. The meaning emerged through the process of working together with the researcher in the classroom—when offering interpretations and talking together—as a shared process. Neither teacher nor researcher remains unchanged. The method focuses on the experience of individual teachers and researchers collaboratively and cooperatively. Once teachers discuss their meanings, they examine their own understanding of lived experience in their teaching communities.

Clandinin (2013) states that personal practical knowledge is to be discovered in teachers' routine practice:

> Personal practical knowledge is revealed through interpretations of observed practices over time and is given biographical, personal meaning through reconstructions of the teacher's narratives of experience. Personal practical knowledge is, therefore, found in practice. It is knowledge which is experiential, embodied, and based on the narrative of experience. (p. 69)

Personal practical knowledge mirrors teacher auto-ethnographical studies as teachers' lived experience includes its context of pedagogy and practice as in autoethnography. Aligned with personal practical knowledge, teacher lore unravels teacher autobiographical knowledge and lived stories as a transformative approach to learning and teaching.

Teacher Lore

> We must come to know how students view their worlds [inner and outer] if we want to teach them.
> (William H. Schubert & Ann Lynn Lopez Schubert, 1981, p. 249)

Pinar et al. (1995) consider William H. Schubert as the principal practitioner of this category of research. Schubert (1991) indicated that teacher lore—learning from our own experience—is "the study of the knowledge, ideas, perspectives, and understandings of teachers. In part, it is inquiry into the beliefs, values, and images that guide teachers' work" (p. 207). Like Richard Butt, Schubert explored the concept of praxis in teacher lore to refer to the combination of theory and practice in teachers' experience. Schubert (1991) strived to disclose the experiential knowledge of teachers by narrating their teaching experience and/or the revealed stories pertaining to such experiences. Considering the combined dimension of theory and practice in teaching experience, teacher lore resembles the personal practical knowledge that Connelly and Clandinin discussed. In "Our Journeys into Teaching," Schubert (1992) considers teacher lore as including "both what I have gained from other teachers for my own teaching and what I can offer other teachers from my experience" (p. 9). Through collaborative conversation, our teaching experience can inform other teachers' practice and their teaching experience can guide our teaching practice as well.

Shulman (1987) defined "pedagogical content knowledge" as the capability of the teacher "to transform the content knowledge he or she possesses into forms that are pedagogically powerful and yet adaptive to the variations in ability and background presented by the students" (p. 15). Shulman asserts that teachers should not only understand "the structures of subject matter" [hard skills], but they have to understand "the principles of inquiry" [soft skills] that helps them answer two types of questions in their practice: "what are the important ideas and skills in this domain? How are new ideas added and deficient ones dropped by those who produce knowledge [e.g. teachers and students] in this area?" (1987, p. 9). Knowing content subject does not suffice successful teaching. Teachers can master pedagogical content knowledge to be able to have a meaningful pedagogical experience in the classroom.

"Pedagogical content knowledge" intersects with the notions of "teacher lore" and "personal practical knowledge". All of them underscore specific knowledge in addition to teacher's knowledge of the subject being taught. Schubert (1991) emphasizes the necessity of a community of practice dedicated to ongoing dialogue and collaborative conversation:

> Through these efforts, we hope to encourage the continued consideration of both the reflective process and the context of teachers' experiential repertoires of knowledge and values that give meaning and direction to their work. We hope, too, that teacher lore ... engages collaborative efforts of teachers, scholars, and interested others to interpret praxis in ways that would not be possible without serious dialogue, conversation, and sharing. (p. 223, cited in Pinar et al., 1995)

Using teacher lore, dialogue as a reflective and collaborative process can facilitate learning and teaching. In my personal experience using teacher lore as an English language teacher in productive conversations with another language educator (referenced at the end of Chapter 3), we exchanged our interfaith knowledge and perspectives to understand the way our shared and different values informed our pedagogy and practice. I personally understand teacher lore as a source of knowledge, belief, value, and pedagogical experience that can be only accessible opening genuine dialogue.

Teachers' Lives

> Historical amnesia allows curriculum reconstruction to be presented as curriculum revolution.
> (Ivor F. Goodson, 1989, p. 137)

Goodson and Walker (1991, p. 139) highlight the importance of life history and narrative writing in educational research. Goodson and Walker suggest that "the singer" is more important than "the song," They refer to Robin Morton's (1973) elaboration of the importance of subjectivity in music: "The opinion grew in me that it was *in* the [subjectivity of the] singer that the song becomes relevant. Analyzing it in terms of motif, or rhyming structure, or minute variation becomes, in my view sterile if the one who carries the particular song is forgotten" (cited in Goodson and Walker, 1991). Teachers and students as the agents of education carry the meaning and rhythm of curriculum, and are interconnected with the subject material they study and teach. As the singer and the song are interrelated, we cannot include the singer and exclude the other.

In reconceptualizing education, teachers can find opportunities to articulate their inner voice which is central to teaching and learning. Goodson and Walker (1991) regard autobiographical research will produce a reconceptualization of teacher development: "Primarily the focus has been on the teacher's practice. What is needed is a focus that listens above all to the person at whom 'development' is aimed" (p. 142). In *Teachers' Professional Lives*, Goodson (2002) shows the significance of studies of the teacher's work and life in restructuring the educational status quo:

> Studies of the teacher's life and work throw new light on the 'language of power' which is used within official rhetorics and discourses of educational change (Goodson, 1992). When we look at teaching as lived experience and work, we often find that seductive rhetorics of change pronounced in policy, break down into cynical, contradictory, or resistant voices within the lives of teachers themselves. . . . If we wish to enhance teachers' professional lives, we have to direct our inquisitive gaze at teachers' own experienced worlds, and from there, pose demanding questions to those who seek to change and restructure the teacher's work from above [in a top-down process]. (Goodson & Hargreaves, 2002, p. 22).

Goodson's inquiry into teachers' experience, Butt and Raymond's research on collaborative autobiography, Clandinin and Connelly's study on personal practical knowledge, and Schubert and Ayers' research on teacher lore all explore the lifeworld and lived experience of teachers biographically and autobiographically. Through such work teachers can transform from within. These forms of autobiographical practice can initiate an emancipatory process for educational, social, and political transformation.

Attunement and Self-Understanding

Heidegger (1996) used the term "*Befindlichkeit*"—translated as *attunement* in English or as *disposition* in French (p. xv)—as a phenomenological element which means "being in a mood" or "being situated in a mood." Heidegger's conception of attunement refers to the ways we sense ourselves in situations, and it encompasses both inside and outside feelings. As human beings, we are always situated in a context and respond to our intrinsic feelings, emotions, and thoughts, as well as external motivations, and triggers. To experience attunement, one's understanding of being is open towards what is yet-to-be-established but is-not-yet-there—a feeling of suspension. For Heidegger attunement is being conscious about one's time and place. Through attunement, I can listen to my students more attentively and non-judgmentally. When my students discuss their inner obstacles (such as their resistance to learning, thriving, and well-being), I attune to their voices and subjective presence meaning to understand their untold stories and unexplored situation. During my attunement, I relate to their deeper levels of discussion once I am open to unravelling meanings and understandings of being.

Sometimes students cannot see the main source of their tension and unease, and they might not be able to overcome their inner obstructions of resistance, transference or projection. My psychoanalytic and hermeneutic knowledge—acquired during my doctoral studies—has contributed to understanding such barriers in my students, the removal of which can facilitate their learning experience and develop their subjectivity. With my doctoral knowledge, I can attune to students more fully as I can suspend my judgment, bracket meaning, and relate to their anxious moments by attentive listening. Once I attune to their existential being, the solutions to their inner obstacles reveal themselves. When subjectivity gets attuned to the experience and meaning of lifeworld, phenomenological understanding of my students' existential reality becomes possible. My mindset provides rewarding moments of empathic care and encouraging opportunities of subjective reconstruction for my students, who become invariably delighted by freeing themselves from the grip of the past.

For Heidegger, all human beings find themselves in the world in a certain way which transforms their beings to experience what is there but not completely manifested yet. This world of meaning is awaiting to be explored by human beings. The mental or emotional state necessary to experience attunement has no specific set of conditions; it does not particularly come from inside or outside world. What it requires is the presence and connectivity of being to one's lifeworld. Heidegger understands attunement as sensitivity to what unfolds: "To be in certain attunement means that we have sensibility to see some aspects of things, or that we are capable of understanding things in a certain way. In this way, we can—'unlock'—things as phenomena so that we can grasp them" (Demuth, 2012, p. 15). In my sessions with certain students, attunement gives me the experience of being watchful and conscious while listening to them attentively. So that what is yet-to-be-established is revealed fully.

One of my students, Niloofar—who also seeks my advice on her self-development—was complaining about how her father repeatedly made disappointing comments concerning her educational achievements, reinforcing her fear that she has always been an incompetent student. This dark image of self has taken away all her hopes and aspirations, even her determination to improve her learning skills. I attuned to her situation and asked her to respect her individuality and study the sources of her dependency.

Becoming attuned to my lived experience, I can understand how painful it is initially to reconstruct one's subjectivity to become independent. For me, subjective reconstruction occurred following the analytic and synthetic phases of *currere* as I attuned myself to the lifeworld. Gadamer's hermeneutic interpretation of the world deepened my knowledge of *currere* so I could disconnect myself from the grip of the past and attune to what was yet to be unfolded. This stage of hermeneutic understanding of the lifeworld is self-exploratory, self-reflective, self-transformative, and self-reconstructive.

To understand their being and lifeworld, teachers can remain open, perceptive, and sensible to what unfolds them, what unravels. Wang (2018) uses attunement too: "Describing my own life history (autobiography) provided a new way of experiencing, of thinking, of theorizing. In a phrase, I became more open to myself. I term this attunement" (p. 76). Wang understands attunement as enabling a new way of learning, understanding, and exploring what is unfamiliar and unknown. This understanding of attunement can contribute to teacher development by encouraging teachers to remain more open to self and others.

My experience of attunement keeps me open to and focused on the meaning animating my students. Being receptive to my students' lifeworld gives me a conscious understanding of their learning experience and educational development. Once certain psychological barriers such as test anxiety or codependency threatens their self-concept, I become attuned to their dilemma, working to help them quiet inner noise preventing them from entering their future. By envisioning and constructing a promising future for my students, I can help them orient their subconscious mind towards not-yet-there fantasies (as in progressive dimension of *currere*). Regressing to the past and progressing to the future can reconstruct my students' self-understanding which is essential for their understanding of their existential reality and educational experience.

Heidegger's attunement reminds me of Husserl's conception of bracketing, a suspension of judgment in order to understand one's existential experience. I am also reminded of Noddings' (1984) understanding of *care* as a "feeling mode":

> [To understand the situation] we enter a feeling mode, but it is not necessarily an emotional mode. In such a mode, we receive what-is-there as nearly as possible without evaluation or assessment. We are in the world of relation, having stepped out of the instrumental world; we have either not yet established goals or we have suspended striving for those already established. We are not attempting to transform the world, but we are allowing ourselves to be transformed. This is, clearly not a degradation of consciousness, although it may be accompanied by an observable change in energy pattern. (Noddings, 1984, p. 34)

Attunement occurs, then, with an openness to our lived experience in a world over which we have little control but from which we can learn and teach. Teachers' autobiographical research can attune their understanding-of-being-in-the-world in ways that enable them to become more open to what occurs to and in them. This unique capability of teachers enables them to reflect on their own thoughts, ideas, pedagogy, practice and professional experience in ways that distinguish them as autobiographical beings. Disturbances such as anxiety, depression, and codependency obstruct attunement, slow down the process of being attentive and living in the moment. *Currere* can give teachers a way to understand, think, and analyze by being open to what occurs to them, what unfolds, what is being manifested but is not-there-yet in their everyday practice. This understanding also attunes teachers to what happens without preconceptions, judgments, interpretations, and expectations.

As meaning-making beings, teachers can remain open to new ways of understanding, envisioning, and analyzing as they are getting repositioned [attuned] by new experiences unfolding to them every single moment. Huebner (1999) considers being open to the internal and external worlds for an attuned learning experience:

> Every mode of knowing is a mode of being open, vulnerable, and available to the internal and external world[s]. The form of a human being is [probably] complete and fixed only at death. Aspects of the self and most of the external world always remain beyond the structures and schemes of knowing. Present forms of knowing are always incomplete, always fallible. Behind every confidence and certainty is residual doubt. (p. 349)

To perceive the meanings of their lifeworld unfolding to them, teachers can remain in the mode of incompleteness which helps them clear their mind constantly from preconceptions and presuppositions to understand the meaning of their own and their students' educational experience. As Lipari (2014) notes one can stay open and attuned by listening to people attentively and trying to understand new meanings receptively and responsively. Lipari draws upon a broad range of fields (such as philosophy, psychology, communications, linguistics, sound studies and quantum physics) to problematize our attention to listening as a way of being: "By changing our thinking about listening, we may be freed to dismantle the linguistic prison houses that confine us to misconceptions of our own making about who we are, what we do, and how we might live peacefully with others on this planet" (p. 3). Attentive listening enables connection to others to achieve an intersubjective meaning and opens curriculum spaces for a "multiplicity of realities" (Miller, 2005, p. 47). Listening attentively is not restricted to the human voice (to decipher its implied meaning), as we can listen to other sounds in nature and interpret their various and not always obvious meanings.

Drawing upon such understanding, my doctoral learning experience was not restricted to my academic study. I was—am—in dialogue with my worlds—inner and outer—to study and interpret new world experiences occurring to me. The inner circle of my reflective dialogue attunes me to listening to my breathing rhythm, heartbeat, and conversation as I am reading and writing this chapter. In the outer circle, I am overhearing the voices, sounds and noises in the Beanery where I am sitting behind a table to render my thoughts into meaning to manifest reflections on the paper.

Temporality of Autobiography

Let us return to the question of time, asking what is time? Is time past, present, or future? In what sense is one's past revealed in present? In what way is future revealed in the present? Can one be at the present moment without being in the past or future? What is the relationship between time and being? Is time a part of being or an external phenomenon to being? As curriculum has intimacy with time—it occurs within time—to understand curriculum, these phenomenological questions are essential for reflection and contemplation.

In his great *The Lure of the Transcendent*, Dwayne E. Huebner (1999) invites us to explore the meaning of time by asking a simple question; "What then is time?" and answers it with delicate care and attention as a philosopher of his caliber would do: "But at any rate this much I dare affirm I know: that if nothing passed, there would be no past time; if nothing were approaching, there would be no future time; if nothing were, there would be no present time" (p.136). Huebner (1999) notes that as being is temporal or historical—past, present, and future exist only through human being's existence. The conceptions of learning, objective, or purpose point to the temporality of human being. Educators (and specifically curriculum specialists) strive to find a way to discuss human temporality that will enhance human's "professional power" in the world. Huebner (1999) discusses the reciprocity of time by regressing to the past and progressing to the future that is typical of autobiography in teacher development:

> Both [past and future] are always found intertwined with the present: in the open circle of future and past, there exists no possibility which is not made concrete by real conditions, nor any realization which does not bring with it new possibilities. This interrelation of reciprocal conditions is a historical process in which the past never assumes a final shape nor the future ever shuts its doors. (Huebner, 1999, p. 137)

In teacher development, understanding the temporality of educational experience can contribute to understanding teaching—a process in which teachers negotiate their pedagogical meaning vis-à-vis their educational experience. Having experienced the tensions of a procedural and test-centered curriculum, it took time for me to be able to break the grip of the past, to find my path forward, and then to relate to the time and place of others also eager to find their futures. Teachers can understand their own time and place after reading others' autobiographical accounts, as these can trigger teachers' self-conscious understanding of themselves. I recall the time I started reading autobiographical studies during my doctoral studies; often I felt the autobiographer must be fragile and weak, as their stories were so personal. Gender was in play I later realized. My educational experience in Iran taught me not to write about my inner feelings and emotions as it was not *manly* to reveal one's personal stories, specifically when others can read them! During my doctoral studies, I faced the dilemma to choose between self-reconstruction using autobiography and sticking to my *manly* disposition encouraged by my upbringing and the gendered Iranian curriculum. When I started writing my autobiography, I was surprised how it empowered me to critique my past, alter undesired outcomes of that curriculum (such as anxiety and fear) and replace them with self-love, self-worth, and self-understanding. I learned that autobiographical research can empower teachers to achieve self-understandings of their lifeworld. This transformative experience can change the meaning of lifeworld for teachers and students as inner obstacles are altered, even removed, and hermeneutic understandings of existential experience are incorporated into the synthesis and analysis of autobiographical accounts.

When interpreting phenomena, autobiographers attune themselves to deeper understandings of self; they feel more grounded in their being and lives. The resistance to understanding one's lifeworld will be weakened and autobiographers contemplate wonderingly as persons who carry the meaning of life within themselves. This understanding of being is the main achievement of autobiography. Autobiographers' understandings of their being-in-the-world intensifies their historical and cultural encounters. After all, one's being is constructed through culture and history. Many autobiographers testify to the importance of this transformative experience occurring in their self-contemplative and explorative journey once the meaning of the *present* changes through using the method of *currere*.

Hongyu Wang (2009) discusses the concept of chronotope (time-space) in curriculum studies. She notes that understanding time-space can transform the present through "historical and cultural" encounters engendering "temporal, spatial, and inter/subjective" emergence so that the *becoming* of the world becomes creative, interactive, and dialogic, a dynamic and ever-emerging relationships between the world and being (p. 1). Wang draws upon Bakhtin's (1986) concept of chronotope (drawn from Goethe's works) to show the reciprocity between self-change and transformation of the world:

> He [the person] emerges *along with the world* and he reflects the historical emergence of the world itself. He is no longer within an epoch, but on the border between two epochs, at the transition point from one to the other. This transition [transformation] is accomplished in him and through him. He is forced to become a new, unprecedented type of human being. What is happening here is precisely the emergence of a new man. ... this is not, of course, the private bio-graphical future, but the historical future. It is as though the very foundations of the world are changing, and man must change along with them .... The image of the emerging man begins to surmount its private nature (within certain limits, of course) and enter into a completely new, *spatial* sphere of historical existence. (pp. 23–24, cited in Wang 2009, pp. 1–2)

Autobiography can thus connect teachers to their historical being. Once autobiographers transcend the boundaries set by their educational experience, time, and place, they can understand their historical being-in-the-world. This emergence occurs as autobiographers transcend the boundaries of the individual self-confined by time and place and surpass the private nature of being. Wang's concept of chronotope depicts teachers as historical beings in a dynamic process of transformation that enables teachers to become, thrive, and prosper. Bakhtin's conception of emergence of being along with the emergence of the world mirrors Aoki's (2004) concept of place once he emphasizes the space in-between the curriculum as planned and the curriculum as lived, a space that can be transformational, emancipatory and awakening for both teachers and students. Our being is emerging with the world, as being and lifeworld are constantly transcending their boundaries to disclose new meanings of existence. As the world is emerging, our being and lifeworld are transcending their limits in a transformational learning experience. Understanding this emerging experience creates an in-between state of mind for autobiographers as they are constantly transforming their concept of time and being. *Currere* can facilitate this transformative and hermeneutic learning experience for autobiographers to emerge into their historical existence.

In her book *The Dialectic of Freedom*, Maxine Greene (1988) believes that an aesthetic awareness of education can awaken reflection, imagination, and possibility. Greene considers human freedom as the "leitmotiv of our time" (1988, p. 25), by which she means our conditioned environment controlled by technology and bureaucracy submerge our subjectivity into a common logic of the *given*. As a response to the conditioning curriculum of our conditioned time, she encourages the educators to cultivate self-knowledge and undertake a constant dialogue between self and society. She encourages us to find freedom from the dominating circumstances and invites educators to reflect on possibilities of change: "What is left for us in this positivist, media-dominated and self-centered time? How, with so much acquiescence and so much thoughtlessness around us, we are to open people to the power of possibility?" (Greene, 1988, p. 55).

Without awakening imagination, fantasy, and possibility, how can educators cultivate reverence in themselves and their students? Our conditioned time and conditioned curriculum take our subjectivity for granted. Self-knowledge can free our subjectivity from technological and bureaucratic forces and open us towards the world of possibility. Understanding in-betweenness—which assumes constant questioning of knowledge, reality, and lived experience—can empower teachers to transcend the boundaries set by their past educational experience. This conscious knowledge provides an entry into teachers' creativity and mindful decision-making despite the dominating circumstances of curriculum. Once teachers understand the dynamics of their temporality, they can emerge into their own lived curriculum.

Concluding Notes

Parker Palmer (2012) explored the teacher's inner life and asked: "How can the teacher's selfhood become a legitimate topic in education and in our public dialogues on educational reform?" (p. 3). To illustrate the landscape of research in teacher education, he outlines three important paths woven neatly together—intellectual, emotional, and spiritual. Palmer emphasizes that teacher selfhood should be a combination of all as a holistic understanding of being and teacher personhood cannot be reduced to only intellect, emotion, and spirit: "They are interwoven in the human self and in education at its best, and I have tried to interweave them in this book as well" (p. 5). In this chapter, I strived to examine teacher's inner life through autobiography and suggest its significance for teacher education.

Autobiographical research in teacher education focuses on teachers' lifeworld and explores it as curriculum. Such new education is humanistic, holistic, creative, transformative and emancipatory. Using autobiographical research, teachers can reveal untold stories, share pedagogical practices, build evolving communities, and transform traditional understanding of curriculum. Once teachers explore their private spheres through biographical and autobiographical research, they can mobilize public and political spheres using dialogue. In the following chapter, I will discuss dialogue in teacher professional development that can nurture teacher professional development and contribute to the formation of a healthy society. At the close of the chapter, I will reference my own dialogic learning experience to explore interfaith understanding of our teaching pedagogy in the field of English language teaching.

References

Aoki, T. T., Pinar, W. F., & Irwin, R. L. (2004). *Curriculum in a new key: The collected works of Ted T. Aoki*. Mahwah, NJ: Lawrence Erlbaum Associates, Publishers.

Bakhtin, M. (1986). *Speech genres and other late essays* (Vern W. McGee Trans.; Caryl Emerson & Michael Holquist, Eds.). Austin: University of Texas Press.

Britzman, D. P. (2009). *The very thought of education: Psychoanalysis and the impossible professions*. Albany: State University of New York Press.

Butt, R. L., & Raymond, D. (1987). Arguments for using qualitative approaches in understanding teacher thinking: The case for biography. *JCT, 7*(1), 63–69.

Butt, R. L., & Raymond, D. (1988). Biographical and contextual influences on an "ordinary" teacher's thoughts and actions. In J. Lowyck, C. Clarke, & R. Halkes (Eds.), *Teacher thinking and professional action*. Lisse, Holland: Swets & Zeitlinger.

Butt, R. L., & Raymond, D. (1989). Studying the nature and development of teachers' knowledge using collaborative autobiography. *International Journal of Educational Research, 13*(4), 403–419. doi: 10.1016/0883-0355(89)90037-2.

Butt, R. L., & Raymond, D. (1992). Studying the nature and development of teachers' knowledge using collaborative autobiography. *International Journal of Educational Research, 13*(4), 402–444.

Chambers, C. (2003). "As Canadian as possible under the circumstances": A view of contemporary curriculum discourses in Canada. In William F. Pinar (Ed.), *International handbook of curriculum research* (pp. 221–252). Mahwah, NJ: Lawrence.

Clandinin, D. J. (2013). *Personal practical knowledge: A study of teachers' classroom images.* (pp. 67–95) Wiley. doi: 10.1108/S1479-3687(2013)0000019007.

Clandinin, D. J., & Connelly, F. M. (2000). *Narrative inquiry: Experience and story in qualitative research* (1st ed.). San Francisco: Jossey-Bass Publishers.

Clarke, A. (2012). Burgeo and back: Catching oneself in the act of being attentive to pedagogy. In A. Cohen & M. Porath (Eds.), *Speaking of teaching: Inclinations, inspirations, and innerworkings,* (pp. 55–62). Sense Publishers: New York.

Clarke, A., & Erickson, G. (2004). The nature of teaching and learning in self-study. In J. J. Loughran, M. L. Hamilton, V. K. LaBoskey, & T. L. Russell (Eds.), *The international handbook of self-study of teaching practices (1 & 2).* Dordrecht: Kluwer Academic Publishers.

Connelly, F. M., & Clandinin, D. J. (1988). Narrative meaning: Focus on teacher education. *Elements, 19*(2), 15–18.

Connelly, F. M., & Clandinin, D. J. (1990). Stories of experience and narrative inquiry. *Educational Researcher, 19*(5), 2–14. doi: 10.2307/1176100.

Demuth, A. (2012). Heidegger's concept of "die Befindlichkeit" and his role in human cognition and self-cognition. Retrieved from: http://www.acarindex.com/dosyalar/makale/acarindex-1423907282.pdf.

Dwyer, K. (1979). The dialogic of ethnology. *Dialectical Anthropology, 4,* 205–224.

Elbaz, F. (1991). Research on teachers' knowledge: The evolution of a discourse. *Journal of Curriculum Studies, 23*(1), 1–19.

Elbaz, F. (2005). *Teachers' voices: Storytelling and possibility.* Greenwich, CT: Information Age Publishing.

Elbaz, F. (2014). *Auto/biography and pedagogy: Memory, and place in teaching.* New York: Peter Lang.

Goodson, I. (1989). Curriculum reform and curriculum theory: A case of historical amnesia. *Cambridge Journal of Education, 19*(2), 131–141.

Goodson, I., & Hargreaves, A. (1996; 2002). *Teachers' professional lives* (1st ed.). London; Washington: Falmer Press. doi: 10.4324/9780203453988.

Goodson, I., & Walker, R. (1991). *Biography, identity, and schooling: Episodes in educational research.* London, England: Falmer.

Greene, M. (1973). *Teacher as stranger: Educational philosophy for the modern age.* Belmont, CA: Wadsworth Publishing Co.

Greene, M. (1988). *The dialectic of freedom.* New York: Teachers College Press.

Greene, M. (2001). *Variations on a Blue Guitar: The Lincoln Center Institute Lectures on Aesthetic Education.* New York: Teacher College Press.

Heidegger, M. (1996). *Being and time: A translation of sein und zeit*. (J. Stambaugh, Trans.). Albany: State University of New York Press.

Huebner, D. E. (1999). *The lure of the transcendent: Collected essays by Dwayne E. Huebner.* Mahwah, NJ: Lawrence Erlbaum Associates.

Husserl, E. (1969). *Ideas: General introduction to pure phenomenology*. New York; London: Allen & Unwin.

Leggo, C. (2012). Poetic inquiry. In A. Cohen, M. Porath, A. Clarke, H. Bai, C. Leggo, & K. Meyer (Eds.), *Speaking of teaching: Inclinations, inspirations, and innerworkings* (pp. 83–108). Sense Publishers: New York.

Lipari, L. (2014). *Listening, thinking and being: Toward an ethics of attunement*. University Park: Penn State University Press.

Miller, J. L. (2005). *Sounds of silence breaking: Women, autobiography, curriculum* (Vol. 1). New York: Peter Lang.

Noddings, N. (1984). *Caring: A feminine approach to ethics and moral education* (2nd ed.). Berkeley: University of California Press.

Noddings, N. (2006). *Critical lessons: What our schools should teach*. Cambridge; New York: Cambridge University Press.

Palmer, P. J. (2012). *Courage to teach*. Wiley.

Schubert, W. (1991). Teacher lore: A basis for understanding praxis. In C. Witherell & N. Noddings (Eds.), *Stories lives tell: Narrative and dialogue in education*. New York: Teachers College Press.

Schubert, W. (1992). Our journeys into teaching: Remembering the past. In W. Schubert & W. Ayers (Eds.), *Teacher lore* (pp. 3–10). New York: Longman.

Schubert, W., & Schubert, A. (1981). Toward curricula that are of, by, and therefore for students. *JCT, 3*(1), 239–251.

Shulman, L. (1987). Knowledge and teaching: Foundations of the new reform. *Harvard Educational Review, 57*(1), 1–23.

Wang, H. (2009). The chronotopes of encounter and emergence. *Journal of Curriculum Theorizing, 25*(1), 1–5.

Wang, W. (2018). *Currere and subjective reconstruction*. Doctoral dissertation, The University of British Columbia, Vancouver, Canada.

Zhang, H., & Pinar, W. F. (2015). *Autobiography and teacher development in China: Subjectivity and culture in curriculum reform*. New York, NY: Palgrave Macmillan.

3

DIALOGUE AND TEACHER PROFESSIONAL DEVELOPMENT

There is no way to love freely, to experience freedom in loving, when you cannot feel your feelings.

(Carol Gilligan, 2002, p. 71)

Break the narrative. Refuse all the stories that have been told so far ..., and try to tell the story differently.

(Jeanette Winterson, 2001, pp. 62–63, cited in Leggo 2012, p. 46)

Introduction

In the second chapter, I introduced teacher development using autobiographical research. Living autobiographically nurtures a mode of being present and attentive to teachers' circumstances and the possibilities of curricular knowledge as lived. I asserted that traditional system of schooling and education might disturb or constrain teacher understanding of self in curriculum. I discussed teachers' autobiography as the most relevant to this project, citing the three streams of autobiographical research in teacher education; that is, autobiographical theory and practice, feminist autobiography, and teachers' biography and autobiography. In teachers' biography and autobiography, I inquired into four streams of scholarships—collaborative autobiography, narrative inquiry, teacher lore, and biographical studies of teachers' lives—all focused on teachers' selfhood, inner life, lived experience, and lifeworld. I discussed attunement and temporality in teacher autobiography and concluded that they can create a mode of attentive being to autobiographical learning in teacher development. My educational experience from autobiographical research and teacher development encourages me to study the way dialogue as an indispensable method for teacher development can nurture teacher professional development. My question for this chapter is: In what sense can dialogue nurture teacher professional development?

Background

Knowing about teachers' personal, professional, and political lives and circumstances, including their pedagogy and practice in the classroom, how they include students' voices and if they are being engaged in doing research to improve their teaching pedagogy and practice—all are accessible through ongoing dialogue with teachers and teacher educators. Being open to teachers' different practices, ideas, thoughts, and (even) fantasies of education can support a more supportive culture of schools wherein the staff and faculty can engage non-judgmentally in their educational experience to improve the quality of education for the students.

Teacher professional development is a responsibility of individual teachers and the schools where they work to ensure that every student receives the highest-quality teaching from the most highly-qualified teachers. Teachers as well as principals, vice-principals, and other team leaders at schools can play an important role in teacher professional development. Teachers can learn to engage with the humanity and selfhood of themselves, and other teachers and students at schools through open and genuine conversations. Recall Clarke's (2012, p. 60) reference to Avaraham's (2009) notion of *inner life* as a monastic, meditative, and contemplative understanding of teacher selfhood transformed by *inner work*. This can produce a more tangible, practicable, and pedagogically livable engagement among teachers. Reflecting on his inner work with other teachers, Clarke seemed to see no limit to the ways their conversations unraveled; quoting Gadamer (1990):

> We say that we 'conduct' a conversation, but the more genuine a conversation is, the less its conduct lies within the will of either partner. Thus, a genuine conversation is

never the one that we wanted to conduct. Rather, it is generally more correct to say that we fall into conversation, or even that we become involved in it. The way one word follows another, with the conversation taking its own twists and reaching its own conclusion, may well be conducted in some way, but the partners conversing are far less the leaders of it than the led. No one knows in advance what will 'come out' of a conversation. (pp. 383–84, cited in Clarke, 2012, p. 60)

Clarke's understanding of genuine dialogue provides a meaningful and humanistic potential of conversations when the interlocutors do not consider a prescribed objective and predetermined goal, as their presupposed thoughts of education might lead them into the vicious cycle. I find this understanding of Gadamerian dialogue as spontaneous, generative, and transformative and strive to inquire into the way such dialogic conversations can contribute to teacher professional development in Chapter 4.

Dialogue in Teacher Professional Development

Understanding curriculum shifts its focus from "the separation of subject and object" to their negotiation, possible integration, and interdisciplinary dialogue (Pinar et al. 1995, p. 502) that can provide a meaningful understanding of our educational experience. Negotiating the dialogic meaning of knowledge shared between teachers and students reveals hitherto unknown meanings of their educational experience. Doll (1993a) notes that in the process of meaning-making, the dichotomy of subject-object or teacher-learner makes sense only once one is embedded in the other. Educational experience is created, facilitated, and supported by dialogue. One needs the other for one's own sense of being, becoming, thriving and transforming. As Doll appreciates, dialogue in curriculum focuses on the process of "traversing the courses of negotiating with self and others" (p. 286) to exchange meanings of our educational experience.

Doll (1993b) uses the term *post-modern* to refer to a paradigmatic shift from rationalism and empiricism to deconstruction of accepted meanings in teacher development. Doll's understanding of dialogue in teacher professional development is transformative, scientific, and experiential during which a dialogic understanding of accepted meaning will arise in collaborative conversations among teachers and educators. Teachers experience new subjectivities as they learn from each other in dialogic conversations to transform their understanding of education. This transformation occurs due to the nature of dialogue that can immerse educators in a collaborative leaning experience.

To open dialogue in teacher professional development is to transform meaning; certain concepts—"truth, language, knowledge, and power" (Slattery, 2006, p. 17)—can be subject to critical re-evaluation and reconstruction once we commit to understand the subjective meanings of teachers' engagement with students. Doll (1993b) suggests that the main advantage of post-modernism is the generation of new knowledge and the transformation of learning, both accented by a shift from "discrete to relational," and from "closed systems to interactive and dissipative systems" (p. 12). Central to these "systems" are participating teachers and students who transform their knowledge and themselves as they align their visions to openness and interactivity.

This conception of curriculum is consistent with Bakhtin's work on dialogism formed in truly transformative conversations (Holquist, 2003), events that evolve to better and deeper understandings of self and other, and not only in teacher professional development. Huebner (1999) asserts that real dialogue is only possible if we are "willing [and ready] to be influenced" by other interlocutors. The willingness to be influenced by others, he continues, demands "an openness toward the world," and acknowledgment that one is never a "completed being" but a curious human in "the process of becoming" who makes "an attempt at … desolitudinizing"... [self] by showing self to others and receiving [self] from others in a conversation (Huebner, 1999, p. 78).

Huebner's understanding of real dialogue for teacher professional development entails conscious understanding of our thinking processes and the possible prejudices we might possess unconsciously. Without self-study, teachers are less likely to achieve this conscious knowledge to overcome their inner barriers of resistance, prejudice, and preconception. Being open to dialogue means a free state of liberated mind. Teachers can use *currere* to understand how their previous lifeworld knowledge and educational experience have conditioned their thinking, feeling, and being in the world so that they become prepared to express themselves to others and receive self from others in a genuine, open-ended conversation.

Following the four phases of *currere* one analyses and synthesizes the meaning of lifeworld; the self can achieve a holistic understanding of existence and its being. This self-reflective study gives depth to the autobiography so that teachers understand the meanings emerging in dialogue. The distance between self and others becomes less, more transparent, and the autobiographer grows more conscious of the inner barriers in each interlocutor. The genuine dialogue can contribute to the meaning constructed spontaneously by interlocutors so the process of meaning-making and mutual fulfilment will replace individual resistance and preconception.

Using dialogue for teacher professional development, a relational understanding of educational experience and a willingness to be transformed and influenced by the professional experience of other teachers and teacher educators are essential so that dialogue can construct teacher professional development. Teacher subjectivity is at the core of this transformative experience. Understanding the meaning of dialogue in teacher professional development opens new possibilities for teachers and teacher educators who are eager to learn and expand on their educational and professional experience by generating collaborative and dialectic knowledge. The preliminary stage in understanding this shared knowledge occurs by being open to one's lifeworld and being willing to understand the meaning intended or conveyed by the interlocutors.

Noddings (2015) invites educators to reflect and engage in an ongoing dialogue, "a never ending vibrant examination of what we mean by a better adult" (p. 54), one who follows a constructive and generative understanding of education to more deeply connect to self and others. By "better adult," Noddings is inviting educators into an ongoing dialogue about how we might reconstruct our notions of self, schooling, and education. Teachers can start by working from within to understand the meaning of their lives so that they can communicate this understanding in transformative dialogue with others.

Self-reflection facilitates genuine dialogue during which interlocutors share their transformative experience of lifeworld. Teachers can be constantly becoming and their being can be in continuous transformation as the world of meaning can be a non-stop transformative experience. Dialogue provides an opportunity to teachers to examine their understanding of the world vis-à-vis the shared understanding of lifeworld. Open dialogue entails teachers' willingness to become conscious of presuppositions and prejudgments as these psychological processes obstruct real meaning-making in genuine dialogue. Once teachers overcome such limitations, they can interpret the ongoing conversations wonderingly and inquiringly to create genuine meaning.

Aoki (2004) notes how teachers ontologically engage in open dialogue through which they explore the "intentions and assumptions underlying their acts" and critically reflect on their conduct in "brackets" to "go beyond the immediate level of interpretation" (Aoki et al., 2004, p. 7). In their reflective moments, teachers bracket their understanding of pedagogy in an inner dialogue. Regarding the dialogic understanding of "explaining," he suggests that the structure of meanings is not accessible to empirical analytic science, researchers; instead, we must use interpretive explanations by entering an "intersubjective dialogue" with those who are in the research situation. This is the essence of hermeneutic understanding in dialogue wherein interlocutors bracket their own judgment to attentively listen to the explanations and interpretations of the other discussants which complete their dialogic understanding. Intersubjective understanding is the merging of ideas, opinions, and lifeworlds disclosed and shared between two or more interlocutors. Intersubjective dialogue can strengthen teachers' pedagogy and practice, and provide a transformative understanding of their phenomenological and existential experience.

In its concentration on the lifeworld and personhood of teachers, Aoki's conception of intersubjectivity in l engagement of teachers in dialogue mirrors Doll's (1993b) relational understanding of dissipative systems and Huebner's (1999) conception of reciprocal understanding of self in conversations with others: all these practices take teachers away from their comfort zones to draw them into unfamiliar and at times uncomfortable intersubjective and dialogic spaces. Zhang (2015) reminds that the educational process is one of "autonomy, cooperation, dialogue, and inquiry," the development of "free personality, social equality, and justice" (p. 59). Regarding education as a "liberal cause and an emancipatory praxis", Zhang appreciates that teachers [and students] can be intellectuals with "free personality, independent spirits, and critical consciousness."

Dialogue contributes to teacher personal and professional development as it concentrates on both personal aspects [autonomy, free personality], and social and political domains [community, equality, justice], to develop supportive spaces of cooperative learning and mutual respect. Teachers can achieve transformative understandings of their own personal and social development in dialogue as they examine unexplored phenomenological and existential aspects of shared meaning.

Focusing on philosophical dialogue to enable teachers to intervene and transform the learning process, Zhenyu (2015) connects a community of philosophical inquiry (CPI) to revised Socratic dialogue (Fisher, 2005) by means of which teachers can engage in dialogic conversations to problematize traditional understandings of schooling in a top-down educational system to transform from within for professional development. Teachers as agents of education can create a dialogic and supportive space to problematize their educational experience and communicate their individual and educational issues in service to their professional development.

Dialogue in Critical Pedagogy

Nathalia Jaramillo (2015) notes that, as an emancipatory practice, "critical pedagogy" encourages the educators to critique the foundations of traditional schooling by replacing rote learning, banking education, and memorization with critical and rational thinking in the classroom. Critical pedagogy resituates teachers and students into dialogic conversations to foster teacher and student agency in support of social change through reflective inquiry, dialogue and collaborative action. Jaramillo (2015, p. 170) emphasizes that "decolonial pedagogy stems from an acknowledgment that the world we inhabit carries the seeds of colonial-capitalism," and can challenge Western conceptions of democracy:

> Decolonial thought is, therefore, anchored in other epistemological frameworks, value systems, and an ethical commitment to caring for others, the environment, and other ways of knowing. Teachers in decolonial pedagogy enter dialogue with suppressed knowledge(s) and voices to advance educational practice in support of diversity. (Jaramillo, 2015, p. 171)

What makes knowledge colonial is not its geographical origin but its intentions and effects. As you can see, Western (specifically North American) knowledge can be— has been—freeing for my cosmopolitan Persian self. Although critical pedagogy critiques some forms of autobiographical approaches as apolitical, students of *currere* know that teacher subjectivity is entangled with public and political spheres. Once teacher subjectivity acknowledges and transcends boundaries of traditional education using autobiography, it enters into the world of politics by analyzing and synthesizing teacher suppressed knowledge(s).

Unlike critical pedagogy, *currere* resituates teacher subjectivity in dialogue with their lifeworld and political circumstances to understand the strength of their voice and personal knowledge in their work in the public sphere (the classroom). Self-education occurs when teachers educate themselves by reflecting on their own educational experience; this is a process that is more analytical and synthetical than critical pedagogy: autobiographical inquiry demands a deeper reflection on teachers' very personal experience and their intertwined relation with social and political spheres.

Dialogue, Freire (2014, p. 17) reminds, is a way of "knowing and learning;" he knows that it helps us to value the collective nature of knowing and learning, as dialogical knowledge is collective and shared. Understanding dialogue as a process of knowing and learning calls for an "epistemological curiosity" about "the element of dialogue" (p. 18). Dialogue in this sense is not an end, but a means to achieve a deeper understanding of self, situation, and academic knowledge. In quest of t meaning, teachers can engage in genuine conversations to understand the suppressed knowledge of themselves and others in order to empower themselves and their students in personal and social transformation. Teachers can decolonize knowledge and thought as they study how they might have been influenced by cultures unconsciously. Dialogue can provide a venue for teachers to express their voice and seeks personal fulfillment as they engage in social action. Understanding oppressed voices of teachers can advance their pedagogy and practice and contribute to a diverse teaching community by mobilizing their knowledge, values, and ideologies.

Freire (2014, p. 19) underscores an engagement of theory and practice in dialogue and asserts that if we "negate practice for the sake of theory," there is a danger of reducing theory "to a pure verbalism or intellectualism," and if we "negate theory for the sake of practice" and consider dialogue as mere conversation, there is a danger of losing ourselves "in the disconnectedness of practice." To minimize such risks, Freire advocates a unity of theory and practice. Teachers and students can transform their educational experience into professional knowledge.

Is dialogue possible without prior theoretical and practical knowledge and without any "epistemological curiosity"? Freire's conception of dialogue can be utilized by teachers and teacher educators as they labor to understand each other. This collective understanding of dialogue in teacher development reminds me (again) of Bakhtin's conception of dialogism during which teacher epistemological quest for understanding dialogic knowledge can lead to better understanding of self and other for teacher professional development. In a Freirian sense, dialogue *is* critical pedagogy. Freire's dialogic understanding can be at the core of teacher personal and professional development as it encourages teacher dialogue as a commitment to collaborative learning of pedagogical knowledge. Freire (2014, pp. 88–89) encourages those whose rights of dialogue have been denied—the oppressed—to reclaim their voice and bring this "dehumanizing aggression" to a halt as dialogue—the encounter between the human being and the world—is human "primordial right."

Human beings can transform the worlds—inner and outer—once they engage in dialogic conversations to achieve a new meaning of their subjectivity and their world. Dialogue is thus "an existential necessity" and provides a medium for interlocutors to reflect on their thoughts and transform their shared reality as they address the world. As an act of co-creation, dialogue should not be monopolized as a "crafty instrument" to dominate and suppress others; it should contain profound love and devotion to the world and its people. In teacher development, dialogue can help teachers to understand the humanity of their voices which might have been oppressed and neglected during their educational experience.

Sharing teacher educational experience opens pathways to teacher knowledge, and works as a humanizing process during which an understandings of teacher subjectivity, ontology and phenomenology can be discussed, critiqued, and elevated. As teachers' primordial right, dialogue brings out the untold stories of teachers' lifeworld with others which can transform understandings of their subjectivity and their pivotal role in the school curriculum. As a caring, humanizing, and empowering process, teacher dialogue can be included in every school's philosophy of education and agenda for curriculum development as it provides invaluable access to teacher knowledge for teacher and student development.

Dialogue as Reflective Practice

Gary Poole (2012) asserts that the single best way to improve pedagogy is by providing opportunities for the teachers to talk to each other about their teaching. In their reflective chapters, six scholars reveal their inner selves and reflections on teaching pedagogy and practice using dialogue. Poole reveals the intricacy of their inner-workings and dialogic discussions: "Discussions of the products of inner work require impressive degrees of honesty and courage. There is little point in discussing simply what we think people want to hear about teaching when we know that the inner work yields more intricate content" (see Cohen & Porath, 2012, p. 9). Facilitating teacher dialogue in school curriculum can encourage teachers to unravel their personal stories and educational narratives.

Dialogue provides a crucial means of self-inquiry as teachers can openly share their understanding and imagined reality with each other. Personal stories can empower marginalized voices in school and unravel the values of spiritual and ethical lifeworld of teachers. Their dialogic stories reflect psychoanalytical, phenomenological, epistemological, and hermeneutic understandings of each individual teacher that can enrich curriculum and even decolonialize knowledge, pedagogy, and ideology.

Poole highlights that the exploration of inner work can render teachers vulnerable as their values, beliefs, teaching pedagogy and practice might be questioned by colleagues and school officials. The degree to which teachers openly accept these risks and reflect on them for their professional development can determine the nature of conversations.

Avraham Cohen (2012) knows that teachers can consciously work on the holes in their wholeness through self-reflections and dialogic conversations. Using dialogue, teachers can understand and control the climate of their own professional development and classroom dynamics. Cohen believes that "anomie and alienation" (p. 21) are pervasive in many schools and that teachers can connect to students by understanding their situation using dialogue. Schools are one of the major places among others—families and communities—where anomic behavior might become endemic. Educators can connect to their students using dialogue to learn about their inner lives and untold stories, then provide caring support to ensure student success.

During my educational experience, I could relate to those teachers who inspired me by opening a genuine dialogue. Those teachers acknowledged my voice and subjectivity by providing possibilities for developing through dialogic conversations. In my bachelor's degree coursework in Language and Literature at Tehran University, I recall the time when one of my professors, Dr. Mollanazar, was open to my ideas, perspectives, and stories. His teaching philosophy and practice included student voice and differences. The students never felt alienated or marginalized in his class. The other instructor I remember was Dr. Tabatabaee who had just returned from the United States upon completion of her doctoral degree. Her educational experience in the United States was really engaging; as she was telling her stories and comparing her lifestyle in Iran and the States, we could raise our questions publicly and discuss our perspectives.

These teachers included students in their curricular conversations and students typically felt worthy in those classes where they could express themselves freely. Such experience provides care, empathy, and humanistic understanding for students as dialogue can be empathetic and caring, contributing to the well-being and even prosperity of interlocutors. Students' personal experiences and other classroom comments can be communicated to the teachers using dialogue enabling teachers to understand the specific strengths and weaknesses of their pedagogy and practice, modifying them accordingly. Each student possesses untapped memories and dialogue can facilitate sharing these unique ideas and opinions with other students and teachers. Connecting to students using dialogue to reveal teacher stories as a caring strategy, teachers share their inner work and mode of being with their students to provide reflective, educational, and humanistic educational experience.

In *Education for Enlightenment*, Heesoon Bai (2012), emphasizes the power of meditation in the classroom; she asserts that meditative thinking and contemplation can bring watchfulness and wakefulness for teachers and students. (Recall that Maxine Greene—referenced earlier—also affirmed the significance of wide-awakeness: see 1973.) Teachers' conscious presence in the classroom facilitates dialogue, so students and teachers become more receptive and welcoming to each other as a result of this meditation and deep thinking. Contemplative and reflective teaching can encourage students to reflect on their educational experience and understand the mechanism of their intellectual growth and academic learning which can contribute to teacher professional development. Bai (2012) notes the influence of dialogue with other teachers who have contributed to her book on active meditation:

> With these colleagues, my heart naturally and easily opens wide; and my intellect comes alive during our lively and joyful dialogue. My whole being resonates deeply with the generosity of their heart and spirit. I would not hesitate to call my manner of being with them an active meditation. (p. 66)

Such dialogue with teachers can unravel unexplored aspects of their lifeworld, personal stories contain powerful lessons and generous teaching moments. Dialogic encounters can invite teachers to share our private and unexcavated dimensions of self as we open ourselves to existential understandings of life through attentive listening and responding to questions. Dialogic exchanges can encourage interlocutors' meditative state of mind as the ontological, phenomenological, epistemological, and hermeneutic understandings take deep thinking and contemplation. Interlocutors can recognize unexplored dimensions of subjectivity and thereby transform thoughts, opinions, ideologies, and perspectives. This transformative experience can help teachers develop their theoretical, pedagogical, and practical understandings of teaching in school. Teacher dialogue can encourage holistic understandings of teacher personal and educational stories once they generously reveal their educational narratives with students and teachers. When we understand teachers' educational, intellectual, emotional, spiritual, cultural, social, political, and personal stories, we can connect with their autobiographical mode of being which, I am suggesting, facilitates their professional development.

Hermeneutic Reflexivity and Dialogue

Kögler (1996) notes that dialogue is not limited to "the communicative form of linguistic understanding between two subjects," but encompasses "specific symbolic-cultural preconditions" (p. 43). Dialogue can only occur once there exist certain pre-understandings among interlocutors. In every communication, this symbolic precondition structures and conditions the understanding and interpretation of the interlocutors engaged in the dialogue. More important than the linguistic meanings conveyed in dialogic conversations, a Gadamerian understanding of dialogue is evident in Kögler's interpretation, as our meaning is symbolically and culturally preconditioned and predetermined invoking a shared experience of life among the interlocutors.

The intimacy and affinity unraveling in dialogic exchanges is a natural outcome of a genuine conversation: "the central concern is not to identify the other's meaning as an expression of her individuality but to relate the possible truth of what she says to one's own perspectives and assumptions" (Kögler, 1996, p. 43). I relate to my students' truth and reality as an attentive listener who is committed to empathetic conversation. Attentive listening contributes to my students' self-concept and self-image as they feel worthy once I relate to their educational experience and attempt to remove their inner barriers in their learning process. Drawing on my hermeneutic studies in my doctoral studies (during which I could explore my educational experience to address inner tensions and reconstruct my subjectivity), I can interpret their preconceived understandings of lifeworld using hermeneutic knowledge. What intrigues me most in my counselling sessions is their humble attitude towards my psychoanalytical and hermeneutic knowledge and the fact that they value my attentive listening and encouraging comments on how to improve their personal and social well-being. To understand the intended message, interlocutors can transcend the limits of the content-oriented dialogue specified and delimited by the medium of language. Genuine hermeneutic experience is only possible once we give ourselves to productive and spontaneous discussions which transcend the pre-structured suppositions.

Kögler (1996, p. 47) considers experience, either hermeneutic or otherwise, as an essentially *negative* disposition in efforts to interpret dialogue. Our experience provides new light to understand, interpret, and predict the phenomenon and can alter perceived meaning. Genuine experience, by its nature, however, cannot always be anticipated, judged or understood. Especially when our expectations and anticipations in dialogue from previous experiences can—this is Kögler's point—obstruct accurate interpretations of meaning. Such projection can be bracketed. Bracketing such expectations (acquired through negating previous experiences) can contribute to more self-conscious experience: "by proceeding through this antithetical negativity, knowledge experiences itself to the extent that, through encountering alterity, it alters itself" (Kögler, 1996, p. 47). Kögler's conception of antithetical negativity mirrors Elbaz's (2014) abstraction of memory when it curves back on itself like a stream for a fuller understanding of lived experience. Confronting alterity can function as a journey toward consciousness in student and teacher development as we reflect on our educational experience to alter it.

Dialogue for Preparation of Teachers

Noddings (2015) identifies elements that should be included in every curriculum, among them dialogue: "Some of the most promising aims in the Common Core emphasize cooperation, conversation (dialogue, communication), and critical thinking" (p. 170). Reflective collegiality achieved through a culture of dialogue among the teachers and students cultivates a rational process of critical thinking. Instead of thinking of a penalty, teachers can open a dialogue with their students to understand the source of possible infractions. Noddings (2015) emphasizes the significance of dialogue:

> Continual reflective, collegial dialogue is necessary, and a wise administration will respect a reasonable range of faculty positions. Teachers in preparation can think deeply about the kind of school atmosphere in which they would like to teach, and they can certainly ask about the school ethos when they are interviewed for a position. Will there be at least a cadre of teachers with whom you can work to establish and maintain an ethos of care and trust? (p. 172).

As teachers make informed decisions by opening a dialogue on school culture prior to their entry into the cadre of educators, they can facilitate their transition into school curriculum and smoothen their future development.

Dialogue can not only facilitate new teachers' informed decisions for choosing the suitable school to join but candid conversations can also contribute to dynamic school if schools can probably remain open and receptive to ethos of new teachers. Using dialogue between the cadre of established educators and new teachers can create enriched meanings and ultimately refresh both the novice teachers' understanding of school sociopolitical atmosphere and the existing teachers' creative engagement with their own curriculum. Such collaborative and dialogic understanding of school curriculum can prepare new teachers to understand school ethos more fully.

Dialogue and Care. Noddings (2015, p. 121) focuses on *care*—a term specific to her contribution to teacher professional development—and asserts that "caring is best construed as a quality of relation, not primarily as a virtue belonging to an individual." She notes that "care theorists" in education underscore the significance of ongoing dialogue in all types of relational ethics. Noddings emphasizes the importance of "continuing intellectual dialogue" among students and their teachers "to establish and maintain personal relations" which is the foundation of "all good teaching" (2015, p. 122).

Students relate to teachers' educational experience and lifeworld and establishing a strong personal relationship is considered important by most of them. During their intellectual dialogue with teachers, they are engaged in empathetic and caring relationships as authentic dialogue is founded on care and empathy. Caring dialogue can contribute to the well-being and self-fulfillment of care givers and receivers, as both are engaged in a caring relationship. So teachers' dialogue can contribute to their own and their students' well-being as dialogic encounters can establish and maintain ongoing support systems for both. Dialogue becomes a method of being and living in human existence.

That is evident in Bakhtin. Holquist (2003) considers dialogue as a key concept in all Bakhtin's career and life: "Dialogue is present in one way or another throughout the notebooks he kept from his youth to his death at the age of 80" (p. 14). Bakhtin considered human beings as engaged in an ongoing dialogue, including through works of literature, for example, dialogues among authors. Human existential experience informs and is informed by previous work of literature. Dialogue extends to both directions in the past and future as characteristic to human being's existential experience. We human beings are temporal phenomena, extending into the past and onto the future, always informed by dialogic conversations with others, face-to-face and, through study, with the works of those still alive and those long deceased. Teachers are in constant dialogue with works of literature which can transform their understanding of learning and teaching.

Jung-Hoon (2016) developed the concept of care autobiographically by juxtaposing *currere* and *Hakbeolism*—a uniquely Korean concept of *symbolic capital* (Bourdieu & Thompson, 1991) obtainable via high test scores on university entrance examinations. In his important and powerful book, Jung-Hoon begins with a deeply sorrowful poem that captured his attention when he noticed that a boy he knew on the elevator he took daily to school was no longer there! It turns out that the boy had thrown himself off a balcony of a high-rise apartment. He left a note behind: "Mom, I cannot endure this pain any more. My brain nibbles my heart. I am sorry." (p. 1).

While admired worldwide for high test scores on standardized tests, Korean education, Jung-Hoon (2016) emphasizes, "structurally, culturally, and indeed psychologically" (p. 2) has installed instrumental rationality in Korean students who risk losing subjectivity. To value subjectivity of students, self-care can replace the demands of education based on "mere absorption of externally imposed information and skills" (p. 3). Jung-Hoon Jung's *Hakbeolism* as symbolic sociocultural capital resonates with me as it animates my schooling experience in Iran and I am wondering if teachers and academic scholars can work closely together—using dialogue—to transform the university entrance examination system, even eliminating this stressful exam from educational system and replacing it with qualitative evaluation and descriptive methods to provide caring support and empathy.

Dialogue as a Pedagogical Practice. Aligned with Bakhtin, Aoki (2004) critiques researchers' "empirical analytical research," and he calls for researchers to enter "into dialogue with the people in the research situation" (p. 104). In such a transformative process, researchers could be involved in an ongoing conversation and interpretative analysis of ideas, perspectives, and viewpoints. Aoki's dialogical understanding of research can provide an important perspective for classroom teachers to consider themselves and their students as the main participants of the inquiry into their teaching and learning. I remember the way dialogue particularly during high school years contributed to my mental and emotional well-being and understanding of self-worth and self-love. In those years, a few teachers of mine were considered just like a friend once they dialogued on different aspects of social life during which we could express our ideas, thoughts, and critical points of view. By reflecting on lived experience, teachers can encourage their students to learn how to develop their subjectivity, understanding which is the main step to establishing a healthy society.

In my bachelor's degree program in English Language and Literature in Tehran University, I have recalled (earlier in this book) that one of my teachers—Professor Mollanazar—who viewed students as key participants in the complicated conversation that is the curriculum, as he supported genuine dialogue that contributed to our well-being and thriving. During my master's degree program in English Language Teaching at Shiraz University, Professor

Sahragard listened to our stories and supported our feeling, thinking, and being. He never judged negatively our incomplete perspectives and stayed open so that the students could express themselves freely, unfold their meaning, and problematize education. From the onset of my doctoral program, I have been engaged in reflective and constructive dialogue with my caring supervisor—Professor Pinar—and later with my supportive committee members—Professors Anthony Clarke and Carl Leggo—to achieve a deeper understanding of my own pedagogy and practice. My subjectivity has been informed and constructed by such encouraging and supportive dialogic exchanges. I realize in what sense my meaning of education is getting reconstructed by new learnings during our dialogic conversations which help me construct powerful and personal understandings of the interrelations among subjectivity, curriculum, and educational experience.

Freire (2014) clarifies that dialogue between teachers and students does not place them in equal positions; however, it can facilitate a supportive space and humanistic relationship, especially when teachers use their institutional authority to care. As a humanistic approach to teaching, dialogic conversations are true learning moments during which teachers and students learn from each other's lived experience. As participants in the dialogue, they can not only "retain" their identity, but also proactively "defend" it, and "thus grow together" (p. 107). Freire underlines the significance of dialogue as transformational educational inquiry and warns teachers to be wary of any authoritarian attitudes such as imposing their own thinking on students: "Pedagogical dialogue implies not only content, or cognoscible [cognizable] object around which to revolve, but also a presentation concerning it made by the educator for the educands" (2014, p. 108). Knowledgeable teachers are those who have explored their subjectivity and lifeworld well and are open to their students' developing understanding of self. They provide supportive space for them to examine themselves during dialogic encounters. Authority for such teachers is expressed in their attentive listening, supportive care, and empathetic conversations during which they attempt to understand their students' being and becoming.

Dialogue and Plurality in Teacher Development

In *Speaking of Learning*, Wang (2014, p. xi) emphasizes "the profoundly touching, humane, and imaginative voices" of students when teaching two books: "My experience of teaching *Speaking of Teaching* (with amazingly positive, even enlightened responses from students) and reading *Speaking of Learning* also forms a tessellation that resonates with a patterned movement of my own temporal and intercultural learning through encounters." As she opens a dialogue with the authors and her students, Wang is engaging in the complicated conversation that is the curriculum. The inner world contains meanings awaiting to be explored by teachers and students prior to their entry into genuine conversations. Using dialogue, educators learn about their teaching moments by inquiring into their own immediate interior world.

Dialogue in this sense, however, is not limited to an inner conversation or an exchange of ideas, theories, methods, and viewpoints with the other educators in the group. More importantly, being open and listening to students while teaching gives a self-understanding to become better educational associates to students and develop professionally. This aspect of dialogue invites educators to engage in self-education during which they can question their own meaning of pedagogy by empathizing with students and accommodating their viewpoints in teaching practices. Clarke (2012) discusses that their book arose from dialogue. He notes that Avraham Cohen invited them to join a conversation regarding "what it means to be an educator" (p. xxv). Sharing their stories, they opened a dialogue to question their teaching pedagogy and practice. By examining their teaching practice, their collective conversation contributed to an *emerging understanding* of their individual teaching and provided a true moment of presence, and reflection.

Plurality is meaningfully practiced once teachers and educators remain open to different realities of students and in continuous dialogue with those realities to understand new dimensions of self in student and teacher educational experience. Pedagogical practices can be influenced, informed, and reconstructed by multiple dialogic meanings emerging from students and teachers' educational experience. Multiplicity is understanding the unique reality of each individual teacher and student. Becoming engaged in such meaning-making process can reconstruct each interlocutor's lifeworld, allowing entry into an emerging space of self-learning, self-value, and self-worth.

Deborah Osberg and Gert Biesta (2008) consider curriculum as such a "space of emergence" and propose that in this sense curriculum "is *not* a space of common ground." For them, human subjectivity can only emerge in one's interactions with others, specifically with those who are different from us. A plural space of emergence provides an opportunity for an educational experience to occur. Osberg and Biesta (2008) contend that plurality as a condition of possibility of education might be dissonant with traditional understandings of schooling in which the teachers are the sole informants:

> However, if plurality is the condition of possibility of education, then this challenges the conventional logic of schooling whereby everything possible is done to *reduce* the differences between the teacher and those being educated on the one hand, and the differences between the various individuals being educated by the teacher (e.g. in terms of age, gender, ability, interests, etc.) on the other. The idea of a 'space of emergence' suggests that difference must be maintained in the classroom. Any reduction of such difference *prevents* education from taking place. (2008, p. 324)

Through ongoing dialogue in a pluralistic context of learning and teaching, informed teachers can create educational moments during which each student becomes able to realize their capabilities and potentials so that unique individuals emerge because of teacher conscious decisions and student collaboration in dialogic exchanges.

Indeed, the transformative understanding of this educational experience will support students who can confidently express their thoughts, imaginations, and fantasies without being too much concerned about judgments of their teachers and peers in educational contexts which will create emerging possibilities for education. This subjective understanding of education can empower each individual student to trust their new understanding of educational experience to transform and emerge new possibilities and can contribute to teacher professional development. Doll and Trueit (2012) affirm that such curriculum can bring new possibilities for students by opening space for "creative emergence of new ideas and procedures" and incorporating plurality and non-linearity into understanding curriculum using conversation as the primary mode of instruction:

> A focus on such challenges calls into question the efficacy of a sequentially ordered curriculum, as well as the common teaching strategy of "teaching-as-telling." While the constructivist movement does help us see the efficacy of paying attention to the learner's frame - his/her schemas; the complexivist movement goes beyond this subjectivization to bring forth the concept and practice of transformation via situational self-organization. (Doll & Trueit, 2012, p. 122)

Understanding pluralistic dialogue in teacher development can bring teachers closer to students not only by simply telling their educational stories but also by understanding the situational space of each individual student in the process of learning.

Situational self-development is essential for transformative learning experience; it can provoke a contextualized and individualized teaching experience and encourages teacher self and professional development. Teachers' primary commitment, then, is to encourage creative moments in their educational and professional experience for students so that they could appreciate plurality in their own otherness and in the otherness of other teachers. What makes creativity and plurality interrelated is that understanding otherness requires coming out of one's comfort zone, and that requires courage. But it can trigger creativity.

Clarke and Phelan (2017) emphasize the significance of plurality in teacher professional development by acknowledging differences. In their evaluation of the Kaye College Active Collaborative Education (ACE) program, Clarke and Phelan noticed that Kaye College invited teachers to construct their professional identity and become agents of social change and transformation. Embracing plurality, the curriculum included students' voices and religious identities:

> The narrative approach used in the programme not only fits with students' cultural backgrounds but also provides rich opportunities for students to recognize that a range of voices exists, to engage with the experiences and perspectives of their peers and to reconstruct their beliefs not only about education but also about religious and political identities. (p. 101)

They continue that the program acknowledges agonistic assumptions: "that a plurality of views on fundamental questions exists; that certain dimensions of human suffering are inevitable and even ordinary; and that conflict is an inescapable feature of the human condition and would exist even in a society better than the ones we have" (p. 102).

Including differing perspectives in curriculum provides support for marginalized individuals to express themselves. As teachers respect each individual student's situation they acknowledge ethnic, racial, religious, and social differences, contributing to the nation's unity. Youthful citizens find supportive and caring space to share their voice and express their different worldviews. Keeping the right balance of differing human conditions is perhaps the most important challenge a teacher faces in plural classrooms. Understanding students' individuality takes effort for teachers and educators to guarantee quality education for everyone—essential for maintaining a healthy society.

Dialogue and Individuation

Jung (2014, p. 448) considers *individuation* as a process through which "individual beings are formed and differentiated" which is distinct from the collective understanding of self. Conformity can conceal subjectivity. Conditioned by my early school experience, my subjectivity was not ready for self-reflection and reconstruction. My doctoral research was a transformative experience during which my caterpillar turned into a butterfly. In my dark stage, in a silky cocoon, I was alone. Nobody could help me to transform my subjectivity into a butterfly. Self-dialogue encouraged me most to transform and understand individuality and individuation.

Individuation is essential to prevent from conformity in public education. Jung asserts that "any serious check to individuality, therefore, is an artificial stunting" and a social group consisting of "stunted individuals" cannot form a healthy society (Jung 2014, p. 448). Perhaps, a society which preserves its cohesion and coherence by connecting people while preserving individuality can thrive and remain more healthy and productive. Jung notes that individuation by itself is by no means the sole end of education: "the educational aim of adaptation to the necessary minimum of collective norms must first be attained. If a plant is to unfold its specific nature to the full, it must first be able to grow in the soil in which it is planted" (2014, p. 449). This apparently paradoxical conception of individuation becomes clear in societies in which individuals affirm their group identity while maintaining their individual integrity.

To understand the individual space of each student, other scholars employ their narrative accounts. For instance, Leggo (2012, p. 43) opens his argument with two simple and provoking questions: "What does it mean to become a teacher? What does it mean to become a learner?" Carl narrates his story as a young boy with a statement from Carol Gilligan (2002, p. 63): "it is difficult for young boys to read the world around them and show the sensitive, soft sides of themselves". Leggo asserts that he was "a boisterous, competitive boy who loved sports and games of all kinds [and]… physically active, seemingly tireless, full of boundless energy" (p. 45). In inner dialogue, he observed his individuality among other boys reflecting on his world and intrinsic feelings, and opened an inner dialogue: "I do not remember much trouble with my being "one of the boys", but I can recall many incidents when I was not especially brave or risk-taking. I was afraid of crazed bullies, loud extroverts, and grinning liars (I still am afraid!)" (p. 45). As individuals, human beings are in a dialogue with themselves and the world they exist in. Leggo's writing exhibits singular characteristics of an active boy who might have been misunderstood and discriminated against. To reiterate Jung's (2014) insight: like plants in soil, we grow through the nourishment of others. A pluralistic education which values individual differences can preserve each individual student by emphasizing self-education to avoid the danger of self-alienation. In pluralistic education, different races, ethnicities, and religions can have specific spaces to express their unique voice.

In teacher professional development, dialogue can enable us to learn more about our differences, knowledge that can contribute to the unity of teaching community. Discussing faith as a personal value with other teachers can provide an intersubjective understanding of teachers' personal and professional identity and individuality. In the following, I provide my interfaith dialogue in Vancouver to show that experiencing this intersubjective space can contribute to teacher individual and professional development.

Dialogue on Faith for Teacher Professional Development: A Narrative

Several years ago, I had an opportunity to open an interfaith dialogue with Joel Heng Hartse from the Department of Language and Literacy Education at the University of British Columbia, now as a lecturer at Simon Fraser University. I remember when I was in an express bus heading home from Vancouver Georgia College—an English language school in Vancouver, downtown. I opened and flipped through the book I had borrowed from Joel; *Christian and Critical Language Educators in Dialogue* co-edited by Mary Shepard Wong and Suresh Canagarajah (2009). I skimmed through the table of contents and read several pages regarding different types of dialogue among Christian and critical English language educators. As I was reading, I was wondering if I could contribute a chapter to a book on interfaith dialogue among English language educators. I was eager to share my teaching experience with other educators who came from different religious backgrounds. I was curious to know how religious educators would respond to my questions and concerns. Had they encountered the same issues I was experiencing as a Shia Muslim educator?

With these questions in mind, I arranged a meeting with Joel in the Blenz Coffee at the University of British Columbia Village in the summer of 2012. Before attending the meeting, I had several email exchanges with Joel and I knew exactly what topics I was going to discuss. I was not quite sure how Joel, as a self-identified Evangelical Christian educator, would respond to my concerns and questions as a Shia Muslim educator. Our first meeting went quite well. We were so engaged in our interfaith conversations that Joel extended his parking time to continue our dialogue. In our very first meeting, I was so passionate about the outcome of our conversations that I proposed to co-edit a book on interfaith dialogue inviting both religious and non-religious scholars into a conversation and it took Joel by surprise. I encouraged him to think of his strong network of scholars in the academe and invite them to contribute to my proposed chapter book.

At the time I had not been admitted into UBC and did not have a strong network of faculty members and scholars. That was why I asked him to initiate the invitations. Joel thought, instead, we could write a chapter for a co-edited book by Mary Shepard Wong and Ahmar Mahboob. He knew Mary from his previous engagement with Christian scholarship. He was going to see her in a conference in the United States two weeks after our meeting and discuss the possibility of including our chapter on interfaith dialogue.

To our surprise, Mary agreed to send an invitation to English language educators who were interested in interfaith dialogue. Her co-edited volume; *Spirituality & English Language Teaching: Religious Explorations of Teacher Identity, Pedagogy, and Context*, encompassed a broad perspective and invited scholars from around the world to contribute. When I received Joel's email confirming that invited us to contribute to Mary and Ahmar's co-edited volume, I became excited as it was my first opportunity to be able to express my voice as a Muslim English language educator. To write our chapter "Attempting Interfaith Dialogue in TESOL: A Duoethnography," Joel and I scheduled monthly meetings when we could engage in dialogue regarding our Christian and Muslim faiths. During each month, we read related books (Wong & Canagarajah, 2009, Wong, Dörnyei, & Kristjánsson, 2013) and articles (Edge, 2003; Pennycook & Coutand-Marin, 2003; Pennycook & Makoni, 2005) and reflected on how we would identify our identities as two religious ESL educators.

Our approach in dialogue was intentionally open-ended. Initially, we inquired into the conflicts involving Christianity and Islam through the literature (see Hadley, 2006; Karmani, 2005, 2006). Interested in interpersonal and transformative aspects of dialogue, we were inspired by Wong and Canagarajah (2009), as the conversations in the volume were formed by scholars who self-identified as Christian, agnostic, spiritual, and atheist. I can remember when Joel asked about the five pillars of Islam in our first meeting in a café on the 4th street. I had learned about the five pillars years back in primary school. I remember I was hesitating to answer this simple question, though. And I was wondering why?

Joel's provocative questions in our first meeting helped me attend my faith more fully. That was a pivotal moment in understanding and valuing my faith. Joel never stopped encouraging me to study and understand my faith. Joel was well aware and critical of Islamophobia in the Western world. He acknowledged the positive aspects of Islam and Muslim faith, and how the radical groups in the United States promoted anti-Islamic ideology.

Our ongoing dialogue was filled with opposing yet transformative views. Coming from the United States, Joel assumed an individualistic religious identity as a Christian ESL educator. My understanding of faith was more collective. I mainly focused on 'us' rather than 'I' as it was the way I had learned about Islam in Iran. Joel had a clear understanding of his Christian faith, I should admit, and he encouraged me to specify the tenets of my faith so I would be able to participate an intersubjective dialogue between two religious faiths. I concentrated on shared values across both faiths. I am now wondering why I was concentrating on shared values. Was it because of my collective understanding of religion, faith, and spiritual values? Did our differing values carry equal sociocultural and sociopolitical status in Vancouver? As a Shia Muslim, I still concentrate on commonalities of Abrahamic religions and understand the differences in these religions are negligible once we focus on peace for the world.

Writing Our Interfaith Dialogue into TESOL

During our regular writing and discussions, it became clear that we had a different understanding of notions like 'Muslim' and 'Christian'—even of 'religion'—and the ways in which these conceptions influence our personalities and teaching careers. We began to look for theoretical models that could accommodate a personal understanding, encompassing autobiography and *currere* (Pinar, 2011), sociological concepts of religious habitus (Mellor & Shilling, 2010), and communication perspectives on interfaith dialogue (Brown, 2013). Finally, duoethnography emerged as the most effective method for us to both engage in and model the type of interpersonal academic dialogue we believed was missing and necessary. We wrote our chapter not as representatives of various religious beliefs, or as TESOL professionals, but ultimately as 'different individuals trying to make meaning of their life histories and then reconceptualizing those meanings' (Norris, Sawyer, & Lund, 2012, p. 178).

Our writing testifies to the powerful influence of dialogue. Even if interlocutors start with certain preconceptions and prefabricated ideologies, by the end of their dialogic encounter, they can transform their understandings of ideology and undergo a transformative learning experience. In our interfaith dialogue, we experienced new understandings of intersubjective dialogue during which our knowledge of our respective lifeworlds transformed substantially. By the end of our dialogic encounter, once we had discussed controversial issues in Islam and Christianity, our intersubjective dialogue opened understandings of our respective educational experience in the United States and Iran. Interfaith dialogue contributed to the development of our religious belief systems as each of us learned of the other interlocutor, and modified previous understandings of Christianity and Islam.

There is scant separation between 'data collection' and 'writing' in duoethnography as the method involves individual life histories. Nonetheless, we generated a 'data set' to aid our analysis which included an 80-page document including every email we sent to each other—and periodically to others, like the editors of the volume—between June 2012 and October 2014. Supplementary data included our original drafts of our first paper (encompassing autobiographical narratives and accounts of our religious values) and our individual notes from the fourteen face-to-face meetings. Characteristic of duoethnography, researchers come from different sociocultural, linguistic, religious, or political backgrounds: for instance, black and white (McClellan & Sader, 2012), immigrant and non-immigrant (Nabavi & Lund, 2012), and in our case, Christian and Muslim (Heng Hartse & Nazari, 2018; Nazari & Heng Hartse, 2018).

My interfaith dialogue made me confident to understand, critique, and strengthen my faith in an intersubjective understanding of belief systems as sharing heart-felt perspectives on religion and faith can empower marginalized voices and enrich joint knowledge. My dialogue with Joel contributed to an increased ethical understanding of lifeworld and universe as we came to know how faith could connect us to ourselves. Clearly, beliefs are an integral part of our subjectivity even rooted in our psyche.

Intersubjective self-reflective dialogue is a medium for self-excavation and contemplative meaning-making process, and our life experience of religion can be explored. Our interfaith dialogue opened a supportive as well as critical shared space during which I could express my religious Muslim voice and listen to Joel's Christian responses. It took honesty and courage to reflect, question, and understand my religious values in the humanistic and intersubjective space of our dialogic exchanges. Duoethnography as a non-intrusive method of self-inquiry provided an open and empathetic arena for both of us to reflect on our verbal and non-verbal exchanges and question our cultural, social, political, and contextual understanding of faith in our life history and lived experience.

Concluding Notes

In this chapter, I have discussed the importance of dialogue in teacher and student development. Transformative dialogue as a relational learning experience can deepen intersubjective space to surface suppressed knowledge and prepare students teachers for a pluralistic world of today. In the concluding section of my chapter on interfaith dialogue, I was asked: "Is it possible to maintain your previous beliefs and welcome new ones?" (Heng Hartse & Nazari, 2018, p. 60). I am still amazed that interfaith dialogue could be important for student and teacher development, and not only in TESOL. Should we keep our questions regarding faith to ourselves, or should we open an interfaith conversation with other educators and our students? And in what way does sharing our inner work on faith contribute to student and teacher development? As Poole discussed in his forward to *Speaking of Teaching*, "digging down into our values" (Cohen & Porath, 2013, p. 9) is essential in teaching and teacher development. He continues further that it is "more challenging than discussions of teaching techniques" and "requires impressive degrees of honesty and courage". The honesty, courage, and integrity Poole highlights are ideal qualities for teachers, specifically when they are responding to questions raised during interfaith dialogue. Without an interpersonal dialogue on values and faiths in teacher development, in what way is it possible to know what beliefs and values are integral for participating teachers?

Once we understand plurality as a condition of possibility of education, dialogue on shared or differing values and beliefs becomes significant for student and teacher personal development—specifically in a multicultural character of Vancouver—and can facilitate intersubjective understandings of ethics and faith in their pedagogical practice. To deepen our understanding of dialogue and its educational significance, I will discuss Gadamer's theoretical framework as articulated in *Truth and Method*.

References

Aoki, T. T., Pinar, W. F., & Irwin, R. L. (2004). *Curriculum in a new key: The collected works of Ted T. Aoki*. Mahwah, NJ: Lawrence Erlbaum Associates, Publishers.

Bai, H. (2012). Education for enlightenment. In A. Cohen, & M. Porath (Eds.), *Speaking of teaching: Inclinations, inspirations, and innerworkings* (pp. 63–82). New York: Sense Publishers.

Bourdieu, P., & Thompson, J. B. (1991). *Language and symbolic power*. Cambridge, MA: Harvard University Press.

Brown, D. S. (2013). *Interfaith dialogue in practice: Christian, Muslim, Jew*. Kansas City, MO: Rockhurst University Press.

Clarke, A. (2012). Burgeo and back: Catching oneself in the act of being attentive to pedagogy. In A. Cohen, & M. Porath (Eds.), *Speaking of Teaching: Inclinations, inspirations, and innerworkings*, (pp. 55–62). Sense Publishers: New York.

Clarke, M., & Phelan, A. M. (2017). *Teacher education and the political: The power of negative thinking*. New York; London: Routledge, Taylor & Francis Group.

Cohen, A., Porath, M., Clarke, A., Bai, H., Leggo, C., & Meyer, K. (2012; 2013). *Speaking of teaching: Inclinations, inspirations, and innerworkings*. Papendrecht: Sense Publishers.

Doll, W. E. (1993a). Curriculum possibilities in a "post"-future. *Journal of Curriculum & Supervision, 8*(4), 277–292.

Doll, W. E. (1993b). *A post-modern perspective on curriculum*. New York: Teachers College Press.

Doll, W. E., & Trueit, D. (2012). *Pragmatism, postmodernism, and complexity theory: The fascinating imaginative realm of William E. Doll, jr*. New York, NY: Routledge.

Edge, J. (2003). Imperial troopers and servants of the Lord. *TESOL Quarterly, 37*, 701–709.

Elbaz, F. (2014). *Auto/biography and pedagogy: Memory, and place in teaching*. New York: Peter Lang.

Fisher, R. (2005). *Teaching children to think* (2nd ed.). Cheltenham, UK: Nelson Thornes Ltd.

Freire, P., & Ramos, M. B. (2014). *Pedagogy of the oppressed: 30th anniversary edition*. USA: Bloomsbury Publishing.

Freire, P., Freire, A. M. A., & Barr, R. R. (2014). *Pedagogy of hope: Reliving pedagogy of the oppressed* (Bloomsbury Revelations ed.). London, UK; New York, NY: Bloomsbury.

Gilligan, C. (2002). *The birth of pleasure*. New York, NY: Alfred A. Knopf.

Greene, M. (1973). *Teacher as stranger: Educational philosophy for the modern age*. Belmont, CA: Wadsworth Publishing Co.

Hadley, G. (2006). ELT and the new world order: Nation building or neocolonial reconstruction? *Issues in Political Discourse Analysis 1*(1), 23–48.

Heng Hartse, J., & Nazari, S. (2018). Duoethnography: An interfaith dialogue on lived experiences in TESOL. In M. S. Wong, & A. Mahboob (Eds.), *Spirituality & English language teaching: Religious explorations of teacher identity, pedagogy and context* (pp. 46–62). UK: Multilingual Matters.

Holquist, M. (2003). *Dialogism: Bakhtin and his world* (2nd ed.). GB: Routledge Ltd. doi: 10.4324/9780203425855.

Huebner, D. E. (1999). *The lure of the transcendent: Collected essays by Dwayne E. Huebner*. Mahwah, NJ: Lawrence Erlbaum Associates.

Jaramillo, N. (2015). Teachers and pedagogy for communal well-being. In M. F. He, & B. D. Schultz (Eds.), *The sage guide to curriculum in education* (pp. 165–173). Thousand Oaks, CA: SAGE Publications Ltd.

Jung, C. G. (2014). *The collected works of C. G. Jung*. New York, NY: Routledge.

Jung, J. H. (2016). *The concept of care in curriculum studies*. New York: Routledge.

Karmani, S. (2005). TESOL in a time of terror: Toward an Islamic perspective on applied linguistics. *TESOL Quarterly, 39*(4), 738–748.

Karmani, S. (2006). Good Muslims speak English. *Critical Discourse Studies, 3,* 103–105.

Kögler, H. (1996). *The power of dialogue: Critical hermeneutics after Gadamer and Foucault.* Cambridge, MA: MIT Press.

Leggo, C. (2012). Poetic inquiry. In A. Cohen, M. Porath, A. Clarke, H. Bai, & C. Leggo, & K. Meyer (Eds.), *Speaking of Teaching: Inclinations, inspirations, and innerworkings* (pp. 83–108). Sense Publishers: New York.

McClellan, P., & Sader, J. (2012). Power and privilege. In J. Norris, R. Sawyer, & D. Lund (Eds.), *Duoethnography: Dialogic methods for social, health, and educational research* (pp. 137–156). Walnut Creek, CA: Left Coast Publications.

Mellor, P. A., & Shilling, C. (2010). Body pedagogics and the religious habitus: A new direction for the sociological study of religion. *Religion, 40*(1), 27–38.

Nazari, S., & Heng Hartse, J. (2018). Duoethnography: Provoking ideology and curriculum in dialogic voices. In E. Hasebe-Ludt, & C. Leggo (Eds.), *Canadian curriculum studies: A Métissage of inspiration/imagination/interconnection* (pp. 165–173). Toronto, Ontario: Canadian Scholars' Press.

Noddings, N. (2015). *A Richer, brighter vision for American high schools.* Cambridge: Cambridge University Press.

Norris, J., Sawyer, R., & Lund, D. (2012; 2016). *Duoethnography: Dialogic methods for social, health, and educational research.* Walnut Creek; Chicago: Left Coast Press, Incorporated. doi: 10.4324/9781315430058.

Osberg, D., & Biesta, G. (2008). The emergent curriculum: Navigating a complex course between unguided learning and planned enculturation. *Journal of Curriculum Studies, 40*(3), 328; 313–328. doi: 10.1080/00220270701610746.

Pennycook, A., & Coutand-Marin, S. (2003). Teaching English as a missionary language (TEML). *Discourse: Studies in the Cultural Politics of Education, 24,* 337–353.

Pennycook, A., & Makoni, S. (2005). The modern mission: The language effects of Christianity. *Journal of Language, Identity and Education, 4*(2), 137–155.

Pinar, W. F. (2011). *The character of curriculum studies.* New York: Palgrave Macmillan.

Slattery, P. (1998; 2006). *Curriculum development in the postmodern era.* London, UK: Routledge.

Wong, M. S., & Canagarajah, S. (2009). *Christian and critical English language educators in dialogue: Pedagogical and ethical dilemmas.* New York: Routledge.

Wong, M. S., Kristjánsson, C., & Dörnyei, Z. (2013). *Christian faith and English language teaching and learning: Research on the interrelationship of religion and ELT.* New York: Routledge.

Zhang, H., & Pinar, W. F. (2015). *Autobiography and teacher development in China: Subjectivity and culture in curriculum reform.* New York, NY: Palgrave Macmillan.

Zhenyu, G. (2015). Philosophy for children in China: Teacher knowledge and teacher development. In Z. Hua, & W. F. Pinar (Eds.), *Autobiography and teacher development in China: Subjective and culture in curriculum reform* (pp. 99–119). New York: Palgrave Macmillan.

4

GADAMERIAN DIALOGUE

> The first condition in the art of conversation is ensuring that the other person is with us.
>
> Gadamer (2004, p. 360)

Introduction

In chapter three, I discussed how dialogue can contribute to teacher professional development as a responsibility of teachers and schools to ensure the highest-quality of teaching in a dynamic society. I studied the ways teachers' selfhood strengthened by engaging in open and genuine conversations, as reflective practice could reveal pedagogical meanings of teaching practice hitherto suppressed. In this chapter, I will focus specifically on a Gadamer-informed conception of dialogue as Gadamer complements a hermeneutical understanding of human being (as discussed earlier in *currere*) with a historically text-oriented consciousness of human subjectivity.

In his inner and outer circles of dialogue, Gadamer concentrates on an interpretive understanding of subjectivity rooted in religious and historical consciousness and human circumstances. I will respond to the following question: In what way can Gadamerian dialogue foster student and teacher development? I note that nowhere does Gadamer explicitly spell out the educational (and specifically pedagogical) implications of his philosophical doctrine. What follows, therefore, are my own inferences of his major work on philosophical hermeneutics and applied hermeneutics as I specify their significance for educational settings, and for student and teacher development.

The main idea that informs the whole of Gadamer's diverse literature is that understanding, interpretation, and application form one unified construct which lays bare our meaning-making process in understanding truth. Gadamer insisted on the hermeneutical foundation of ontology through text-based reading, re-reading, understanding, interpretation, and re-interpretation. Our diverse interpretations of the world around us and our judgments about the world inform our values, ethics, and decisions which are recurrent themes in Gadamerian hermeneutics. Our understanding of who we are and our meaning in the world are intrinsic to our interpretations of new ideas, thoughts, and belief systems.

Students and teachers appreciate this hermeneutic understanding once they evaluate their own reality and meaning-making through their interactions with students. As teachers inquire into their own reality and determine if it is interconnected with the unfamiliar world of students in different educational settings, they can unfold their horizons of meaning, comprehension, and hermeneutic understanding. As hermeneutics was developed as an interpretive methodology for understanding and interpretation of religious texts (in particular, within the Judeo-Christian canon), this meaning-making methodology is historically text-oriented. To interpret the meaning of the text, Gadamer (2006) emphasizes that keeping a hermeneutical distance from the text as that can facilitate our scientific understanding of the text:

> According to the self-understanding of science, then, it can make no difference to the historian whether a text was addressed to a particular person or was intended "to belong to all ages." The general requirement of hermeneutics is, rather, that every text must be understood according to the aim appropriate to it. But this means that historical scholarship first seeks to understand every text in its own terms and does not accept the content of what it says as true, but leaves it undecided. Understanding is certainly concretization [actualization], but one that involves keeping a hermeneutical distance. Understanding is possible only if one keeps oneself out of play. This is the demand of science. (p. 330)

In their interpretation of text—understood broadly to include not only written text but as also subjective and social experience—teachers can understand it according to its aim without their prejudgment of its content. Is it possible to keep ourselves out of play in our hermeneutic efforts to concretize our understanding of the written or oral discourse? To understand students' written and oral discourse, teachers need to keep a hermeneutical distance to interpret meaning. In my counselling sessions, I keep distant hermeneutically and strive to be as non-judgmental as possible to understand the reality of my students' educational experience.

One of my clients, Omid, felt hopeless and pressured regarding his decision-making for future achievements. In his first session, he lamented for 1.5 hours about his circumstances; I listened attentively and distanced myself for a hermeneutic understanding of his lifeworld. By the end of our session, the answers to his questions occurred to me as I stayed open and non-judgmental. Teachers can learn to suspend their own prejudgments and preconceptions in their hermeneutic understanding for the sake of student development.

Human beings can be curious creatures who inquire into the world to make sense of it and interpretation is an essence of our human condition once dealing with sources of meaning—either textual or non-textual. Teachers can be engaged in efforts to interpret and understand their students' lifeworld, but understanding students' human conditions and circumstances takes hermeneutic listening. Hermeneutic listening is closely connected to understanding of being; we can look within themselves and question own realities and possibilities in relation to the world wherein we exist. Interpreting the meaning of written or oral discourse can reflect and express one's existential and ontological understanding of being. The hermeneutic meaning of a text does not reside outside intellect; it is related to live experience and requires dialogue with human understanding for its interpretation.

Gadamer (2006) indicates that Husserl's understanding of human subjectivity is universal [and collective] so that he uses the term "life" for this understanding of "transcendental subjectivity":

> Husserl calls this phenomenological concept of the world "life-world". . . . This world horizon is a presupposition of all science as well and is, therefore, more fundamental. As a horizon phenomenon "world" is essentially related to subjectivity, and this relation means also that it "exists in transiency." . . . The concept of the life-world is the antithesis of all objectivism. . . . Certainly, one can inquire into the structure embracing all the worlds that man has ever experienced, which is simply the experience of the possibility of world, and in this sense we can indeed speak of an ontology of the world. (Gadamer, 2006, pp. 238–39)

This understanding of Husserl's ontology accords a historical dimension to human subjectivity and expands human horizon as being transcends its historical past and future in the present.

In our interpretation of the world, we can open a hermeneutic dialogue with the text within our personal-historical subjectivity. Nixon (2017) explains that Gadamer considers this understanding of life-world as significant as it establishes the ethical basis of hermeneutics on this connection: "it is by making sense of the world—and of ourselves in the world—that we realize our full human potential as ethical agents" (p. 15). For Gadamer the possibility of understanding the world and new beginnings is grounded in an interpretative understanding of our origins, and meanings rooted within those origins. Hermeneutical questions—such as who am I as a teacher? What is my reality and possibility in education? In what way is my understanding teachable and transferable? How should I live my teaching life? In what sense can I understand my true self through my teaching profession?—emphasize our being and becoming as educators in the world. These aspects of self-examination render Gadamerian hermeneutics distinctively ethical and can contribute to student and teacher self-fulfillment when studied wonderingly.

Gadamer (2004, p. 298) emphasizes that dialogue can occur once we pose a question towards the ontological reality of being, thereby opening new possibilities. Emphasizing the Socratic method of inquiry, he considers questions as leaps into the dark to explore new meanings. Students and teachers can become encouraged to also leap into the dark as they become their own questioners in their educational experience. Gadamer promotes asking "open" questions which do not presuppose a "yes" or "no" response to unfold new options and possibilities which extend our horizons and reality. Pedagogical questions give us an opportunity to inquire into the possibilities of education in the present and future and support our being and becoming in our educational experience.

Gadamerian Hermeneutics and Questions

Questions explore the ontological reality of our unique trajectories as they inquire into our sense of purpose, meaning of life, and new possibilities of leaning. Using questions, teachers shift the level of exploration and inquiry from the horizontal plane of unlimited possibility to the vertical plane of focused inquiry and investigation. Questions focus our concentration, priorities, and preferences in daily life, and they assume a questioner who is engaged with us in communications. Learning about the world and ourselves in it can start with asking open questions, questions not always with answers but which contribute to the being of the questioners as well as to the engagement of other interlocutors. Gadamer (2004, p. 360) maintains that questions should be genuine: "Every sudden idea has the structure of a question. But the sudden occurrence of the question is already a breach in the smooth front of popular opinion. Hence, we say that a question too occurs' to us, that it 'arises' or 'presents itself' more than that we raise it or present it."

Gadamer (2004, p. 484) confirms the arena of questioning and inquiring as an order of discipline that "guarantees truth." For Gadamer, hermeneutics enables true understanding of what we are saying as well as what others are saying. Questions can facilitate this hermeneutic process and open up the possibility of respectful agreement and disagreement based on mutual understanding and respect. Gadamer (2004) argues that deciding the question for the teachers and students is the path to understanding:

> Insofar as a question remains open, it always includes both negative and positive judgments. This is the basis of the essential relation between question and knowledge. For it is the essence of knowledge not only to judge something correctly but, at the same time and for the same reason, to exclude what is wrong. Deciding the question is the path to knowledge. What decides a question is the preponderance [predominance] of reasons for the one and against the other possibility. But this is still not full knowledge. The thing itself is known only when the counterinstances are dissolved, only when the counterarguments are seen to be incorrect. (2004, p. 358)

Students and teachers can decide on their questions when their pre-understandings do not foreclose their open questions. Gadamer (1992, p. 152) underscores the transformative power of hermeneutics: "To understand someone else is to see the justice, [and] the truth of their position. And this is what transforms us [as teachers and students]". The primary question hermeneutics raises is: in what ways do we understand the human world, human being, and our relation to the natural world we inhabit? The way we interpret questions in a dialogue is pivotal as understanding involves interpretation of the meaning of the perceived ideas, thoughts, and belief systems. The meanings revealed usually transcend what is exchanged in the conversation and can include our interpretation, analysis, and judgment as an integral element of our human condition. It is important to understand what we perceive and what is intended to be conveyed might be different as the interlocutors' realities vary based on their sociocultural, political, economic, educational and linguistic backgrounds.

Gadamerian hermeneutics provokes our understanding of conversations by questioning our perceived meanings to understand embedded realities and our probable preconceptions. Gadamer (1977, p. 8) emphasizes the need for a "hermeneutics of trust" rather than a "hermeneutics of suspicion"—a healthy and respectful skepticism—that concentrates on understanding rather than misunderstanding and misinterpretation of the meanings conveyed. Teachers have an especially important role in encouraging the students to ask open questions by establishing some hermeneutics of trust. In the following, I will discuss this communicative aspect of student and teacher development.

Gadamerian Questions and Teacher Role. Teachers have a substantial role in encouraging students to formulate and raise their questions. For instance, if the primary open question is "Why is it important to study Social Sciences and why should students know about the historical and political aspects of this academic discipline?", a secondary question can be "What should Social Sciences teach us?" and the third question might be "In what sense can Social Sciences improve our understanding of life?" Teachers can elicit the secondary and tertiary questions to guide students towards the primary question starting with "Why?" Learning about the uses of Social Sciences and what this subject teaches the students can encourage them to find an answer for their primary question. Teachers do not necessarily provide answers to these questions; however, they do encourage students' learning and thriving through guiding their open questions. They become like a navigator to suggest the students where the students are heading, emphasizing the significance of the primary question and the unforeseen future possibilities along their way of learning. Understanding the students' mood once dealing with questions can become the primary focus of the teachers. In his *Heidegger and Gadamer's Question of Being*, Regan (2016, pp. 380–381) explains Heidegger's presentation of Dasein's analysis of itself, specifically its awareness of the moods it meets:

> Heidegger places *Dasein*'s analysis of itself into a practical, everyday meaning of life where dasein becomes aware of the moods in which it meets and engages the world (Gadamer, 1994). Moods have a time element to them too: the young boxer who in the midst of training visualises his hero or enemy and willing him on to train harder, or the adult son holding his baby spurred on to be a good father, and to be kind, caring and considerate just like his own father or because his father had not been. This mood is evident in Heidegger's choice of Being as a consistent career long focus for study.

Helping students and teachers to become aware of their moods as they engage with the curriculum underlines how reciprocally related teacher and student development are. Recall that Gadamer understands teaching as a hermeneutic questioning of being alive, and the meanings such questioning includes. He structured his lectures and teaching with a series of questions to clarify his argument. Nixon (2017) reflects on Gadamer's teaching in Gadame's own authoritarian era:

> He was in effect modelling what it is to think. 'The student', as Nicholson (2012, 70–71) puts it, 'is invited to think because the teacher does not merely think but fosters thinking through acting out thinking in the course of a class.' There was nothing obviously charismatic or inspirational about Gadamer. He was not that kind of teacher. . . . Reading one of Gadamer's lectures or addresses is much more like sitting in on an ongoing conversation than attending a formal lecture or political rally. It is not even as if Gadamer were seeking to persuade. He is more often than not simply trying to show - to exemplify or figure-forth - what it means to understand. (Nixon, p. 34)

Gadamer's teaching was focused on a dialogic understanding of questions that encouraged students to explore their own meaning-making, requiring an intersubjective dialogue with themselves, with the other students, and with the teacher (and absent presuppositions or determined answers to the questions). During such organic dialogue, self-understandings of teachers and students can merge—the phenomenon I will discuss in the following.

The Fusion of Horizons and Teacher Role. To develop our understanding of each other, we need a supportive space for dialogic conversation, exchanges of information, and authentic negotiation of meaning. Teachers can encourage their students to find their path towards understanding; to work through their partly formed ideas, thoughts, and meanings; and to risk being misunderstood. Teachers' positive and inclusive attitude towards students' open questions allows their inquiry into unexplored aspects of meaning and subjective understanding of learning. Acknowledging the differing and opposing perspectives of students presupposes a disposition of open-mindedness.

In *Truth and Method*, Gadamer formulates the notion of "horizon" to indicate that we can transcend our perspectives, ideas, meanings, and visions to understand the differing ideas in dialogic conversations. Gadamer (2004) emphasizes the dynamic status of our horizons and insists on "the fundamental non-definitiveness of the horizon in which [teacher or student's] understanding moves" (p. 366). He underscores the significance of understanding the meaning of horizon and everything within that horizon for educators and their attempt at mutual understanding through continuous mediation, rethinking, and readjustment of their perceptual field:

> In fact the horizon of the present is continually in the process of being formed because we are continually having to test all our prejudices. An important part of this testing occurs in encountering the past and in understanding the tradition from which we come. Hence the horizon of the present cannot be formed without the past .... Rather, understanding is always the fusion of these horizons supposedly existing by themselves. ... In a tradition [,] this process of fusion is continually going on, for there old and new are always combining into something of living value, without either being explicitly foregrounded from the other. (Gadamer, 2004, p. 305)

In this ongoing fusion, students and teachers are expanding their historical horizons as they make sense of themselves and their educational experience. Engaged in dialogue, teachers and students' horizons can merge. As the interlocutors' [teachers and students] horizons expand and transform beyond their scope in dialogic conversations, they are no longer the same as they were prior to the dialogue. Each interpretation of dialogic conversations is unique and open to other reinterpretations; the fusion of horizons is a continuous process of understanding rather than an achieved state and a final objective. Gadamer (2001) emphasizes the mobile nature of our interpretations in this process: "horizons are not rigid but mobile; they are in motion because our prejudgments are constantly put to the test" (p. 48). Teachers' self-conscious understandings of their horizons and prejudgments can provide a supportive space for their students to notice their possible prejudices and misunderstandings. By understanding the mobile horizons of students, teachers can encourage them to expand their understanding of self in dialogue and their reinterpretation of their ongoing meaning-making process which contributes to student well-being as well as teacher professional development.

Hermeneutic Understanding and Subjectivity

In sharp contrast to scientific ideals of objectivity, Gadamer believes in the "productive power of prejudice" in hermeneutic understanding (Nixon, 2017, p. 19). He emphasizes the implicit value of "the subject" and "subjectivity" and reinforces the "necessity of *trusting* to the subject and to the 'subjectivity' [emphasis is mine] in all understanding". Arguing that hermeneutics cannot be confined to "a technique for avoiding misinterpretation" using inappropriate bias and prejudice, Gadamer (1977, p. 8) contends that "avoidance technique does not in itself constitute understanding." Gaining understanding follows once we use our own prejudices properly to connect with what we are seeking to understand. Although teachers work from their own prejudices when dealing with questions, constant avoidance of inappropriate prejudice and employing positive prejudice—that students can learn, for instance—can provide pedagogic moments during which students and teachers realize that their subjective engagement with the curriculum includes each other, creating moments of insight in the classroom.

Gadamer (2004) uses *play* as an ontological explanation and indicates that the mode of being of the work of art is different from the subjectivity engaged in play:

> When we speak of play in reference to the experience of art, this means neither the orientation nor even the state of mind of the creator or of those enjoying the work of art, nor the freedom of a subjectivity engaged in play, but the mode of being of the work of art itself. In analyzing aesthetic consciousness, we recognized that conceiving aesthetic consciousness as something that confronts an object does not do justice to the real situation. This is why the concept of play is important in my exposition. (p. 102)

Gadamer's (2004) explanation of the playful nature of art can clarify the role of teacher subjectivity that it can transform during educational experience. He asserts that it is the personal experience of the person who experiences the work of art that changes not the work of art itself: "The work of art is not an object that stands over against a subject for itself. Instead the work of art has its true being in the fact that it becomes an experience that changes the person who experiences it" (Gadamer 2004, p. 103). He continues that just as play has its own essence and individual identity independent of players, art works also have their own individual identity independent of subjective experience of people who observe the artifact. Simms (2015) discusses Gadamer's analogy of art and play emphasizing the aesthetic consciousness of the player: "It is the player, or the aesthetic consciousness, who changes during the course of a game or the experience of an artwork; the essence of art, or of play, is immutable" (p. 59). He continues that metaphorical examples of the word play by Gadamer (2004, p. 104) such as "the play of light, the play of the waves, the play of gears or parts of machinery, the interplay of limbs,. . ., even a play on words" make a non goal-directed state emphasizing aesthetic consciousness is at play: "there is a to-and-fro movement that is not intended to bring the activity to an end" (Simms, 2015, p. 60).

Once we understand the significance of aesthetic consciousness, teachers and students as the primary player of the game [curriculum] become highlighted in our understanding and interpretation of the play. In understanding curriculum, teachers can continuously interpret the art of education by attuning their mode of being in conscious and unprejudiced decisions they are making. Understanding Gadamer's teaching experience can open a dialogue to developing teacher professional identity.

Gadamerian Hermeneutics and Teaching

As a teacher Gadamer (1992) asserts that his writing, lectures, seminars, and symposia are his secondary forms of self-manifestation:

> My work comes from my teaching ... Writing is my secondary form of self-presentation, as Plato thought it should be ... I am a dialogical being. When teaching, I was very shy at first, I never looked at the students. This was the case in lectures. But when I held seminars, I myself was present from the first day: I had a real talent for listening and replying and believe that that remains my talent; to listen even to the silent voice of an audience. (Gadamer, 1992, pp. 65–6)

To me, Gadamer's power of listening is the foundation of his hermeneutic philosophy, as he can listen to silent moments of an audience which reminds me of bracketing instances in phenomenology.

Gadamer premised teaching on the possibility of mutual understanding and mutual trust. Acknowledging human differences, Gadamer believes in the commonality of understanding and recognizes human beings as ethical beings who are morally responsible for each other. The main motive of education for Gadamer is to provide an emancipatory and liberating opportunity for the students to free them from constraints imposed by educational institutions which "implement assessment regimes that focus on selective differentiation and that fail to provide positive and formative feedback to students regarding their achievements and their potential" (Nixon, 2017, pp. 24–25). This purpose is only achieved through a subjective understanding of students' individual and unique possibilities emphasized in transformational education which concentrates on providing a medium for flourishing and fulfilling these potentials.

Gadamer (1992) regards teaching as *mediation* during which teachers enter history as participants in a dialogic conversation that constitutes what he termed as hermeneutic *tradition*. Education provides an opportunity for students who enter the historical moment to ensure this dialectic conversation with *tradition*, thinking of teachers as an interpreter and mediator of it. From hermeneutical perspective, therefore, education is considered as a truly "transcultural practice, at the core of communication across difference" between the teacher and students (Grau, 2014, p. 79). Understanding the nature of this dialectic and communicative aspect of education is an important aspect of student and teacher development.

Dialectic Nature of Knowledge

Knowledge is a dialectic phenomenon, as it always includes opposites. The dialectic nature of knowledge is manifested in questions and answers so both the person who has a question and the one who attempts to provide an answer to the question manifest knowledge. Gadamer (2004) confirms the dialectical nature of knowledge: "Knowledge is dialectical from the ground up. Only a person who has questions can have knowledge, but questions include the antithesis of yes and no, of being like this and being like that" (p. 359). For Plato and Aristotle, knowledge shares a common meaning. Gadamer (1986a, p. 34) notes his task as "to make comprehensible what Aristotle shares with Plato even when he critically separates himself from him". Simms (2015, p. 47) notes that Plato uses the word *phronesis* more loosely than does Aristotle as it can at times be interchangeable with either *techne* (skill, art) or *episteme* (scientific knowledge). There still exists a noticeable difference in Plato between *technical-theoretical* reasonableness and *practical* reasonableness. As Gadamer (1986a) indicates, in the exercise of practical reason Plato contends:

> One cannot rely on previously acquired general knowledge, and yet one still claims to reach a judgement by one's own weighing of the pros and cons and to decide reasonably in each case. Whoever deliberates with himself and with others about what would be the right thing to do in a particular practical situation is plainly prepared to support his decision with nothing other than good reasons. (pp. 35–6)

Plato underscores the significance of subjective understanding of knowledge which is first-hand and argues that previously acquired knowledge [objective understanding] cannot always be helpful.

For their mutual development, students and teachers can explore their subjectivity using hermeneutic understanding and reasoning; this transcends any objective understanding of knowledge. Gadamer (2004) relates Aristotle's analysis of moral knowledge to hermeneutical problem of the human sciences:

> Admittedly, hermeneutical consciousness is involved neither with technical nor moral knowledge, but these two types of knowledge still include the same task of application that we have recognized as the central problem of hermeneutics.

> Certainly, application does not mean the same thing in each case. There is a curious tension between a techne that can be taught and one acquired through experience. The prior knowledge that a person has who has been taught a craft is not, in practice, necessarily superior to the kind of knowledge that someone has who is untrained but has had extensive experience. (p. 313)

Although Aristotle distinguished between knowledge [*techne*] gained through practice and knowledge gained through extensive experience, he poisted no superiority between the two.

Lived experience can contain *techne* and for teacher development, teacher educators rely on their extensive experience and academic study maybe more than upon skills (although the three can coalesce). Indeed, for Aristotle true mastery of knowledge is acquired through *techne* nurtured by the life-world which can be the source for moral knowledge. *Techne* or extensive experience can never be sufficient for making right moral decisions; must one open hermeneutic dialogue to achieve a deeper understanding. Simms (2015, p. 48) emphasizes that Plato at times uses dialectic *"phronesis"* that is neither general nor teachable knowledge: "Dialectic is not something that one can simply learn. It is more than that. It is 'reasonableness'" (Gadamer, 1986a, p. 37). I personally understand dialectical knowledge as a latent talent or wisdom not unlike Gadamer's uses of the term *disposition*. For Plato dialectic is not a *techne* but a "way of being" [and becoming] as Gadamer contends (1986a, p. 39). According to Gadamer's (1986a) understanding of Plato, self-knowledge is dialectic:

> Plato gives self-understanding a more general meaning: wherever the concern is knowledge that cannot be acquired by any learning, but instead through examination of oneself and of the knowledge one believes one has, we are dealing with dialectic. Only in dialogue - with oneself or with others - can one get beyond the mere prejudices [and preconceptions] of prevailing conventions. (Gadamer, 1986a, p. 43)

Gadamer seems to understand dialectics in Platonic sense, as hermeneutics is at once a form of dialogue, self-reflexive, and a philosophy in themselves.

In contrast, Aristotle considers understanding as applying something universal to a specific situation. The reason and knowledge Aristotle discusses can be said to be determined by Dasein, so they are attached to one's being [self]. Gadamer (2004) considers Aristotle as "the founder of ethics as a discipline independent of metaphysics" (310), while Heidegger was suspicious of Aristotle as "metaphysical" (cited in Simms, 2015, p. 50). Considering these perspectives, teacher dialectic knowledge is an ongoing hermeneutic understanding which can be self-reflective, self-explorative, unprejudiced, and ethical. Teachers can enrich and broaden a hermeneutic understanding of their professional identity using the art of dialogue in concert with other stakeholders.

The Art of Conversation

Gadamer's (1986b, p. 114) contribution to hermeneutics shifts its concentration from a traditional linguistic understanding of language to social, cultural, and communicational aspects which facilitate our understanding of the world. Language as a dialogic means of communication presupposes an addressee and an addressor. Nixon (2017, p. 29) notes that neither addressee nor addressor is precisely definable:

> For example, the kinds of founding religious texts with which hermeneutics had traditionally been concerned are shrouded in obscurity regarding their authorship and likely readership. Indeed, one of the prime tasks of hermeneutics had been to provide a philologically grounded interpretation of specific texts that would offer more general insights into questions of textual transmission and reception. Gadamer built on this legacy of philological hermeneutics to focus on what he saw as the dialogical and conversational nature of all human understanding.

This dialogic understanding of hermeneutics reflects Bakhtin's conception of dialogism as human beings are in ongoing dialogue with other works of literature and their authors to make their own meaning.

Our existential experience, then, is informed by preceding work of literature so our dialogic experience extends to the past and future. Works of literature are informed by dialogue of the present, and future literary texts will represent dialogic understandings of self, existence, place, and time.

Past and future are extensions of human beings, and the previous as well as the future literature are also informed by our extended experience of lifeworld. The idea of conversation recalls the open-ended nature of knowledge and understanding. It is essential to keep the conversation going by ensuring that it stays open. None of the interlocutors knows and predicts the direction of the conversation. There is no competition for *succeeding in* the conversation as the flow of exchanges would cease then. Gadamer (2004, p. 360) underscores the art of questioning in the Socratic-Platonic dialectic:

> the Socratic-Platonic dialectic raises the art of questioning to a conscious art; but there is something peculiar about this art. We have seen that it is reserved to the person who wants to know - i.e., who already has questions. The art of questioning is not the art of resisting the pressure of opinion; it already presupposes this freedom.

> It is not an art in the sense that the Greeks speak of techne, not a craft that can be taught or by means of which we could master the discovery of truth.

Gadamer views the art of questioning in a dialectic conversation as the art of thinking and conducting intense dialogue which typically occurs between two people as he draws on the nature of dialogue in Plato and of dialectic in Hegel compared to conversation: "For Gadamer, dialogue was not just a means of passing the time in pleasant but aimless conversation; it was an intense, restless, and unending quest for truth" (Gadamer, 2001, p. 10). Gadamer writes in a conversation "one does not know beforehand what will come out of it, and one usually does not break it off unless forced to do so, because there is always something more you want to say" (2001, p. 59), so conversations occur genuinely with no forced control of human factors.

Terminating a conversation represents a respectful agreement in which all interlocutors acknowledge the pause. Gadamer (2004) notes that real conversations encompass disagreements and differences in which interlocutors explore new realities, and writes "The first condition in the art of conversations is ensuring that the other person is with us" (2004, p. 360). Among the participants of the conversation, there is a tacit agreement about the subject and an enthusiasm to value the opinions of the other interlocutors: "To conduct a conversation means to allow oneself to be conducted by the subject matter to which the partners in the dialogue are oriented. It requires that one does not try to argue the other person down but that one really considers the weight of the other's opinion" (pp. 360–61).

Once the interlocutors respond to the differing opinions, the art of questioning can encourage deeper understanding of personal opinions and possibilities. Gadamer (2004) encourages the discussants to bring out the real strength of ideas and opinions in dialectic exchanges by understanding the art of questioning:

> But the art of testing is the art of questioning. For we have seen that to question means to lay open, to place in the open. As against the fixity of opinions, questioning makes the object and all its possibilities fluid. A person skilled in the "art" of questioning is a person who can prevent questions from being suppressed by the dominant opinion .... Dialectic consists not in trying to discover the weakness of what is said, but in bringing out its real strength. It is not the art of arguing (which can make a strong case out of a weak one) but the art of thinking (which can strengthen objections by referring to the subject matter). (Gadamer, 2004, p. 361)

Although the art of questioning is rooted in a subjective intervention in dialogic exchanges, Gadamer provides a sympathetic understanding of questioning to protect it from being suppressed by dominant opinion.

What teachers can understand within the context of their practice for professional development is that their personal judgment and understanding play a crucial role in preventing questions from being suppressed, weakening the power of questioning and the quality of dialectic understanding. Hermeneutics and language are intertwined, as meaning is conveyed through the language of discussants which is an essential aspect for understanding Gadamerian dialogue in student and teacher development.

Gadamerian Hermeneutics and Language

Influenced by Heidegger, Gadamer (2007) manifests his sensitivity to the question of Being as a feature of his thought in different phenomena including language:

> When I wrote the sentence 'Being that can be understood is language', what was implied by this was that what is can never be completely understood. This is implied insofar as everything that goes under the name of language always goes beyond whatever achieves the status of a proposition. That which is to be understood is that which comes into language, but of course it is always that which is taken as something, taken as something true. This is the hermeneutical dimension - a dimension in which Being 'shows itself'. (Gadamer 2007, p. 162)

As being is manifested in language, its attributes are translated and transferred into language.

Gadamer's final chapter of *Truth and Method* concerns language as the medium of hermeneutic experience. His understanding of language is centered on hermeneutics while as Simms (2015, p. 36) writes "Heidegger's purpose is to propose a corrective to philosophy itself, to replace 'metaphysics' by a fundamental ontology (the enquiry into being as such). The difference between Heidegger and Gadamer here is that Gadamer is less radical, less keen to 'destroy' metaphysics". For Gadamer, hermeneutics is fundamental to philosophy as it is to any other mode of being. Philosophy is a phenomenon orchestrated through language which is essential for hermeneutics:

> In fact, historical consciousness too involves mediation between past and present. By seeing that language is the universal medium of this meditation, we were able

to expand our enquiry from its starting point, the critiques of aesthetic and historical consciousness and the hermeneutics that would replace them, to universal dimensions. For man's relation to the world is absolutely and fundamentally verbal in nature, and hence intelligible. Thus, hermeneutics is, as we have seen, *a universal aspect of philosophy*, and not just the methodological basis of the human sciences. (Gadamer, 2004, pp. 470–71)

So, hermeneutics is embodied in language as a universal medium of mediation between past, present and future. Teachers can learn to interpret students' language as it is a verbal window opening towards their reality, being, and intellect. Students' language can contain intended messages that mindful and attentive teachers can interpret using hermeneutic understanding. Literature and hermeneutics are in a symbiotic relationship:

> It is universally true of texts that only in the process of understanding them is the dead trace of meaning transformed back into living meaning. We must ask whether what we found to be true of the experience of art is also true of texts as a whole, including those that are not works of art. We saw that the work of art is actualized only when it is "presented," and we were drawn to the conclusion that all literary works of art are actualized only when they are read. Is this true also of the understanding of any text? Is the meaning of all texts actualized only when they are understood? (Gadamer, 2004, pp.156–57)

Gadamer's hermeneutic understanding of artwork and literature can be reflected in human lived experience. Both literary work and art work are only actualized when they become human experience and understanding. Teachers can understand their students only once they can trace back the meaning of their language as students "present" themselves which takes teachers' mindful decisions to facilitate this opportunity. When referring to literature, Gadamer (2004, p. 156) contends written word is so strange as well as demanding that raises a particular problem of translation to human understanding:

> Nothing is so strange, and at the same time so demanding, as the written word [or oral discourse]. ... The written word and what partakes of it - literature - is the intelligibility of mind transferred to the most alien medium. Nothing is so purely the trace of the mind as writing, but nothing is so dependent on the understanding mind either.

Understanding students' written and oral discourse is only possible once teachers can trace it to their intellect. Understanding students' intellectual meaning that appears in their verbal or non-verbal discourse using hermeneutics becomes possible once teachers understand their presence and accomplish historical consciousness as discussed earlier. Gadamer underscores that hermeneutic interpretation requires transformation:

> The remnants of past life - what is left of buildings, tools, the contents of graves - are weather-beaten by the storms of time that have swept over them, whereas a written tradition, once deciphered and read, is to such an extent pure mind that it speaks to us as if in the present. That is why the capacity to read, to understand what is written, is like a secret art, even a magic that frees and binds us. In it time and space seem to be superseded. (Gadamer, 2004, p. 156)

Reading literature is understanding the lived experience of the people in the past who present themselves through the artwork of words and letters.

Deciphering and interpreting our written tradition is living in the past and understanding their reality and possibility. Gadamer considers hermeneutic understanding of language as a miracle of human being and is an enthusiastic supporter of literary work as a means to understand the human condition. Simms (2015, p. 69) writes "being literate is also, and thereby, a precondition of hermeneutics, of being the hermeneutic being who understands others and, through that understanding, also understands himself." Note that Simms's understanding of hermeneutics is dialogic and provides an organic understanding of human conditions and circumstances. Understanding this organic and dialogic aspect of literature embedded in the complexity and novelty of language can help teachers and teacher educators to connect with new horizons of their being and to bridge this understanding to their student life-world.

Language and Prejudice. When interpreting a language, one can overcome one's fore-meanings and misinterpretations of the discourse encountered. Hermeneutic understanding of reading the text involves an understanding of the linguistic usage of the time of the author. Gadamer (2004, p. 270) writes when reading, we are "pulled up short by the text. Either it does not yield any meaning at all or its meaning is not compatible with what we had expected. This is what brings us up short and alerts us to a possible difference in usage." Our preconceived understandings of meanings of the words and phrases or misunderstanding of a text are partly rooted in the fact that the text was written by an author with different meanings of life, reflective perhaps, of his or her time and place. Staying open to the meanings, allowing them to unfold, can perhaps facilitate understanding the language. Gadamer (2004, p. 294) notes hermeneutics can help us to become conscious of our fore-understanding: "understanding means, primarily, to understand the content of what is said, and only secondarily to isolate and understand another's meaning as such. Hence the most basic of all hermeneutic preconditions remains one's own fore-understanding, which comes from being concerned with the same subject." There is a continuous dialogue between the content of the text and the reader.

Acknowledging fore-understandings as the creator of the content and receiver of the message resemble peeling off the skin to understand the content of life-world. Regarding the meanings of our fore-understanding, Simms (2015) asserts:

> The task of understanding - hermeneutics - is to get from the meanings of our fore-understandings to the meaning of the text, and then to incorporate this recovered meaning into our own meaning (so that, ultimately, our own meaningfulness is enhanced and we have a greater understanding of ourselves). How is this achieved? (p. 69)

Engaged with pre-understanding, receivers of textual or verbal messages might have a biased understanding. Hermeneutics provokes our initial understanding [fore-understanding] of the text for a greater understanding. Knowing that prejudice can disturb our true understanding, teachers and students can focus on a conscious interpretation of each other's language to understand it precisely, impartially. Gadamer (2004) highlights the significance of being open to such understanding of the text:

> All that is asked is that we remain open to the meaning of the other person or text. But this openness always includes our situating the other meaning in relation to the whole of our own meanings or ourselves in relation to it. Now, the fact is that meanings represent a fluid multiplicity of possibilities (in comparison to the agreement presented by a language and a vocabulary), but within this multiplicity of what can be thought - i.e., of what a reader can find meaningful and hence expect to find - not everything is possible; and if a person fails to hear what the other person is really saying, he will not be able to fit what he has misunderstood into the range of his own various expectations of meaning (p. 271).

In relational understanding of the text, the reader situates the meaning derived from the text vis-à-vis his or her pre-understanding of meaning.

In hermeneutics, openness to the message conveyed [bottom-up processing] and the fore-meanings of the text [top-down processing] both interact to help us make sense of the text. For hermeneutic understanding, students and teachers can use their parallel processing of meaning-making during which both the intended message of the text and fore-understanding collaborate to make an understanding of the text or verbal language of the students. Gadamer (2004) underscores this parallel processing of discourse as being aware of our own biases once reading and interpreting messages:

> A person trying to understand a text is prepared for it to tell him something. That is why a hermeneutically trained consciousness must be, from the start, sensitive to the text's alterity. But this kind of sensitivity involves neither "neutrality" with respect to content nor the extinction of one's self [fore-understanding], but the foregrounding and appropriation of one's own fore-meanings and prejudices. The important thing is to be aware of one's own bias, so that the text can present itself in all its otherness and thus assert its own truth against one's own fore-meanings. (Gadamer, 2004, pp. 271–72)

Being aware of our prejudices is the point of entry into understanding the text, as our biases can obstruct our hermeneutic understanding of the text.

Recall that Gadamer (2004) contends that the hermeneutic task is not necessarily to eliminate our biases but rather to recognize them in our open encounter with the discourse so that they do not occlude or obstruct our genuine understanding of the text:

> It is not at all a matter of securing ourselves against the tradition that speaks out of the text then, but, on the contrary, of excluding everything that could hinder us from understanding it in terms of the subject matter. It is the tyranny of hidden prejudices that makes us deaf to what speaks to us in tradition. (p. 272)

In what way is it possible for teachers to know that their understanding of the text is prejudiced and biased? In what sense can an understanding of their hidden prejudice contribute to teacher self and professional development? Responding to these self-reflective questions can render an in-depth hermeneutic understanding for teachers and contribute to their continuous self-education and professional development.

Prejudice and the Enlightenment. Gadamer (2004, p. 273) affirms the hermeneutical problem of prejudice and the role of the European Enlightenment in the command to bring conscious understanding of our prejudices, noting that "the fundamental prejudice of the Enlightenment is the prejudice against prejudice itself, which denies tradition its power." He considers prejudice as a fact, and notes that "The history of ideas shows that not until the Enlightenment does the concept of prejudice acquire the negative connotation familiar today."

To provide a more impartial understanding of prejudice, Gadamer (2004, p. 273) recovers a pre-Enlightenment conception of prejudice as "a judgement that is rendered before all elements that determine a situation have been fully examined" and writes prejudice does not necessarily mean an erroneous judgment but it can have either a positive or negative value. In the Enlightenment, the idea that prejudice was irrational and illogical became prevalent and rationalism confirmed the idea that prejudice should actually be corrected. Prejudice lacked rational grounding was therefore irrational:

> The only thing that gives a judgment dignity is its having a basis, a methodological justification (and not the fact that it may actually be correct). For the Enlightenment, the absence of such a basis does not mean that there might be other kinds of certainty, but rather that the judgment has no foundation in the things themselves - i.e., that it is "unfounded." This conclusion follows only in the spirit of rationalism. It is the reason for discrediting prejudices and the reason scientific knowledge claims to exclude them completely. (Gadamer, 2004, p. 273)

Being unfounded does not necessarily mean being baseless and unscientific, and students' and teachers' journeys from scientific knowledge to subjective understanding of their prejudice can be the point of entry into enlightened decisions, as well as personal and professional development.

Understanding that we might have bias or prejudice due to our human conditions and circumstances is crucially important. More significantly, humans are able to critique and revise the influencing and rational power of their prejudice. Gadamer (2004) strives to turn those ideas that the Enlightenment and modern science assign as negative values into positive concepts and he starts with prejudice:

> Reversing the Enlightenment's presupposition results in the paradoxical tendency toward restoration - i.e., the tendency to reconstruct the old because it is old, the conscious return to the unconscious, culminating in the recognition of the superior wisdom of the primeval age of myth. But the romantic reversal of the Enlightenment's criteria of value actually perpetuates the abstract contrast between myth and reason. All criticism of the Enlightenment now proceeds via this romantic mirror image of the Enlightenment. (2004, p. 275)

Gadamer does not intend to use a Romantic view as Romanticism hardly attempted to restore an undetermined past of earlier times.

Gadamer (2004, p. 276) critiques what he seems to regard as the prejudice of the Enlightenment: that it is as opinionated and abstract to accept there was a "mysterious darkness" in which there was a mythological consciousness preceding all thought as that of "a state of perfect enlightenment or of absolute knowledge." Hence understanding hermeneutics to overcome the Enlightenment prejudice implies mastering all other prejudices, one can be conscious of not falling into romanticizing the past, that of mythology. A conscious return to the unconscious, however, can help students and teachers critique their previous knowledge and reconstruct their understanding of prejudice and bias that can have a positive and empowering influence on their informed decisions.

Prejudice, Authority, and Tradition. Humans are historical beings that are situated within traditions as an inescapable part of that being. Gadamer (2004, p. 278) notes that considering the historical dimension of our being, we belong to history rather than to ourselves:

> Long before we understand ourselves through the process of self-examination, we understand ourselves in a self-evident way in the family, society, and state in which we live. The focus of subjectivity is a distorting mirror. The self-awareness of the individual is only a flickering in the closed circuits of historical life. That is why the prejudices of the individual, far more than his judgments, constitute the historical reality of his being.

Thus, our historical understanding of being-in-the-world (family, society, state) precedes our understanding of subjectivity.

Thus, history precedes autobiography, as history is public and autobiography is history made private, therefore "history does not belong to us; we belong to it." Gadamer (2004, p. 278) formulates two fundamental epistemological questions for historical hermeneutics to rehabilitate the concept of prejudice: "What is the ground of the legitimacy of prejudices? What distinguishes legitimate prejudices from the countless others which it is the undeniable task of critical reason to overcome?" Since Gadamer considers prejudices as "conditions of understanding," he acknowledges that there are legitimate prejudices.

In the light of Gadamerian understanding of subjectivity vis-à-vis historical life, can students and teachers distinguish their legitimate prejudices form their illegitimate ones? This question invites students and teachers (and teacher educators) to reflect on their practice, as prejudice, subjectivity, and history all influence teacher philosophy. Gadamer (2004, p. 280) differentiates between two types of prejudice:

> that of 'authority' and that of 'overhastiness'. In each case, it is the task of reason to overcome them: overhastiness is the incorrect deployment of reason, whereas

authority is the result of not using one's reason at all ....' The Enlightenment's distinction between faith in authority and using one's own reason is, in itself, legitimate', Gadamer says, since 'if the prestige of authority displaces one's own judgement then authority is in fact a source of prejudices'. (cited in Simms, 2015, p. 72)

Gadamer highlights that the Enlightenment overlooked the fact that authority is based on the recognition of knowledge: "the knowledge, namely, that the other is superior to oneself in judgment and insight and that for this reason his judgment takes precedence - i.e., it has priority over one's own" (2004, p. 281). Basing authority on knowledge, Gadamer insists that acknowledging authority is not blind obedience:

> Acknowledging authority is always connected with the idea that what the authority says is not irrational and arbitrary but can, in principle, be discovered to be true. This is the essence of the authority claimed by the teacher, the superior, the expert. The prejudices that they implant are legitimized by the person who presents. (2004, p. 281)

This apparently paradoxical understanding of authority sounds legitimate in teacher education as those teachers who assume authority, have achieved this distinguishing power because of their knowledge and experience, so it is not an arbitrary practice, and to some degree it is embedded in tradition. To overcome the prejudice of tradition, Gadamer (2004, p. 282) writes:

> Even the most genuine and pure tradition does not persist because of the inertia of what once existed. It needs to be affirmed, embraced, [and] cultivated. It is, essentially, preservation, and it is active in all historical change. But preservation is an act of reason, though an inconspicuous one.

Once we understand subjectivity by Gadamer as a mere flickering in the circuit of historical life, understanding tradition and our subjectivity in relation to that becomes tradition. This understanding can make teachers more committed to confirming their own and others' traditions and view their subjectivity in continuous dialogue with those traditions and historical meanings.

Concluding Notes

Understanding Gadamerian hermeneutics recalls my previous understanding: dialectic knowledge, art of conversation, language, prejudice, the Enlightenment, tradition, and authority in teacher professional development.

Learning about the dialectic nature of knowledge encourages educators to invite their students to ask their open questions. Mastering the art of questioning and respectful termination of conversations by overcoming the pressure of opinion contributes to student and teacher development.

In their hermeneutic understanding of literature, teachers live in the past and interpret such reality and possibility using language as a miracle of human beings to understand the human condition. Acknowledging fore-meanings and fore-understanding will enable teachers and educators to interpret textual and non-textual discourses unprejudiced by their past. Recovering the meaning of prejudice as not necessarily erroneous judgment but as having a negative or positive value can support teachers' confidence with subjective understanding of their own belief systems. Teachers can encourage legitimate prejudices, such as the inestimable value of each person.

Understanding historical dimension of being can complement teachers' knowledge of self and subjectivity in the community, society, and state wherein they live; it underlines the historical reality of their being. Acknowledging that authority is not always irrational and arbitrary, but can in principle be legitimate, specifically when claimed by teachers, supervisors, and experts. Understanding the nature of Gadamerian dialogue can contribute to students' and teachers' personal well-being and scholarly development. In Chapter 1, I explored the autobiographical method of *currere* in my efforts to understand my educational experience. That autobiographical research could contribute to teacher development I explored in Chapter 2. I emphasized dialogue and the way it nurtures student and teacher development in Chapter 3. My autobiographic learnings from the first three chapters encouraged me to study Gadamerian dialogue and hermeneutic understanding of knowledge which provoked my previous knowledge by adding hermeneutic understanding of dialogue to self-education for student and teacher development in Chapter 4. In Chapter 5, I will inquire into the way Gadamerian dialogue can encourage teachers to include student voice in their teaching practice.

References

Gadamer, H. G. (1977). *Philosophical hermeneutics* (D. E. Ling, Ed. and Trans.). Berkeley, Los Angeles and London: University of California Press.
Gadamer, H. G. (1986a). *The idea of the good in platonic-Aristotelian philosophy*, (P. Christopher Smith, Trans.). New Haven, CT, and London: Yale University Press.

Gadamer, H. G. (1986b). *The relevance of the beautiful and other essays* (N. Walker, Trans.). Cambridge: Cambridge University Press.

Gadamer, H. G. (1992). *Hans-Georg Gadamer on education, poetry, and history: Applied hermeneutics* (D. Misgeld & G. Nicholson, Eds.; L. Schmidt & M. Reuss, Trans.). Albany, NY: State University of New York Press.

Gadamer, H. G. (2001). *Gadamer in conversation: Reflections and commentary* (R. E. Palmer, Ed. and Trans.). New Haven and London: Yale University Press.

Gadamer, H. G. (1990/2004). *Truth and method* (2nd ed.) (J. Weinsheimer & D. Marshall, Trans.). New York: Crossroad. (Original work published 1960).

Gadamer, H. G. (2006). *A century of philosophy: A conversation with Riccardo Dottori* (R. Coltman & S. Koepke, Trans.). New York and London: Continuum.

Gadamer, H. G. (2007). *The Gadamer Reader: A bouquet of the later writings*, trans. and ed. Richard E. Palmer, Evanston, IL: Northwestern University Press.

Grau, M. (2014). *Refiguring theological hermeneutics*. New York: Palgrave Macmillan.

Nixon, J. (2017). *Hans-Georg Gadamer: The hermeneutical imagination*. New York: Springer. doi: 10.1007/978-3-319-52117-6.

Regan, P. (2016). This thinking lacks a language: Heidegger and Gadamer's question of being. *Meta: Research in Hermeneutics*, (2), 376–394.

Simms, K. (2015). *Hans-Georg Gadamer*. London; New York: Routledge, Taylor & Francis Group. doi: 10.4324/9780203068816.

5

GADAMERIAN DIALOGUE AND STUDENT VOICE

> [Good will] has nothing to do with an "appeal", and nothing at all to do with ethics. Even immoral beings try to understand one another.
>
> Gadamer (1989, p. 55)

Introduction

In Chapter 4, I studied the significance of Gadamerian hermeneutics for student and teacher development, emphasizing dialogue. I discussed that, in their ethical understanding of hermeneutics, teachers can realize their full personal and professional potentials, understand their fore-meanings and prejudices, and inquire into their development as educators by forming self-reflective questions to study their academic, historical, and professional life. Understanding questions in hermeneutics allows us to enquire into the truth and justice of the questioners. Teachers have an essential role in scaffolding students' learning process to construct their questions as they engage in their intersubjective dialogue. Students' horizon of the present is continuously being formed as they test their prejudices and preconceptions in classroom dialectics, and as these merge into other horizons, either personal or textual.

In this chapter, I will inquire into the way Gadamerian dialogue can encourage teachers to value students' voice in their teaching pedagogy and practice. My question here is: Could Gadamerian dialogue encourage teachers to value student voice? As background, I will start by using Gadamer's response to Derrida's questions regarding *good will* to value and strengthen student voice as understanding good will, as this point of entry will help with bracketing teacher fore-understanding in the classroom.

Background

In his response to Derrida, Gadamer (1989, p. 55) writes that *good will* has nothing to do with the metaphysical conception of *will*; good will means that one does not typically focus on "identifying the weaknesses of what another person says in order to prove that one is always right, but one seeks instead as far as possible to strengthen the other's viewpoint so that what the other person has to say becomes illuminating."

Gadamer's insight is my point of entry into understanding student voice in dialogic conversations. Gadamer continues that good will has nothing to do with ethics since "even immoral beings try to understand one another". Gadamer complains that Derrida understands the concept of "living dialogue" as metaphysical while Gadamer (1989) considers understanding each other as a natural aspect of human condition and writes with acerbic frustration:

> Is [Derrida] really disappointed that we cannot understand each other? Indeed not, for in his view that would be a relapse into metaphysics. He will, in fact, be pleased, because he takes this private experience of disillusionment to confirm his own metaphysics. But I cannot see here how he can be right only with himself, be in agreement only with himself. (Gadamer 1989, pp. 56–7)

Gadamer understands dialogue as a down-to-earth aspect of human beings rather than a metaphysical phenomenon.

This understanding can encourage teachers to understand students, as he asserts that the solidarities that bind human beings together and make them partners in a genuine dialogue do not always achieve mutual agreement and understanding. Gadamerian dialogue encompasses both inner and social circles intermingling with one another:

> Just between two people this [establishing solidarity] would require a never-ending dialogue. And the same would apply with regard to the inner dialogue the soul [self]

has with itself. Of course, we encounter limits again and again; we speak past each other and are even at cross-purposes with ourselves. But in my opinion we could not do this at all if we had not traveled a long way together, perhaps without even acknowledging it to ourselves. (Gadamer 1989, p. 56)

Gadamer's understanding of dialogue—inner or otherwise—assumes a never-ending exchange of ideas, thoughts, and viewpoints which will not necessarily achieve mutual agreement.

Acknowledging their dialogic circles, teachers can enter students' personal space—caringly and wonderingly—to understand student circumstances as an initial step to take care of their education and personal fulfillment. Simms (2015) confirms that this never-ending aspect of dialogue entails an incomplete understanding of self-presence as acknowledged by Heidegger and Gadamer:

> When Heidegger and, following him, Gadamer speak of self-presence, self-understanding or self-consciousness, it is already understood that these terms do not denote a self-assurance, a presence to oneself that is complete, and that the self smugly knows itself in a totality. The presence to oneself that self-consciousness or self-understanding entails is always incomplete; the search for understanding is a continuous process. That we are thus limited is itself a universal phenomenon. (Simms, 2015, p. 132)

This dialogic aspect of self can fulfill teachers' understanding of self/other by providing doubt, suspension, and incompleteness. Teachers can always practice good will by identifying the strength of students in school dialectics, and by encouraging students to know their capabilities and to value their self-presence in open conversations in the classroom.

Language and Open-Mindedness

Once elaborating "fusion," Gadamer (2004, p. 370) contends that "the fusion of horizons" taking place in our understanding of dialectics is "the achievement of language." In all communications, we attempt to find common ground. This fact might be more noticeable when we are communicating across languages; even communicating within a shared mother tongue we normally are speaking across our distinctive positionings, reflecting different cultures and world experiences.

Gadamer (2004) notes that when we examine the hermeneutical reality using the model of conversation between two people, we try to make sense of the "subject matter" before us either in its textual or oral form. As teachers and students attempt to reach an agreement on the meaning of the discourse, they are engaged with their individual interpretations of the discourse (or curriculum). Gadamer (2004) writes this understanding of the subject matter takes the form of language:

> It is not that the understanding is subsequently put into words; rather, the way understanding occurs - whether in the case of a text or a dialogue with another person who raises an issue with us - is the coming-into-language of the thing itself .... Whereas up to now we have framed the constitutive significance of the question for the hermeneutical phenomenon in terms of conversation, we must now demonstrate the linguisticality of dialogue, which is the basis of the question, as an element of hermeneutics. (Gadamer, 2004, pp. 370–71)

Language in Gadamer's hermeneutics is what constitutes dialectic knowledge and understanding.

Finding a common language coincides with understanding and reaching an agreement working with dialogic knowledge. Language provides a common space for discussion, creation, collaboration, and dialogic exchange between teachers and students. Gadamer (2004) continues that:

> Our first point is that the language in which something comes to speak is not a possession at the disposal of one or the other of the interlocutors. Every conversation presupposes a common language, or better, creates a common language. Something is placed in the center, as the Greeks say, which the partners in dialogue both share, and concerning which they can exchange ideas with one another. (p. 371)

Language is no private possession at the exclusive disposal of teachers or students; it should be placed in the center of dialogic exchanges so that all interlocutors can have an equal chance to participate through it.

Students can use their language in collaborative conversations in school freely and teachers' open-minded attitude can facilitate this process. Nixon (2017) asserts that open-mindedness can communicate knowledge in educational institutions using students' sometimes faulty language and too often half-formed arguments which can nonetheless be partially understood:

> We need to be able to feel our way towards understanding, to be allowed to work through half-formed ideas and arguments, to risk being misunderstood or only partially understood. If such spaces of open-mindedness are disallowed - through, for example, a pedantic over-insistence on 'correctness' or an all-too-familiar obsession with outcomes - then education stalls. (p. 31)

Understanding students' mistakes and erroneous language as a positive aspect of learning experience can ensure their participation, enabling them to construct a fulfilling learning experience as they feel supported and cared for.

This empathetic gesture can reflect teacher authority and nuanced decision-making once they value the student's *human condition* and position it before their learning experience. Nixon (2017) contends that open-mindedness is the most essential condition of successful learning experience: "Educational success ... cannot be read off against 'what one knows', but has to be understood in terms of a disposition to open-mindedness: a willingness to acknowledge the differing perspectives that inform and enlarge the open mind" (p. 32). Teacher-student dialectics can be based on open-mindedness because without a tendency to understand and value opposing ideas, thoughts, and belief systems, teacher and student intersubjective dialogue would cease to progress and understanding will vanish.

As noted, throughout my educational experience I largely remember those teachers who were open to my mistakes and could hear my voice intertwined with, sometimes submerged in, an erroneous language. They became my encouragement throughout my learning experience from primary school to doctoral studies. What is teaching if devoid of empathy, passion, tolerance, and encouragement?

Teacher Intervention

Following the publication of *Truth and Method* in 1960, Gadamer concentrated on what he called applied hermeneutics. Nixon (2017, p. 53) asserts that the phrase is a "tautology" as Gadamer points out "application is never an add-on to that which has already been understood." In developing the idea of applied hermeneutics, Gadamer concentrates on particular domains of professional and institutional practice, very much relevant here. Application becomes pivotal to understanding as we only learn something once we have found a way of applying it to our own circumstances and have tested it against our own preconceptions. Gadamer specifically concentrated on "how understanding informs professional values and practices and the institutional conditions necessary for those values and practices to be encouraged and sustained (Gadamer 1992, 1996)". For true interpretation of the traditions, students and teachers can become self-conscious about their educational experience as well as their own biases and prejudices during that experience. Once teachers overcome their illegitimate prejudice, they can help students with their educational transformation.

Gadamer (1992) regards education as a process of intervention and mediation between the strange and the familiar than a process of knowledge transfer, and views education as:

> A 'free space' within which we make sense of things, learn how to communicate with one another, gain the confidence to move from the familiar to the strange, and become at home in the world. His work presents a major challenge to current orthodoxies: the belief, for example, that a combination of standardised testing, target-setting, and pre-specified learning outcomes constitutes some kind of educational panacea. (Nixon, 2017, pp. 53–4)

Gadamer's understanding can pave the path for supportive education with empathy and love for the students in the classroom and kindle curiosity after they trust their educational experience.

Students will move voluntarily to the strange once they feel at home in this lifeworld experience, and teachers can intervene by providing a free and non-judgmental space to facilitate a voluntary learning experience. Gadamer considers pre-structured learning as the problem of education as it imposes a mode of rationality that overlooks the complexity of the educational process since it assumes a product-oriented understanding of education. As Gadamer notes in his hermeneutical philosophy, education should not be governed by such restrictions; it is an open-ended process of learning, thriving, becoming, and engaging with the world we inhabit.

Therefore, the fact that education contributes to economic growth as it develops a skilled work force or it provides the accreditation needed for the employment market is not considered as the sole or even primary goal of education. Nor is it the primary basis of teacher intervention. Gadamer's writings and speeches confirm that ethical formation is the prime purpose of education:

> What we take from Gadamer's scattered writings and speeches on education - and from his philosophical writings as a whole - is that education is a process of ethical formation .... It is an attempt to square up to our 'sovereign ethical responsibility to make something of our own lives, as a painter makes something valuable of his canvas' (Dworkin 2011, 13). (cited in Nixon, 2017, p. 54)

Teachers can intervene to encourage students to make something valuable and meaningful of their own canvas and to create their unique masterpiece by understanding their ethics, their meaning of life, and their possibility of education by providing a *free space* in which students can understand the true meaning of transformative, creative, aesthetic, emancipatory, individualistic, and collective educational experience.

Becoming Attentive

To understand our students' reality and meaning of life, we need to attend to their personal differences and their individual distances from us. Understanding their meaning of life demands initially the recognition of such differences and distinctions once interacting with students in the educational contexts we are teaching. Nixon (2017) writes it is essential to understand the whole strangeness of that and whom we experience:

> We have to receive the object of understanding in all its strangeness in order to render it familiar. This insight is as relevant to texts and works of art as it is to people and the social groupings they comprise. It has relevance, in other words, across the human sciences: anthropology, history, psychology, sociology, etc. But it also pertains to the natural sciences, which are increasingly located within a broader epistemological frame that includes the humanistic .... As human creatures, we live in symbiotic relation with nature. (Nixon, 2017, p. 35)

In this symbiotic relation with nature, teachers can enter into continuous dialogue with students, enacting their attentive and perceptive awareness as listening and interpretation.

Gadamer (1992, p. 66) reports that he found his voice as a teacher when he learned how to listen. For him, the dialectic nature of teaching requires attentive listening prior to learning what we should say and in what way we should say it. Gadamer (1992) maintains truth is achieved through mutual understanding not through what the teacher believes to be true: "It is more important to find the words which convince the other than those which can be demonstrated in their truth, once and for all" (p. 71).

Dialogue provides the disciplinary framework within which students and teachers become attentive to each other. Nixon (2017) writes Gadamer viewed the process of becoming attentive as getting involved in a particular experience of time:

> There are, he argued, 'two fundamental ways of experiencing time'. The first may take the form of either boredom or bustle .... Both these extreme cases are instances of 'empty' time, in which 'time is not experienced in its own right, but as something that has to be 'spent'.... There is, however, a totally different experience of time, which Gadamer terms 'fulfilled' or 'autonomous' time. 'This fulfilment', he states, 'does not come about because someone has empty time to fill .... This is the experience of time within which we achieve autonomy. (Nixon, 2017, p. 36)

Students can achieve autonomy in their educational experience by favoring their fulfilled time scheduled by informed educators to allow students to experience a more conscious and attentive educational journey which can then open new horizons toward their subjective understanding of lifeworld(s). Attentive teaching means inquiry into students' worlds, along with an ability to interpret their reality.

Interpreting Students' World Meaning

In our hermeneutical understanding of students' pedagogical meaning, we can learn to interpret the discourse embedded in their common or ordinary language. Gadamer associates interpretation and understanding and writes that interpretation is the act of understanding:

> Interpretation is not something pedagogical for us either; it is the act of understanding itself, which is realized - not just for the one for whom one is interpreting but also for the interpreter himself - in the explicitness of verbal interpretation. Thanks to the verbal nature of all interpretation, every interpretation includes the possibility of a relationship with others. There can be no speaking that does not bind the speaker and the person spoken to. This is true of the hermeneutic process as well. (Gadamer, 2004, p. 399)

In our hermeneutic understanding of students' discourse, teachers are making a strong bond with students, contributing to mutual understanding and trust.

Teachers' relationship with the students does not dictate the interpretive process of understanding since interpretation is a fusion of meaning. To understand students, we always apply their discussion to our own meaning-making, the same as the time when we understand a text by applying it to our conditions and circumstances. Gadamer (2004) notes that our verbal understanding of our interpretation fades away naturally and does not generate a second meaning other than the one which is interpreted by the interlocutor:

> The verbal explicitness that understanding achieves through interpretation does not create a second sense apart from that which is understood and interpreted. The interpretive meanings are not, as such, thematic in understanding. Rather, it is their nature to disappear behind what they bring to speech in interpretation .... The possibility of understanding is dependent on the possibility of this kind of mediating interpretation. (Gadamer, 2004, p. 399)

The evanescent and instantaneous nature of interpretation of students' speech is contained within the understanding of their life-world and lived experience.

In *Being and Time*, Heidegger (1962, p. 189) discusses the relationship between understanding and interpretation indicating that Dasein deals with what is ready-to-hand [familiar] circumspectively: "We 'see' it as a table, a door, a carriage, or a bridge". For Heidegger, we always see things specifically as they are, and never just see things in the abstract. He continues that the relationship between interpretation and understanding is that in interpretation understanding "becomes itself" (p. 188). As an interpreting animal, human beings understand phenomena through interpretation, itself already the interpretation of others.

Simms (2015) highlights that in our interpretive understanding of something in the world, we see it as something and understand it in terms of this relationship. The only change in our understanding of something in the world is that what was implicit now becomes explicit:

> I implicitly understand the world always already, and my encounters with aspects of it make that understanding explicit. But this circularity is precisely Heidegger's point. For him, 'circumspective interpretation' is grounded in something we have in advance, something we see in advance, and something we grasp in advance: fore-having, fore-sight and fore-conception. It is this structure of the 'fore' that is essential to understanding for Heidegger. (Simms, 2015, p. 33)

In our circumspective interpretation, it is important to be conscious of our fore-concepts when communicating with students and overcome our illegitimate prejudice in order to let the true meaning and understanding of students to emerge. In their bracketing space, teachers can be conscious of their foresight to interpret student meaning—understanding which presupposes knowledge of students' common language.

Understanding Students' Language. As discussed earlier, to reach a horizon of understanding and interpretation, we need to acquire a fusion either in our textual or oral interpretation of discourse. Gadamer (2004) confirms that this fusion occurs in the verbal aspect of interpretation:

> The text is made to speak through interpretation. But no text and no book speaks if it does not speak a language that reaches the other person. Thus, interpretation must find the right language if it really wants to make the text speak . . .. The historical life of a tradition depends on being constantly assimilated and interpreted. An interpretation that was correct in itself would be a foolish ideal that mistook the nature of tradition. Every interpretation has to adapt itself to the hermeneutical situation to which it belongs. (Gadamer, 2004, p. 398)

Like the way in which interpretation finds the 'right' language, teachers can communicate in a language that is interpretable for the students, to encourage them to generate their own individual language.

Teachers' legitimate and unprejudiced "authority"—which is based on the recognition of knowledge (Simms, 2015, p. 72) rather than on blind obedience—can nurture students' open and candid oral exchanges in the classroom. Students can learn to decipher the hermeneutical situation they belong to in their interpretation of common language with their teachers and other students. Gadamer (2004) notes that understanding a text entails applying it to ourselves, and he asserts that the same text may present itself in different ways that are changed once they are activated. In their verbal understanding of students' discourse, teachers can pay attention to the instant understanding of messages as they are not going to have a second sense except for what is primarily understood, and can act as mediators who use their legitimate prejudice and appropriate authority to interpret students' language:

> When we are concerned with understanding and interpreting verbal texts, interpretation in the medium of language itself shows what understanding always is: assimilating what is said to the point that it becomes one's own. Verbal interpretation is the form of all interpretation, even when what is to be interpreted is not linguistic in nature - i.e., is not a text but a statue or a musical composition. We must not let ourselves be confused by forms of interpretation that are not verbal but in fact presuppose language. (Gadamer, 2004, pp. 399–40)

Assimilating students' language—even once it is not linguistic in nature—to the point that it becomes our own is a process of hermeneutic understanding which can be acknowledged as the main linguistic achievement of educators in their communication with students. For interpreting students' language, teachers can also recognize the individuality of students and their unique conditions and circumstances.

Acknowledging Students' Individuality. Understanding unique differences of students is essential to Gadamerian philosophical and applied hermeneutics. This understanding is rooted in each individual student's idiosyncratic circumstances and histories which needs a quality of education attuned to such differences. Nixon (2017) critiques that in the past students were categorized within broad *bands* or *sets* for specific subjects as a means of distinction:

> One of the favoured means of differentiation in the past has been to categorise students within broad ability 'bands' and/or into ability 'sets' for specific subjects or

> groups of subjects. The system of 'setting' is clearly a more sophisticated system of differentiation, since it acknowledges that students may perform differently in different subjects. But neither system acknowledges the full range and complexity of difference within and across categories. As a result, the unique individuality of the individuals comprising those categories falls outside the system's field of vision. (Nixon, 2017, p. 24)

Acknowledging individual differences is essential for hermeneutics as understanding begins with attending to the unique circumstances and historical life of each individual student. Gadamer (2004) writes, "Hence, the hermeneutically trained mind will also include historical consciousness. It will make conscious the prejudices governing our own understanding, so that the text, as another's meaning, can be isolated and valued on its own" (p. 298).

Understanding begins once a text or an idea communicates with the circumstances and historical life of the individual student. This is the "first condition of hermeneutics" as Nixon (2017, p. 24) confirms: "The prime task of the educator is to ensure that—whatever system of differentiation is in place and whatever pedagogical practices are employed—the 'first condition of hermeneutics' is met and upheld and that the student thereby becomes the agent of her or his own understanding". In what sense is acknowledging each student's circumstances and historical life as the first condition of hermeneutics possible in the classroom? Nixon (2017) critiques the way education normalizes students and endorses Gadamer's solution for this problem:

> Education fulfils various functions: it prepares people (mainly but not exclusively *young* people) for the world of work; it *'normalises'* them with regard to societal norms and expectations; it operates as a system of academic and indeed social selection. It can offer greater equality of opportunity, but also serves to reproduce existing inequalities and social hierarchies . . . .. But Gadamer reminds us that education is also a way of becoming ourselves, of flourishing as intelligent and sentient beings, of being alive to the world. (Nixon, 2017, p. 24)

Normalizing young people by education is asserted similarly by Pinar (2004, p. xiii) once he affirms the "public sphere [as] a "shopping mall" in which citizens (and students) have been reduced to consumers" and by Apple (2004, p. xxii) who emphasizes that institutions "produce the type of knowledge (as a kind of commodity) that is needed to maintain the dominant *economic, political, and cultural* arrangements that now exist." Nixon (2017) argues that institutions of education can set the students free from the constraints that inhibit learning and "refuse to implement assessment regimes" that are unsuccessful in providing formative and constructive feedback to students:

[Educational institutions] root out not only overt discriminatory practices but hidden biases in the system and in everyday interactions between students and between students and teachers; and to discourage forms of competition that exclude or alienate particular students or groups of students. They would need to provide students with an institutional environment within which to flourish and fulfil their potential; to encourage them to form and voice their own opinions and define their own individual ends and purposes; to help them turn mistakes and mishaps into opportunities for learning and transform problems into challenges. (Nixon 2017, p. 25)

Student and teacher development using self-education can result in empowering student voice as teachers can create opportunities for students to thrive and flourish. Students can find confidence in themselves to see their mistakes as a developmental stage of learning experience without feeling nervous and intimidated in a competitive environment. I remember those teachers who turned my mistakes into opportunities, giving me a learning chance. And I remember those who focused on my mishaps to prove I was wrong. I feel indebted to those who made ethical decisions in converting my mistakes into opportunities for learning. To understand students' individual voices, teachers can also be able to interpret their language rhetoric and facilitate educational opportunities during which students can express their free and open viewpoints in the classroom.

Understanding Students' Rhetoric of Language. In our pedagogical engagement with students, it is imperative to maintain a sound and positive judgment of their viewpoints when interpreting their language, valuing their mistakes as a necessary stage of their learning experience. Education can play a substantial role in encouraging students to express their free and uncensored worldviews once they try out their ideas and articulate their visions. Gadamer (2006) expresses that teachers' positive endorsement of students' speculative language can create an atmosphere in which *getting it wrong* is completely acceptable.

Gadamer writes a good society is based on common reasoning regarding the nature of common good and emphasizes—following Aristotle's understanding of rhetorical skills—on participating effectively in arguing, drawing conclusions, and speaking persuasively; he confirms "the art of persuading without being able to prove anything" (Gadamer, 2006, p. 55) embedded in rhetorical skills. Nixon (2017, p. 58) elaborates:

Rhetoric has been taught in one form or another since antiquity and had a vital role to play in the curriculum of the European Latin Middle Ages (see Curtius 1990, 62–78). However, Gadamer is concerned less with rhetorical skills than with the dispositions associated with the art of rhetoric. The question then arises as to what these dispositions are and how best to acquire them.

Understanding Gadamer's perspective on rhetorical skills can help teachers create conditions or dispositions that are conducive to relaxed, supportive, and safe learning atmosphere.

Nixon (2017, p. 58) comments on Gadamer's conception of the quality of the dispositions: "Rhetoric, Gadamer (2006, 56) insists, is *not* a competitive game of discourse played for the sake of winning a contest with the other." He asserts that what is important is to ensure that we are enabling someone to understand our point of view without an intention of being able to prove it. The point of not being able to prove our opinion necessitates an unbiased and fair control of dialectic exchanges in our communication with students as Nixon (2017) confirms:

> To achieve that end, [Gadamer] continues, 'we need to put ourselves in the place of the other without desiring to wage war on him'. There is, then, a clear relation between rhetoric and ethics since rhetoric assumes a respect for the other's point of view and aims at shared understanding based on that mutuality of respect: 'The point of rhetoric is to teach one how to deliver or compose a speech so as to make possible a genuine understanding *(synesis)* and an authentic communication *(syggnome)*, which constitute the basis for an actual consensus' (p. 57). (Nixon, 2017, p. 58)

For Gadamer, the dispositions of rhetoric are adjacent to ethical purposes practiced by teachers in their dialogical relationships with students to understand their human conditions and circumstances. Once teachers put themselves in the place of students, they will be able to view their life-world and understand their language rhetoric to make ethical judgments based on their hermeneutic understanding of the situation.

Nourishing Students' Individuality. Understanding students' dialogue includes a complicated process of hermeneutics. Gadamer conceives of understanding as an event in which interlocutors apply their general understanding (insights, visions, ideas, etc.) to specific situations (human experience, texts, discourse, etc.). Gadamer (1992, p. 233) recounts understanding as an event and emphasizes the lasting unity of understanding and application:

> It is through the event of understanding that we express our agency, distinguish our own life-course from that of others, and achieve individuality. Understanding, therefore, is a prerequisite for self-fulfilment: what Aristotle called *eudaimonia* or human

flourishing. Since we all share this potential for self-fulfilment—and rely upon one another for its realization—individuality cannot and should not be confused with self-interest. On the contrary, Gadamer's philosophical hermeneutics is premised on the assumption that we must all 'learn to respect others and otherness'. (cited in Nixon, 2017, p. 60)

For Gadamer, understanding and application are jointly reflected to shape our individuality.

Understanding self is reflected in respecting otherness. This self-fulfillment can be observed in the manners of teachers who respect the individuality and otherness of their students by understanding their different perspectives, worldviews, and belief systems and applying this understanding to their decisions. Our individual understandings both characterize our life histories and inform our entire worldview. Education can transform both student's lifelong learning experience and their being. Nixon (2017) writes such education system would focus on achievement than attainment:

> Any such education system would focus on achievement rather than attainment . . . . Attainment provides a broad categorisation, while achievement reflects the individual - and individualising - effort of the student given her or his particular circumstances. Two students may achieve the same attainment grades, but the achievement of the one may vastly outweigh that of the other. It is to achievement that we must look for an indication of the dispositions and qualities that differentiate students and that are invaluable in later life: determination, perseverance, patience, etc. (Nixon, 2017, p. 61)

To acknowledge the achievement of students, education must recognize the specific and continually changing circumstances of students.

Assessment regimes are based on attainment and overlook the value of achievement as vital to individual student's flourishing. From a Gadamerian perspective *good teachers* know the way to acknowledge the achievement of individual students and maneuver around assessment regimes. Good teaching entails understanding the students' circumstances and application of teacher informed knowledge to those unique circumstances. Auerbach (2014, p. 7) suggests that:

> The task of humanistic scholarship is one requiring 'a passionate devotion, much patience, and something that may well be called magnanimity', then the teacher must exemplify devotion, patience and magnanimity within the teaching situation.

> The task - the very difficult pedagogical task - is not to posture or preach, but simply to express these dispositions through one's commitment to the relevant subject matter and one's respect for one's students. (cited in Nixon, 2017, p. 61)

Nurturing each student's unique individuality triggers an interconnection between teachers' unprejudiced knowledge of the individual student's circumstances and skillful application of the attained knowledge to their teaching and learning.

Pring (2004, p. 81) recognizes that the teacher is both an interpreter and a go-between, as teaching "is essentially a transaction between, on the one hand, the 'impersonal knowledge' which is publicly accessible in books and artefacts, and, on the other, the 'personal ways of thinking' of the students. The art and the skill of the teacher is to make the connections between the two" (cited in Nixon, 2017, p. 62) which can be facilitated through hermeneutic understanding of teachers to flourish the individuality of students.

Concluding Notes

Nourishing students' voice becomes a possibility once teachers maneuver around obstacles such as assessment regimes—which categorize students within 'bands' or into 'sets'—to empower students' voices by strengthening their unique viewpoints, ideas, and perspectives so that what they say becomes illuminating. When teachers practice open-mindedness, students are encouraged to work through their half-formed arguments. True, students and teachers risk being misunderstood. Gadamer (2006) asserts that teachers' positive endorsement of students' language can create an atmosphere of trust in which *getting it wrong* can be alright. Within such *free space*, students learn to effectively communicate with one another, feel more comfortable to move from the familiar to the strange, and become at home in the world.

Students through the event of understanding—as a prerequisite for self-fulfilment [what Aristotle called *eudaimonia*]—can express their agency, distinguish their own life course, and achieve individuality. Good teachers are those who are devoted, patient, and humble and who can communicate individual students. Their primary obligation is not to preach or impress or cajole the students, but to truly respect them.

References

Apple, M. W. (2004). *Ideology and curriculum*. Routledge. https://doi.org/10.4324/9780203487563.

Gadamer, H. G. (1989). *Reply to Jacques Derrida*, trans. Diane Michelfelder and Richard Palmer, in Michelfelder and Palmer 1989: 55–7.

Gadamer, H. G. (1992). *Hans-Georg Gadamer on education, poetry, and history: Applied hermeneutics* (D. Misgeld & G. Nicholson, Eds.; L. Schmidt & M. Reuss, Trans.). Albany, NY: State University of New York Press.

Gadamer, H. G. (1990/2004). *Truth and method* (2nd ed.) (J. Weinsheimer & D. Marshall, Trans.). New York: Crossroad. (Original work published 1960).

Gadamer, H. G. (2006). *A century of philosophy: A conversation with Riccardo Dottori* (R. Coltman & S. Koepke, Trans.). New York and London: Continuum.

Heidegger, M. (1962). *Being and time: A translation of sein und zeit*. New York: Harper & Row.

Nixon, J. (2017). *Hans-Georg Gadamer: The hermeneutical imagination*. New York: Springer. doi: 10.1007/978-3-319-52117-6.

Pinar, W. F. (2004). *What is curriculum theory?* Mahwah, NJ: Lawrence Erlbaum Associates.

Simms, K. (2015). *Hans-Georg Gadamer*. London; New York: Routledge, Taylor & Francis Group. doi: 10.4324/9780203068816.

6
CONCLUSION

Summary

This book began with recalling my educational experience using the autobiographical method of *currere* which creates "a self in relationship to others" (Ng-A-Fook, 2005, p. 55). It continued with hermeneutical understandings of existential experience, and concludes in teacher professional development and student fulfilment inspired by Gadamerian dialogue (Gadamer, 2004). Both *currere* and hermeneutics enable us to study our existential and educational experience wonderingly. *Currere* facilitates self-development, connects self to social sphere using existential and interpretive understanding of being. The analytic and synthetic phases of the method of *currere* are hermeneutical as we interpret autobiographical accounts to understand concealed meanings of lifeworld and selfhood. Gadamerian hermeneutics invokes our interpretative, historical, and textual understanding of our existential experience.

Gadamerian dialogue is rooted in history, text, and (religious) values and ethics. For student teacher development, *currere* awakens teachers' subjectivity, facilities social interactions, and attunes self to lifeworld through existential, educational, and spiritual experience. Gadamerian hermeneutics complements this educational experience with a historical, interpretive, and textual understanding of subjectivity. William F. Pinar developed the method of *currere* in 1974 to design "an architecture of the self" (1994b, p. 219), to reconnect to self to education and to the public sphere, thereby, transforming education. My academic work with *currere*—my Persian *currere*—has provided an awakening experience, enabling me to explore and mobilize my subjectivity as a student, researcher, and teacher who seeks to help other educators and students in their educational experience.

When starting my doctoral program, I was truly skeptical of my progress in this new terrain of education. Coming from a procedural curriculum and being exposed to quantitative methods of thinking, living, and being in the world, I was looking for numbers and figures in a phenomenological understanding of the world around me and of my being in the world! It took me nearly three years of rethinking and reconstructing my past educational experience prior to understanding the way to connect with my lived experience. Tolerance of ambiguity has always been a key to my academic success.

I remember the time when I was getting prepared for a Master of Arts Entrance Exam [MA Konkour] in Teaching English as an Additional language in Tehran. During my Bachelor's program in English Language and Literature in Tehran University, I did not have a chance to grasp the rudimentary knowledge of Language Testing Methodology. I took an MA Entrance Exam preparation course on Teaching Methodology coordinated by Professor Hossein Farhadi who was an expert in Language Testing and Assessment in Gisha Street in Tehran. Lacking the basic knowledge, it was only after seven times of reading a simple popular textbook on Language Testing called *Fajab* that I then started to understand it. Perseverance pays off. In exam session, I answered the questions including those in Testing Methodology section and passed the entrance exam with a satisfactory final score [ranked 56 among all MA candidates] to be able to choose the high-ranking University of Shiraz among others for my MA studies.

With my doctoral studies, the transition, challenges, and achievements I experienced were quite different. Memorization of prefabricated subject materials was not the issue at all. Understanding the lived experience of people in their narratives and connecting with them provoked a qualitative and psychoanalytic [not psychometric] approach to thinking and being in the world. It took me almost three years of non-stop inquiry to overcome my *resistance*—as an outcome of my procedural schooling—and to become accustomed to my new ways of learning and being, and I am grateful for this accomplishment I could ultimately achieve. Still, I might be thinking in fragments and chunks at times. A broader corpus of my doctoral research contributes to students' and teachers' personal and professional development using dialogue, specifically Gadamerian dialogue.

Transformed by the autobiographical method of *currere*, students and teachers can question their existential reality and attune these questions towards their ontological and epistemological understanding of universe using hermeneutic analysis. Putting forth metaphorically, if I were an unlit candle before commencing my doctoral program in Curriculum and Pedagogy at the University of British Columbia, inquiring into *currere* in Chapter 1 ignited me once I recollected my educational experience, envisioned new possibilities, analyzed the accounts for a hermeneutic understanding of present, and synthesized them to mobilize self. A glowing candle adding light and warmth to my circumstances and communicating with my educational and pedagogical community in Chapter 2, I studied autobiographical research in student and teacher development to understand the way other educators unraveled their transformative educational experience using their lifeworld as curriculum to mobilize teacher knowledge and create educational communities. This was just the beginning of an enlightening journey from within contextualized in teacher community of practice and lifeworld. Teacher and student development for me was simply illuminating other candles [teachers] that might have been unlit [suffocated] or half-lit due to certain circumstances such as an exposure to a procedural curriculum.

Dialogue as a pluralistic condition of education opened new possibilities for student and teacher development in Chapter 3 once teachers entered into an intersubjective space of *currere* to exchange their pedagogical, professional, and spiritual experience and to mobilize their shared knowledge and understanding. Following self-education, student and teacher development [or leadership] using Gadamerian dialogue in Chapter 4 means spreading the light and warmth within ourselves to our circumstances—our existing curriculum—which could become outdated [smothered] if unattended. Hermeneutic understanding of the teaching profession could open an inner space of attunement, as in *currere* for teachers to understand creative dimensions of self, pedagogy, and practice by overcoming fore-understanding in interpreting discourse.

Once teachers understand their lifeworld using *currere* and Gadamerian hermeneutics, they can open an engaging dialogue with students to empower their voice—the focus of Chapter 5. Connecting to inner life and interpreting pedagogical meaning, teachers can create an atmosphere of trust to strengthen students' unique ideas, perspectives, and worldviews. Once the autobiographical method of *currere* opened my inner life and contributed to my intersubjective and analytic understanding of lifeworld as curriculum, Gadamerian hermeneutics complemented this understanding by an interpretative approach to educational experience. Analyzing and synthesizing the related literature, I have ordered answering my questions starting from self-education to teacher professional development and student fulfilment using Gadamerian dialogue.

Return to Research Questions

Question (1) In what way has the autobiographical method of currere encouraged an understanding of my educational experience?
In Chapter 1, I studied my educational experience using the autobiographical method of *currere*. I am an Iranian-Canadian educator who has experienced two approaches to curriculum and pedagogy; a traditional curriculum burdened with "predetermined, sequential, skills-oriented, and measurable versions", and an creative curriculum which encouraged me to look "inquiringly and wonderingly on the world" (Miller, 2005, p. 46) through being attuned to the lifeworld through self-reflection, self-inquiry, and self-education.

Although in tension with each other, these two manifestations of curriculum can be considered complementary. Skills-oriented learning at an earlier stage can precede an inquiry into and wondering on one's learning experience. Knowing that many educators and scholars (Chen, 2014; Darling-Hammond, 2012, pp. 149–150; Day, 2012; Rodgers & Raider-Roth, 2012, p. 149; Zhang & Pinar, 2015), use autobiography to understand their positionality and voice among university and school teachers confirms a possibility for teachers like myself. *Currere* encourages teachers to work from within and confirms inner freedom within structures of authority to constitute professional development as lived.

Currere has contributed to understanding my being-in-the-world and becoming-in-the-world as an educator. I have made *currere* my own; it is Persian *currere*. Engaged more proactively with the lifeworld of an educator, I feel, think, judge, and critique the sociopolitical aspects of education for a development of self/other. My narrative has invited me to be present for self-development, teacher empowerment, and school transformation by attuning to the present non-judgmentally and attending to my circumstances consciously. By disclosing my story, I create new possibilities and release tensions [test anxiety] of a traditional curriculum as the literature confirms and my transformative educational experience reveals itself. Using *currere*, my memory runs as a stream that curves back and deepens itself through an interactive dialogue I open with my context of practice to gain new pedagogical understanding and meaning, and to recognize the internal [psychoanalytical] and external [contextual] sources of feeling estranged and distant.

My place—either physical or psychological—interacts with my subjectivity and connects it with new boundaries as well as creative possibilities. My autobiographical experience of a cross-contextual curriculum reveals itself in its in-betweenness. My experience with *currere* was a rebirth to distance self from the non-ego [curriculum] which occurred to me as my academic and intellectual freedom. During four dimensions of *currere*; regressive, progressive, analytic and synthetic, I recollected my educational experience, envisioned new possibilities in education, analyzed the accounts for the present meaning, and synthesized the themes for a deeper understanding of lifeworld and educational experience.

As self can be connected to society through our educational experience, the curriculum can include both subjective and sociopolitical aspects of self which resonate with my *currere* experience. As an unassisted method of self-inquiry, *currere* has both connected me to my existing social and political spheres in teacher education, and has attuned me to my understanding-of-being-in-the-world. *Currere* has helped me to understand the psychoanalytical obstacles of *transferring* emotions I might have for one person to a different person, *projecting* my own qualities to a different person, and *resistance* to certain feelings or memories of early educational experience by removing an undesired aspect of curriculum—test anxiety.

Another technique employed by *currere* that has helped me to achieve a non-judgmental understanding of lived experience is bracketing or "disconnecting" (Husserl, 1969, p. 58) as a process of phenomenological reduction that has contributed to my well-being in everyday routines by improving my intellectual, emotional, and spiritual capacity. I constantly bracket my mode-of-being—as far as it is possible to do so—to understand its psychoanalytical content and to remove undesired aspects of attitude towards life, being, and educational experience. I immerse myself in my existential being to understand my "lived body, lived space, lived time, and lived other" (van Manen, 1977, cited in Palmer, 2018) and I find curriculum-as-being, as-time/space, and as-consciousness. As for the psychoanalytical transformation experienced in *currere*, release from tensions of the past and present [I call it constant rebirth] occurred to me following four dimensions of the method. Once my past educational experience manifested both encouraging [teacher dialogue] and challenging [test anxiety] memories for reflection, my present education fostered moments of contemplation, innovation, and creation for future possibilities. This is the art of working from within as William Blake confirms aesthetically:

> To see a world in a grain of sand
> And a heaven in a wild flower
> Hold infinity in the palm of your hand
> And eternity in an hour

Question (2) How can autobiographical research contribute to teacher development?
Autobiographical research helps student teachers to examine their life-world and invites them to explore their reality. As the educational experience confirms itself in our life-world and "permeates our meaning of education" (Britzman, 2009, p. 28), it can disturb our judgment and understanding as it is present in psychoanalytic understandings of self, of the psyche. Once teachers reconstruct their pedagogical meaning and reevaluate their philosophy of life in teaching, they can articulate their meanings, and become engaged in a dialogical space with others—especially their students—to invite them to expand their meaning-making. Shifting to phenomenological models of learning can be more instructive, constructive, and transformative for specifically those teachers who have experienced a merely behavioristic and procedural school of thought (Miller's, 2005, p. 46).

In their self-conscious practice, teachers experience moments of being attentive to teaching which can contribute to their personal and professional development. Using collaborative autobiography, teachers can inquire into the development of the knowledge. Involved in autobiographical praxis, teachers can inquire into the deep meaning and understanding of both their work life experience and professional future (Butt & Raymond, 1989). Repositioned at the center of thinking narratively, effective working relationships play an essential role in teacher development and can contribute to teacher well-being in classrooms individually and collectively.

Relationships practiced as collaboration and cooperation in learning experience in mutual exchanges with other students, teachers, and teacher educators. Teachers can attend to the details of learning process in their autobiographical development to include both the structure of subject materials and the methods of inquiry to mobilize knowledge. Listening to teachers and understanding their selfhood in their stories are emphasized in the literature for teacher development. Autobiographical research enacts a reconceptualization of teacher development as the focus is not only on teacher's practice, but on the personhood of teachers as the canvas of learning experience which allows them to work from the creative sources within teacher life-world. Biographic and autobiographic research on teachers' lived experience creates an emancipatory and transformative process resulting in teacher development as well as social and political enactment. In their self-inquiry, teachers become attuned to educational experience by being open and receptive to what is yet-to-be-established but is-not-yet-there—a world of meaning awaiting to be explored by all humans through presence and connectivity to life-world. Once attuned to life-world, teachers can overcome their misconceptions by understanding plurality through opening an intersubjective dialogue with others, as they inquire into intersubjective and collaborative meaning of life. Teachers can emerge along with the world to a new human to realize their (auto)biographical as well as future by transcending their personhood and by entering historical existence once they work from within and develop new understanding of their possibilities, as autobiographical research can begin with self-development and land in social and historical spheres. Understanding these dimensions of teacher autobiography and self-knowledge, teachers can form their communities of practice to transcend public and political spheres to mobilize self and other knowledge and transform education (Butt & Raymond, 1987, 1988, 1992).

Question (3) In what sense can dialogue nurture teacher professional development?
Dialogue creates an understanding of teachers' personal and professional lives, and their circumstances to improve their teaching pedagogy and practice, and to develop enthusiastic students for dynamic schools. Understanding the inner life of teachers—a meditative understanding of their personhood—can transform to inner work—a more pedagogically oriented practice—using conversations which connect us with the inner life as well as the pedagogical orientation of teachers and teacher educators. In the process of meaning-making, the relationship of teacher-student makes sense only if one includes the other facilitated by dialogue which makes teachers and students learn from shared educational experience as it provides an opportunity for a collaborative and constructive meaning-making process. New understanding of dialogic conversations shifts from rationalism to constructivism incorporating a scientific, collaborative, experiential, and transformative approach to teacher professional development. Using dialogic conversations, teachers' professional knowledge can be transformed and a deeper understanding can be acquired which demands a willingness for teachers to be influenced by other interlocutors and

"an openness toward the world" (Huebner, 2008, p. 78), overcoming their inappropriate prejudices and irrational authority.

Entering into intersubjective dialogue with others, teachers become ethically engaged with their pedagogical practices to reconstruct the notions of schooling. That requires going beyond "immediate level of interpretation" (Aoki et al., 2004, p. 7). Through dialogue, teachers can replace "banking education" and mindless memorization with rational and critical thinking to foster teacher and student agency, thereby mobilizing knowledge of the oppressed to support social change. Students and teachers can use friendly and mutually supportive conversations as a collective and humanistic way of knowing and learning to achieve a deeper understanding of the object of knowledge and to transform educational experience.

Resolving misunderstandings and miscommunications arising from diverse social, cultural, and political backgrounds can provide a mutual and collaborative focus for teachers' professional development. In the process of meaning-making, experienced teachers can engage in productive and spontaneous discussions, thereby overcoming their negative attitudes in interpretations of dialogue. In the name of professional development, teachers can continue reflective and collegial dialogue using their rational processes of critical thinking and reasoning to understand the sources of possible infractions; they can assert that caring is best interpreted as a quality of relation not only as goodness belonging to an individual. Dialogue can become a key concept in teacher and student development; educational life as human being's existential experience informs and is informed by reflective dialogue.

Using dialogic conversations, teachers can listen attentively to students, a humanistic process of attunement that can give them insights into students and themselves. Considering plurality as a possibility of education, teachers can use ongoing dialogue to maintain difference in their classrooms. Using mindful conversations, teachers can understand the specifications of the soil in which each student is planted (Jung, 2014, p. 449), encourage individuality, avoiding the danger of conformity.

Question (4) In what way can Gadamerian dialogue foster teacher professional development?
In teacher development, dialogue can start with posing a question towards the ontological reality of being, so teachers can begin their dialogue with an open question of "Who am I as a teacher?" as initiated in Chapter 2. Making a sense of the world as well as ourselves in the world provides an understanding of our full human potential as ethical beings. This understanding is facilitated

through asking gentle questions by teachers and teacher educators to make sure that we avoid the "sudden occurrence of the question" which is a violation of the ethics of Gadamerian dialogue (Gadamer, 2004, p. 360). Questions can facilitate our hermeneutic consciousness of what teachers are saying and what other interlocutors [students] are saying.

Perhaps our first step in posing a question is deciding on a question, a step which requires teachers' unprejudiced judgment and a hermeneutic understanding of correct and incorrect counterarguments. Given a transformative power of hermeneutics, teachers might be able to see the justice of their own position and the truth of others. Teachers can focus on a dialogical understanding of questions to encourage students to explore their meanings using intersubjective dialogue with themselves, other students, and other teachers. This dialogic understanding assumes a disposition of open-mindedness for teachers who can transcend their perspectives and visions to understand the differing and opposing ideas.

Teachers can become able to transform their perspectives to understand the horizon of the students using continuous meditation, rethinking, and reflection on their perceptual field. This understanding can expand to a merging of horizons of the past, present, and future during which teachers can continuously make sense of their subjectivity as well as their own professional development. Of note, our horizons can be flexible as our prejudgments and presuppositions are incessantly put to the test to develop dynamic understandings of our pedagogical practices. Employing productive understanding of prejudice and overcoming inappropriate prejudice during dialogic exchanges can help teachers provide pedagogical possibilities for students through which teachers' subjective engagement creates educational moments. Teachers can improve their power of listening once in dialogue with other students; that is the foundation of hermeneutic understanding. Teachers are mediators who intervene the historical trajectory of students using dialectics that constitute what Gadamer (1992) terms hermeneutic traditions within which teachers and students practice education. Educators can use dialectics as a form of self-reflexive and self-explorative hermeneutic understanding which helps students explore their potentials and possibilities. Teachers and teacher educators can ensure that the students are 'with them' during genuine conversation through conscious listening, valuing their differing opinions, and highlighting the strength of what is said. For their personal and professional development, educators can remain open to the meaning of the other person or text by situating that meaning in relation to their own meaning and circumstances and recognizing their biases and prejudgments using a hermeneutic understanding of the person or text. Using Gadamerian dialogue, teachers can master the art of questioning, overcome their fore-understandings, control the pressure of opinion, perceive unprejudiced meanings, and practice rational authority which will foster their professional development in schools where they are teaching.

Question (5) Could Gadamerian dialogue encourage teachers to value student voice?
Understanding student voice begins with our positive, even empathetic, attitude to identify the strength and power of their perspectives, ideas, and worldviews so that what they say shines out. Understanding self-presence and self-consciousness is always incomplete and a continuous process. Teachers can find a common ground in their hermeneutic understanding of dialectic with students to ensure an agreement on the meaning of the written or oral discourse taking the form of language.

Finding common language and therefore shared understanding—with an equal chance for the interlocutors to contribute to—coincides with reaching an agreement in a shared space with students for discussions and exchange of meanings and thoughts. Open-minded teachers provide opportunities for the students to work through half-formed and incomplete ideas and arguments with a risk of being misunderstood or partly understood as a natural outcome of learning process. Teachers can attune themselves to students so that they can establish a rapport and mutual understanding, using words which unravel truth [only]. Once students become attentive to the particularity of *their* experience of *their* time, they can experience "fulfilled" or "autonomous" time rather than "empty" time and even achieve autonomy (Nixon, 2017, p. 36).

Teachers can become aware of each student's custom and culture as these are embedded in their language, requiring hermeneutic understanding of their oral and textual discourse. Educators can learn not to be compelled to prove their opinion; instead teachers can assume an unbiased and caring position vis-à-vis students, everyone understanding the circumstances of each other. Through hermeneutic understanding of students, teachers can respect their agency, strengthen their voice, and help them to achieve their unique individuality. Understanding students is therefore a precondition for the students' self-fulfillment, self-worth, self-wellbeing, and self-education. Teachers can value students' otherness by providing opportunities for students to express and reconstruct their individuality, acknowledge their achievement, create personal ways of thinking, and expand their life-world in their educational experience.

Research Achievements and Contributions

The autobiographical method of *currere* is not only an educational method but a conscious approach to life. As an Iranian-Canadian educator, my engagement with *currere* created new understandings of my subjectivity, time, and place. *Currere* is akin to interplay with time and place in the course of lived experience. In my academic study, *currere* freed and liberated my subjectivity from the undesired attachments such as test and stage anxiety inculcated in me due to a traditional test-centered assessment regime. It inspired me with new possibilities. *Currere* invoked a conscious and constant reconstruction of self and expanded my traditional understanding of subjectivity. My subjectivity—now released and awakened—is an infinite source of inspiration; it enables me to create a transformative curriculum by connecting to unlimited sources of knowledge, meaning, and understanding *within* and outside of myself. This educational freedom is the primary achievement and contribution of my research to self-education, the field of curriculum studies, to other educators, and students.

In "Sanity, Madness, and School," Pinar (1975a) worries that "we graduate, credentialized but crazed" (p. 381). The degree and depth of "madness" in traditional schooling is not measurable unless one *in person* takes a *currere* journey within to recover past educational experience and to re-educate self. Without taking an autobiographical journey, it is impossible to understand the degree and depth of this madness. In what way can other scientific fields of study provide a subjective understanding of our educational experience and the madness ingrained in our subjectivity? It is only through subjective and autobiographical research on educational experience that we can excavate our buried subjectivity under the burden of traditional schooling, banking education, and assessment regimes. Acknowledging this madness manufactured by traditional schooling and the demand for self-study and self-education "take impressive degrees of honesty and courage" (Poole, 2012, p. 9, cited in Cohen et al., 2012) as another valuable achievement and contribution of my autobiographical study.

Understanding the ways "banking education" and assessment regimes can craze and cripple our students, it is crucial that teachers, teacher educators, and policy makers to open a dialogue to remove such inner obstacles in self-education, one of which is the Iranian University Entrance Exam—Konkour—elimination of which is the most important step in transforming the quality of education in Iran. The Ministry of Science, Research, and Technology which establishes the Education Evaluation Organization to oversee all aspects of the test can open a dialogue with public-school teachers and university scholars to examine the ways they can eliminate Konkour and modify the means of university selection criteria by using a qualitative evaluation system. Knowing that the selection method provides advantages to those candidates who belong to upper and upper-middle class favoring a higher quality of education, Konkour works as a discriminatory selection method by maintaining "the dominant economic, political, and cultural arrangements that now exist" (Apple, 2004, p. xxii). Eliminating this admissions method and replacing it with a more efficient and humanistic approach of screening takes genuine dialogue among educational stakeholders and specifically teachers to understand what is at stake for students (see Fenstermacher, 1994).

Limitations of the Study

In my Master of Arts degree program in Teaching English as an Additional Language in Shiraz State University in Iran, I conducted quantitative research on Language Learning Strategies. I used Statistical Package for the Social Sciences (SPSS) for statistical analysis of data. My statistical understanding of data during MA research coupled with traditional schooling experience endorsing marketing understanding of "accountability, competitiveness, and performativity" (Autio, 2003, p. 302). This experience inculcated in me a statistical and numerical understanding of knowledge. This educational experience formed a quantitative *habitus* of education (see Bourdieu & Thompson, 1991) in me; therefore, acknowledging alternative, innovative, and creative methods of understanding took me a long time. It took until the middle of the third year of my doctoral studies that I could achieve new conceptual and theoretical understanding and was able to meaningfully reconnect with my personal stories. I consider my transition from a procedural curriculum to alternative aspects of my doctoral research as both a limitation (considering the challenges I encountered to reconstruct my fore-understanding of education) and as an advantage as my doctoral journey opened new possibilities and horizons of knowledge towards me.

The second limitation of my study is that unlike quantitative measures using which researchers analyze and synthesize data, my autobiographical and conceptual study lacks data which I consider as its strength as well. Although data can provide information in psychometric studies, during psychoanalytical analysis and synthesis of *currere*, I retrieve my educational experience and expand on my inner world and life-world. Understanding this conceptual and theoretical approach to research might seem unfamiliar and strange for those researchers coming from quantitative fields of study such as Educational and Counselling Psychology as they belong to different schools of thought which deals with external data as numbers and figures rather than internal accounts of their educational experience that I find closer to the meaning of being and life.

The third limitation of my study is that I did not specify professional activities to be undertaken. This study has intentionally not elaborated on the traditional concept of teacher professional development as genuine dialogue embraces the notion of teacher professional development within itself.

A final limitation of this study is perhaps the nature of autobiographical method of *currere*. Although this method connects the autobiographer to the social and political spheres, the educational journey that the autobiographer involves in takes mostly an unassisted and individualistic effort. This fact prevents generalization, as each autobiographer must follow his or her own way. Specifically, in retrieving the memories in the regressive dimension of *currere*, the autobiographer might encounter inundating currents of unpleasant accounts and an overflow of emotions. Once attuned, understanding and interpreting such accounts take the observer's reflective moments of watchfulness, carefulness, and composure. In this hermeneutic understanding, it is crucially important to be patient with such interpretive work so that the meaning of one's lifeworld unravels itself. Invoking one's autobiographical memory and understanding one's educational experience using *currere* takes courage.

Further Research

Understanding self is perhaps the most complicated knowledge acquired in one's academic pursuit. Before commencing my doctoral studies, I was engaged with at least two dimensions of self—spiritual and intellectual. Using *currere* and learning about other autobiographical studies, I have now achieved a solid and fluid understanding of self. I understand self as a unified and unique embodiment of intellect, emotion, and spirit. As Jung-Hoon Jung confirms: "self is a totality of intellect, emotion, and spirituality, all of which are always embodied" (2016, p. 130). Huebner (2008) contests the false assumption that "there is something special that can be identified as moral or spiritual" can be eliminated from understanding curriculum as "Everything that is done in schools, and in preparation for school activity is already infused with the spiritual" (Huebner, 1993, p. 11, cited in Pinar et al., 1995, p. 627).

Understanding the mystery of self as simultaneously spiritual, intellectual, and emotional needs more scrutiny. Such scrutiny that educators further examine their educational experience, using the autobiographical method of *currere* so that they can experience "shattering or evaporation of the ego" (Pinar, 2004, p. 10) prior to mobilizing personal and public knowledge.

Also, missing in the larger project creating a personalized and individualized curriculum is dialogue. How much dialogue is actually included and actively practiced in school curriculum? To what extent are stakeholders committed to this dynamic approach able to transform their educational standards? Can student subjectivity be illuminated in the curriculum once authentic dialogue is missing? In what sense can our educational experience create an understanding of dialogic knowledge in students? Is it possible to design a dialogue-based curriculum? These questions can provoke our critique of a traditional schooling system that follows a top-down processing of knowledge and understanding. Viewing *habitus* (Bourdieu & Thompson, 1991) as ingrained habits and dispositions constructed through years of educational experience, overcoming our traditional understanding of knowledge is not easy; however, dialogue—through the method of *currere*—can create a new and fresh pathway for self-education, and in turn, the education of those in one's care.

References

Aoki, T. T., Pinar, W. F., & Irwin, R. L. (2004). *Curriculum in a new key: The collected works of Ted T. Aoki*. Mahwah, NJ: Lawrence Erlbaum Associates, Publishers.

Apple, M. W. (2004). *Ideology and curriculum*. Routledge. https://doi.org/10.4324/9780203487563.

Autio, T. (2003). Postmodern paradoxes in Finland: The confinements of rationality in curriculum studies. In W. F. Pinar (Ed.), *International handbook of curriculum research* (pp. 301–328). Mahwah, NJ: Lawrence Erlbaum Associates.

Bourdieu, P., & Thompson, J. B. (1991). *Language and symbolic power*. Cambridge, MA: Harvard University Press.

Britzman, D. P. (2009). *The very thought of education: Psychoanalysis and the impossible professions*. Albany: State University of New York Press.

Butt, R., & Raymond, D. (1987). Arguments for using qualitative approaches in understanding teacher thinking: The case for biography. *JCT*, 7(1), 63–69.

Butt, R., & Raymond, D. (1988). Biographical and contextual influences on an "ordinary" teacher's thoughts and actions. In J. Lowyck, C. Clarke, & R. Halkes (Eds.), *Teacher thinking and professional action*. Lisse, Holland: Swets & Zeitlinger.

Butt, R. L., & Raymond, D. (1989). Studying the nature and development of teachers' knowledge using collaborative autobiography. *International Journal of Educational Research, 13*(4), 403–419. doi: 10.1016/0883-0355(89)90037-2.

Butt, R. & Raymond, D. (1992). Studying the nature and development of teachers' knowledge using collaborative autobiography. *International Journal of Educational Research, 13*(4), 402–444.

Chen, Y. (2014). From follower to creator: The past, present and future of the school as a reform subject. In William F. Pinar (Ed.), *Curriculum studies in China* (pp. 69–82) New York: Palgrave Macmillan.

Cohen, A., Porath, M., Clarke, A., Bai, H., Leggo, C., & Meyer, K. (2012; 2013). *Speaking of teaching: Inclinations, inspirations, and innerworkings*. Papendrecht: Sense Publishers.

Darling-Hammond, L. (2012). Teacher preparation and development in the United States. In L. Linda Darling-Hammond & A. Lieberman (Eds.), *Teacher education around the world. Changing policies and practices* (pp. 130–150). New York: Routledge.

Day, C. (2012). Introduction: Connecting teacher and school development: Policies, practices and possibilities. In C. Day (Ed.). *The Routledge international handbook of teacher and school development* (pp. 1–11) London: Routledge.

Fenstermacher, G. D. (1994). The knower and the known: The nature of knowledge in research on teaching. *Review of Research in Education, 20,* 3–56. doi: 10.2307/1167381.

Gadamer, H. G. (1992). *Hans-Georg Gadamer on education, poetry, and history: Applied hermeneutics* (D. Misgeld & G. Nicholson, Eds.; L. Schmidt & M. Reuss, Trans.). Albany, NY: State University of New York Press.

Gadamer, H. G. (1990/2004). *Truth and method* (2nd ed.) (J. Weinsheimer & D. Marshall, Trans.). New York: Crossroad. (Original work published 1960).

Huebner, D. E. (1999/2008). *The lure of the transcendent: Collected essays by Dwayne E. Huebner.* Mahwah, NJ: Lawrence Erlbaum Associates.

Husserl, E. (1969). *Ideas: General introduction to pure phenomenology.* New York; London: Allen & Unwin.

Jung, C. G. (2014). *The collected works of C. G. Jung.* New York, NY: Routledge.

Jung, J. H. (2016). *The concept of care in curriculum studies.* New York: Routledge.

Miller, J. L. (2005). *Sounds of silence breaking: Women, autobiography, curriculum* (Vol. 1). New York: Peter Lang.

Ng-a-fook, N. (2005). A curriculum of mother-son plots on education's center stage. *Journal of Curriculum Theorizing, 21*(4), 43–59.

Nixon, J. (2017). *Hans-Georg Gadamer: The hermeneutical imagination.* New York: Springer. doi: 10.1007/978-3-319-52117-6.

Palmer, L. L. (2018). *Streams that run into the river of lived experience: A phenomenological study of intern teachers using currere to understand curriculum.* ProQuest Dissertations Publishing.

Pinar, W. F. (1975a). Sanity, madness, and the school. In W. Pinar (Ed.), *Curriculum theorizing: The reconceptualists* (pp. 359–383) Berkeley, CA: McCutchan.

Pinar, W. F. (1994b). *Autobiography, politics and sexuality: Essays in curriculum theory 1972–1992.* New York: Peter Lang.

Pinar, W. F. (2004). *What is curriculum theory?* Mahwah, NJ: Lawrence Erlbaum Associates.

Pinar, W., Reynolds, W. M., Slattery, P., & Taubman, P. M. (1995). *Understanding curriculum: An introduction to the study of historical and contemporary curriculum discourses*. New York: Peter Lang.

Rodgers, C. R., & Raider-Roth, M. (2012). Presence in teaching. In C. Day (Ed.), *Routledge international handbook of teacher and school development* (pp. 149–158) London: Routledge.

Zhang, H., & Pinar, W. F. (2015). *Autobiography and teacher development in China: Subjectivity and culture in curriculum reform*. New York, NY: Palgrave Macmillan.

INDEX

Abundantlee 1, 11
Abram, J. 44, 55
Aoki, T. 31, 32, 34, 50–51, 55, 82, 89, 99, 109, 160, 166
Apple, M. 33, 41–42, 55, 147, 151, 164, 166
   institutionalized knowledge 41
   legitimate knowledge 42, 44
Aristotle 11, 123–124, 149, 151
   eudaimonia 11, 149, 151
Autio, T. 33, 55, 164, 166
autobiography 6, 15, 17–20, 24, 27–29, 31, 33, 39, 44, 46, 50, 57, 63, 67–70, 74, 76, 79–80, 82–86, 88, 91, 107, 133, 156, 158–159, 167
   autobiographer 2, 17, 28, 37, 39, 40, 43–44, 50, 53, 64, 79, 88, 165
   autobiographical 1–3, 8–11, 13–14, 17–20, 23–25, 27–32, 34–39, 41–43, 45–46, 49–50, 53–55, 59–65, 67–72, 74, 77, 79–80, 82, 85–86, 91, 95, 108, 135, 153, 155–159, 163–166
   autobiographical knowledge 10, 30, 41, 46, 53, 72

autobiographical method of *currere* 1, 3, 8–10, 13–14, 18, 27, 34, 36–37, 39, 49, 55, 59, 69, 135, 153, 155, 156, 163, 165–166
autobiographical research 9–10, 17–18, 28, 31, 45, 53, 55, 59–61, 63, 68, 70, 74, 77, 79, 82, 85–86, 135, 155, 158–159, 163
autobiographical understanding 2, 32, 41, 46
biographical 13, 18, 46, 59, 67–71, 82, 86, 159
biographic situation 20–21, 25
emancipatory 37, 55, 64, 69, 74, 81–82, 90–91, 122, 142, 159
epistemological 20–21, 91–93, 95, 155
epistemological curiosity 91–92
existential 16–17, 27, 32–34, 38–39, 49–52, 54, 62–64, 75–76, 80, 90, 92, 95, 98, 115, 125, 153, 155, 157, 160
ontological 20, 29, 33, 38, 56, 95, 115–116, 121, 155, 160
ontology 54, 93, 114–116, 127

phenomenological 14, 17, 20–21, 33–34, 38, 49–50, 54, 56, 58, 60, 63–64, 74–75, 78, 90, 93, 95, 115, 154, 157–158, 167
philosophy 5, 45, 56, 62, 78, 83, 93–94, 110–111, 122, 124, 127–128, 133, 135–136, 142, 152, 158
political a, 7, 9, 10, 15, 20, 22, 24–25, 29–30, 33–34, 36, 37, 39, 41, 42–44, 60, 63, 68, 74, 82, 86, 91, 95, 103, 108–110, 117–119, 147, 157, 159–160, 164–165, 169
subconscious 36, 40, 43, 46, 53, 76
temporality 14, 39, 52–55, 58, 60, 79, 81, 86
time 3, 6–7, 9–10, 13–16, 18, 22, 25–27, 31, 35, 38–40, 42, 44–46, 52–56, 61, 64–66, 71, 75, 78–81, 84, 94, 106, 111, 117–118, 125–126, 128–129, 143–144, 152, 154, 157, 162–164, 169
voice xvii, 9–10, 13, 17–24, 32, 40, 43, 53, 55, 57, 59, 63, 65–67, 74, 78, 91–92, 94, 103, 105–106, 108, 122, 135, 138, 141, 143, 148, 151, 155–156, 162

Bai, H. 56, 84, 95, 110–111, 167
Bakhtin, M. 82, 98–99, 110
Barane, J. 6, 11, 27, 55
Baszile, D. 1, 2, 11
Bourdieu, P. 98, 110, 164, 166
Britzman, D. 2, 11, 60, 82, 158, 166
Brown, D. 107, 110
Butt, R. 59, 68–70, 82–83, 166–167
Butt and Reymond 68–70, 74, 82–83, 158–159, 166–167
  collaborative autobiography 68, 70, 74, 83, 86, 158, 167

Canagarajah, S. 105–106, 111
Chambers, C. 70–71, 83
Chan, Z. 49, 56
Chen, Y. 156, 167
Clandinin and Connelly 18, 68, 70–72, 74, 83

narrative ix, x, 3, 9, 24–25, 30, 33, 68, 70–71, 73, 83–86, 103–105, 156
narrative inquiry 68, 70, 83, 86
Clarke, A. a, xiv, xvii, 33, 56, 63–64, 82–84, 86–87, 100–101, 103, 110–111, 166–167
Cohen, A. 56, 83–84, 94, 101, 110–111, 163, 167
Cohen & Porath 33, 93, 109
Connelly, F. 68, 70–71, 83
Currere a, iii, iv, ix–x, xiii– xiv, 1, 2, 3, 8–11, 13– 19, 21, 23, 25, 27, 29, 31, 33–39, 41, 43–47, 49–55, 57–61, 77, 81, 84, 153, 156–157, 163
  analytic 11, 20, 39, 47, 76, 90, 153, 156–157
  analyzing 16, 39, 42, 46, 70, 74, 77, 111, 141
  attitude xiii, 43, 50–51, 62, 67, 96, 119, 140, 157, 162
  connectivity 18, 37, 46, 75, 159
  cross-contextual 13, 17, 31, 47, 157
  dialectic xi, 19, 38, 81, 83, 89, 122–127, 134–135, 140, 143, 149, 162
  educational experience 4–5, 7, 9–11, 13–18, 20, 23–27, 29, 33–37, 39–40, 42–43, 45–47, 49–52, 54–55, 59–67, 70, 76, 77, 79–81, 86–98, 100–102, 108, 115–116, 120–121, 135, 141–142, 144, 153–160, 162–166
  ego 36–39, 42–46, 48–49, 157, 166
  emerge 13, 18, 30, 32, 40, 63, 71, 81, 101–102, 107, 145, 159
  empowerment 21, 56, 156
  envisioning 9, 14, 16, 54–55, 76–77
  erudition 29, 44, 46–47, 53
  fantasies 2, 14, 27, 34, 37, 39–40, 47, 54–55, 76, 86, 102
  faith x, 41, 65, 105, 107–109, 111, 134
  imagination 2, 30, 35, 65, 81, 111, 136, 152, 167
  immigrant 26, 47, 108
  individualistic 47, 107, 142, 165
  individuality 11, 18, 22, 24, 36, 41, 76, 96, 103–105, 146–147, 149–151, 160, 162

inner call 1–2
inner life 63, 65, 82, 86, 155–156, 159
inner work 60, 63–66, 86, 93–95, 109, 159
integrity 44, 46, 104, 109
intellect 32, 82, 95, 115, 128, 165
intellectual 2, 23–24, 38, 44, 82, 95, 98, 128, 157, 165–166
learning experience 3, 11, 15–16, 20, 27, 29, 35, 41, 46–47, 52, 62–63, 75–78, 81–82, 103, 108–109, 141–142, 148, 150, 156, 158–159
mobilize 10, 39, 44, 82, 154–155, 158–159
non-ego 37–39, 42, 48–49, 157
pedagogical 10, 23–24, 41, 52, 60, 65, 68, 72–73, 79, 82, 92, 95, 99–101, 109, 111, 113–114, 116, 144, 147–148, 150, 155, 157–161, 169
Persian iii, iv, xiv, 5, 17, 91, 154, 156
professional judgment 2
progressive 7, 9, 11, 22, 31–32, 39, 50, 53, 55, 76, 157
psyche 6, 16, 23, 26, 38, 43, 45, 108, 158
psychoanalytical 16–17, 29, 31, 42, 46, 51, 53, 63, 66, 93, 96, 157, 164
psychological 5–6, 20, 25–26, 28, 31, 35, 37–38, 42, 49, 63, 76, 89, 157
psychological development 2
psychological tensions 5
regress 9–10, 23, 29, 42, 52
regressive 11, 27, 30, 39, 50, 52–54, 61, 64, 157, 165
synthetic 11, 39, 47, 76, 153, 157
visualizing 9, 14, 17, 22, 54
watchfulness 64–65, 95, 165
wellbeing 1, 68, 162
working from within 89, 158
Curriculum iv, xvii, 3–20, 22–23, 29–48, 51, 55–59, 61–63, 68–70, 73, 78–85, 87–88, 93, 97–103, 110–111, 118, 121–122, 140, 148, 151–152, 154–157, 163–164, 166–169
anxiety 16–17, 26, 35–37, 40–41, 45–46, 48, 52–53, 55, 61–63, 66, 76–77, 79, 156–158, 163

anxiousness 37
cognitivist movement 2
collectivity 18
conformity 18, 104, 160
credentialized 5, 35, 163
curriculum and pedagogy 47, 156
formulaic learning 20–21
meaningful understanding 2, 5, 45, 63, 87
memorization 5, 15–16, 20, 22, 91, 160
memorizing 4, 15, 42
nonconformist 6
normalizing 147
predetermined 15–16, 87, 96, 156
predetermined structures 16
procedural education 2, 23
procedural schooling 4, 154
rationalism 87, 132, 159
reconceptualization 32–33, 57, 74, 159
recollecting 16
reflective practice 113
shopping mall 39, 67, 147
standardized tests 3, 33, 99
test anxiety 16, 35, 37, 40–41, 46, 52–53, 61–63, 66, 76, 156–158
traditional 6, 10, 21, 23, 34–35, 45, 55, 60–61, 65, 82, 85, 90–91, 102, 125, 156, 163–166

Darling-Hammond, L. 156, 167
Day, C. 156, 167–168
Demuth, A. 75, 83
Dewey, J. 40, 56
democracy 40, 9
dialogue a, i, iii, ix–xi, xiii–xiv, xviii, 2–4, 6–10, 14, 16, 18– 20, 22–28, 30–32, 34, 36, 38, 40–42, 44, 46, 48, 50–52, 54, 56, 58, 60, 64–68, 70, 72–74, 76, 78, 80–82, 84, 86–111, 113–166, 168
genuine conversation 7, 10, 86, 92, 96, 113, 161
interpersonal 106–107, 109
interfaith 9–10, 73, 82, 105–110
intersubjective dialogue 90, 107–108, 119, 137, 141, 159–161

pluralistic 102, 105, 109, 155
plurality 21, 101–103, 109, 159–160
religious 47, 65, 103, 105–108, 111, 113–114, 125, 153
transcendent 56, 84, 110, 167
transformation 1–2, 19, 26, 34, 41, 43, 52, 74, 80–81, 88–89, 92, 102–103, 129, 141, 156–157
transformative 3, 14–15, 21, 26, 29, 30–31, 36, 41, 43, 46, 48, 52, 55, 62–64, 72, 76, 79–82, 87–90, 95, 99, 102–104, 106–108, 117, 142, 155–156, 158–159, 161, 163
Doll, W. 87–88, 102, 110
Dwyer, K. 71, 83

Edge, J. 106, 110
Edgerton, S. 28–29, 56
Elbaz, F. 56, 68, 83, 110
Elbaz-Luwisch 27

Fenstermacher, G. 164, 167
Fisher, R. 90, 110
Freire, P. 91–92, 100, 110
  decolonial pedagogy 91
  colonial 91
  critical pedagogy 91–92
Freud, S. 47–48, 56
  free association 14, 47, 49, 53, 59
  resistance 38, 48–49, 53, 63, 66, 75, 80, 88–89, 154, 157
  transference 48, 75

Gadamer, H. 86, 111, 113–153, 161, 167
  authority 10, 100, 133–135, 141, 146, 156, 160, 162
  enlightenment 95, 110, 131–134
  fore-understanding 130–131, 135, 138, 155, 164
  Gadamerian dialogue 9–10, 87, 114, 127, 135, 138, 153, 155–156, 160–162
  Gadamerian hermeneutics x– xi, 10, 114, 116, 118, 122, 127, 134, 137, 153, 155
  hermeneutic dialogue 10, 116

history a, 7–8, 16–17, 24, 28, 53, 64–66, 69, 71, 73, 76, 80, 109, 122, 131, 133, 136, 143, 152–153, 167
interpretive understanding 10, 45, 50, 113, 145, 153
intervention xi, 23, 48, 127, 141–142, 169
judgment 2, 23, 49, 51, 60, 75–76, 90, 117, 127, 132, 134–135, 148, 158, 161
Plato 122–124, 126
preconditioned 96
prejudice 10, 88, 120–121, 130–135, 141, 145–146
rhetoric 56, 148–149
spiritual 42, 65, 82, 93, 95, 106–107, 153, 155, 157, 165–166
student voice 9, 22, 94, 135, 138, 148, 162
Truth and Method 109, 119, 127, 136, 141, 152, 167
Gilligan, C. 85, 104, 110
Goodson, I. 68, 73–74, 83
Grau, M. 123, 136
Greene, M. 22–23, 34, 56, 62, 81, 83, 95, 110
Grumet, M. 19–20, 24, 34, 37, 50, 56, 57
  marginalization 19

Hadley, G. 106, 110
Hasebe-Ludt, E. 30–31, 56–57, 111
Heidegger, M. 11, 54, 56, 74–75, 84, 118, 124, 127, 136, 139, 145, 152
  attunement 74–77, 84, 86, 155, 160
  lebenswelt 11, 49
  lifeworld 8, 16, 18, 20, 23, 27, 38–39, 41–46, 48–53, 61, 65–66, 74–77, 79–82, 86, 88–91, 93, 95–96, 98, 100–101, 108, 115, 125, 142, 144, 153, 155–157, 159, 165
  life-world xvii, 1, 8, 115–116, 124, 129–130, 144, 149, 158–159, 162, 165
Heng Hartse, J. 9, 105, 108–111
  Christian 65, 105–108, 110–111, 114
Holquist, M. 82, 88, 98, 110
Huebner, D. 34, 53–54, 56, 77–79, 84, 88, 110, 160, 165–167
  Dasein 54, 124, 145

INDEX

Husserl, E. 50, 56, 84, 115, 157, 167
   bracketing x, 49, 51, 56, 58, 97
   non-judgmental 7, 39, 49–52, 115, 142, 157
   preconception(s) 50, 77, 88–89, 107, 115, 118, 124, 137, 141
   preconceptual 11, 35, 49
   suspend 23, 50, 75, 115
   suspension 75–76, 139

Jaramillo, N. 91, 110
   banking education 5, 7, 38, 40–42, 61, 66, 91, 160, 163
Jung, J. 11, 104–105, 110, 160, 167
   individuation 42, 104
Jung, J-H. 2, 98–99, 165
   Hakbeolism 98–99
   self-care 2, 11, 99
   symbolic capital 98

Karmani, S. 106, 111
Kincheloe, J. 56
Kincheloe & Pinar 28, 30
Kögler, H. 96–97, 111
Konkour 3, 154, 163–164
   entrance exam 3–4, 154, 163
   university entrance exam 3

Leggo, C. xvii, 33, 56, 65–67, 84–85, 100, 104, 110–111, 167
   attentive listening 65, 75, 95, 96, 100, 143
   reverence 65–67, 81
Lipari, L. 77–78, 84

Magrini, J. 34, 56
McClellan, P. 108, 111
Mellor, P. 107, 111
Miller, J. 17–19, 23, 34, 36, 46, 56–57, 78, 84, 156, 167
Morris, M. 15, 43, 57

Nazari, S. a, iii, iv, xv, 108–111
   Muslim 105–108, 110–111
Ng-A-Fook 13, 153

Nixon, J. 116, 119–120, 122, 125, 136, 140–143, 146–152, 162, 167
Noddings, N. 60, 76–77, 84, 89, 97–98, 111
   care xiii, 2, 11, 38, 53–54, 66, 75–76, 78, 94, 97–100, 110, 139, 166–167
   care-for-others 2, 11
   empathy 94, 98–99, 141–142
Norman, R. 31, 57
Norris, Sawyer, & Lund 37, 107, 111

Oakeshott, M. 23, 57
Osberg, D. & Biesta, G. 101, 111

Palmer, P. 82, 84, 136, 151, 157, 167
Pennycook, A. 106, 111
Phelan, A. a, xviii, 20–21, 57, 103, 110
   democratic 21
Pinar, W. ii, xvii, 7, 11, 18, 20, 28, 30, 33–35, 37–39, 41, 43–45, 48–50, 53, 55–58, 67–68, 70, 72–73, 82–84, 87, 100, 107, 109, 111, 147, 152, 154, 156, 163, 166–169
   complicated conversation ii, iv, 7, 8, 44, 99, 169
   conversation iv, 7–8, 10, 23, 25, 32, 44, 57, 72–73, 78, 86–88, 92, 96–97, 99, 101–102, 106, 109, 113, 117, 119, 122, 125–126, 134, 136, 139–140, 152, 161, 169
Pinar & Grumet 20, 34, 50
place ix, xiii, 4, 6, 10–11, 13–14, 17–18, 24–33, 40, 45–47, 50, 55–59, 65–68, 75, 79–81, 83, 100, 102, 110, 125–126, 129, 139, 147, 149, 157, 163, 169
   Arsanjan 16, 26, 35, 45, 66
   Canada a, xiv, 11, 14, 26, 36, 66, 83–84
   Iran 3, 6, 9–10, 14, 16, 25, 28, 35, 41–42, 48, 61–62, 66, 79, 94, 99, 107–108, 163–164
   Iranian-Canadian 28, 47, 156, 163
   revolution ix, 6, 9–10, 14, 73
   Shiraz 16, 25–28, 31, 40, 61, 99, 154, 164
   social space 11, 28–30, 40
   UBC 26–27, 31, 35, 106

University of British Columbia a, xiv, 8, 11, 14, 84, 105, 155, 169
Vancouver a, xiv, 11, 14, 26, 28, 61, 84, 105, 107, 109, 169
Poole, G. 93–94, 109, 163

Regan, P. 118, 136
Robert Frost 4, 11

Schubert, W. 57, 84
Schubert and Ayers 68, 74
Shulman, L. 72, 84
Simms, K. 121, 123–124, 127, 129–130, 134, 136, 139, 145–146, 152
  phronesis 123–124
Slattery, P. 57, 88, 111, 168
Socrates vii, 60
subjectivity x, xviii, 7, 10–11, 14, 17–20, 22–24, 27–47, 52–53, 58–60, 62, 66–67, 73, 75–76, 81, 84, 89, 91–96, 99–101, 104, 108, 111, 113, 115–116, 120–121, 123, 133–135, 153–154, 157, 161, 163, 166, 168
  identity 24, 28, 30, 83, 100, 103–105, 107, 110, 121–122, 125
  self-alienated 35
  self-conscious 23, 51–52, 79, 97, 120, 141, 158
  self-education xvii, 1–2, 5, 21, 30, 36, 40, 44, 63, 67–68, 101, 105, 131, 135, 148, 155–156, 162–163, 166
  self-exploration 1, 5
  self-explorative 8, 124, 161
  self-exploratory 2, 47, 61, 76
  self-fulfillment 1, 5, 11, 98, 116, 150, 162
  selfhood xiii, 2, 5, 7, 10, 82, 86, 113, 153, 158
  self-knowledge xiv, xvii, 3, 8, 17, 20, 60, 81, 124, 159

self-love 35, 66, 79, 99
self-reflective 2, 16–18, 20, 40–43, 46–47, 60, 64–65, 76, 88, 108, 124, 131, 137
self-transformation 1
self-wellbeing 1, 162
self-worth 7, 66, 79, 99, 101, 162
shattered self 2
Szafran, Y. 35, 58

teacher development a, iv, xiv, xvii, 9–10, 55, 58, 60–61, 68–70, 74, 76, 79, 84–87, 92–93, 97, 102, 109, 111, 114, 118, 123–124, 127, 135, 137, 148, 153, 155, 158–160, 168
  English language educator 9, 13, 55, 60, 106
  English language practitioner 2, 14
  IELTS 16–19, 22, 27, 35, 40, 42–43, 46, 52, 61–64
  teacher autobiographical knowledge 72
  teacher educator 2
  teacher lore 68, 72–74, 86
  teacher professional development xiv, 3, 9–10, 82, 86–89, 92, 95, 98, 102–103, 105, 113, 120, 134, 153, 156, 159–160, 165
TESOL x, 10, 106–107, 109–111
Trigg, D 47, 58
Tufford, L & Newman 50, 58

van Manen, M. 34, 49, 58, 157

Wang, H. 43, 52, 58, 76, 80, 84, 100–101
Wilcox, E. 4, 11
Wong, M. 105–106, 110–111

Zhang, H. 33, 58, 60, 84, 90, 111, 156, 168
Zhenyu, G. 90, 111

COMPLICATED CONVERSATION

A BOOK SERIES OF CURRICULUM STUDIES

Reframing the curricular challenge educators face after a decade of school deform, the books published in Peter Lang's Complicated Conversation Series testify to the ethical demands of our time, our place, our profession. What does it mean for us to teach now, in an era structured by political polarization, economic destabilization, and the prospect of climate catastrophe? Each of the books in the Complicated Conversation Series provides provocative paths, theoretical and practical, to a very different future. In this resounding series of scholarly and pedagogical interventions into the nightmare that is the present, we hear once again the sound of silence breaking, supporting us to rearticulate our pedagogical convictions in this time of terrorism, reframing curriculum as committed to the complicated conversation that is intercultural communication, self-understanding, and global justice.

The series editor is

>Dr. William F. Pinar
>Department of Curriculum Studies
>2125 Main Mall
>Faculty of Education
>University of British Columbia
>Vancouver, British Columbia V6T 1Z4
>CANADA

To order other books in this series, please contact our Customer Service Department:

>peterlang@presswarehouse.com (within the U.S.)
>orders@peterlang.com (outside the U.S.)

Or browse online by series:

>www.peterlang.com

www.ingramcontent.com/pod-product-compliance
Ingram Content Group UK Ltd.
Pitfield, Milton Keynes, MK11 3LW, UK
UKHW021838210426
5322IPUK00021B/355